Critical Reflections on the Fiction of Ernest J. Gaines

Critical

Edited by David C. Estes

Reflections on

The University of Georgia Press

the Fiction of

Athens and London

Ernest J. Gaines

$1 - 1040$

© 1994 by the University of Georgia Press
Athens, Georgia 30602
All rights reserved
Designed by Erin Kirk
Set in 10/13 Sabon by Tseng Information Systems, Inc.
Printed and bound by Thomson-Shore, Inc.
The paper in this book meets the guidelines for permanence
and durability of the Committee on Production Guidelines for
Book Longevity of the Council on Library Resources.

Printed in the United States of America

98 97 96 95 94   C   5 4 3 2 1

Library of Congress Cataloging in Publication Data

Critical reflections on the fiction of Ernest J. Gaines / edited by
    David C. Estes.
        p.   cm.
    Includes bibliographical references and index.
    ISBN 0–8203–1607–5 (alk. paper)
    1. Gaines, Ernest J., 1933–   —Criticism and interpretation.
    2. Pastoral fiction, American—History and criticism.
    3. Southern States in literature. 4. Afro-Americans in literature.
    I. Estes, David C., 1950–
    PS3557.A355Z64   1994
    813'.54—dc20   93-5333
                                                                 CIP

British Library Cataloging in Publication Data available

Contents

Critical Reflections on the Fiction of Ernest J. Gaines

Introduction

In 1948, at the age of fifteen, Ernest J. Gaines left rural Oscar, Louisiana, because there were no high schools for blacks near his home. Five generations of his family had lived there, in the former slave quarters of a plantation. He traveled alone from Pointe Coupee Parish to Vallejo, California, to be with his mother and stepfather, who had moved there during World War II to find work. Gaines left behind the aunt who had raised him, the old people for whom he had read and written letters, and the hard work in the fields. In California he lived alongside families of diverse nationalities and, on the playground, learned the complexity of discrimination. Reflecting on that time in his life in the third person in the essay "A Very Big Order: Reconstructing Identity," Gaines says, "He had never thought himself less than anyone else, nor better. He had come from a world where the two races, white and black, were separated but he had never thought he was less than anyone else. He had always carried his share of the load" (247).

At his stepfather's suggestion, Gaines soon began to visit the public library, an institution that had not been open to him in Louisiana because he was black. There he discovered the novels that inspired him to write about the rural way of life he missed so much. First he read Southern writers. Although these white authors depicted "unrecognizable" black characters, Gaines still found their books to contain "something about earth, trees, and water" (248). Soon he was enjoying John Steinbeck and Willa Cather because they "wrote about nature or about people who worked the land" ("Miss Jane and I" 27). Next he turned to such great nineteenth-century Russians as Ivan Turgenev and Anton Chekov, "who seemed to understand the serfs, and often made them better than their masters" ("A Very Big Order" 249).

Yet these books left Gaines unfulfilled in his search for something familiar and failed to alleviate his homesickness for Louisiana. They were about lives quite different from his own.

> I wanted to see on paper those Louisiana black children walking to school on cold days while yellow Louisiana busses passed them by. I wanted to see on paper those black parents going to work before the sun came up and coming back home to look after their children after the sun went down. I wanted to see on paper the true reason why those black fathers left home—not because they were trifling or shiftless—but because they were tired of putting up with certain conditions. I wanted to see on paper the small country churches (schools during the week), and I wanted to hear those simple religious songs, those simple prayers—that true devotion. ("Miss Jane and I" 28)

As Thadious M. Davis has commented, "few contemporary African American writers have been as candid as Gaines in asserting the formative power of race- and region-specific experiences" ("Ernest J. Gaines" 129).

After about a year in Vallejo, at age sixteen or seventeen, Gaines recalls, he took up the challenge to put his Louisiana on paper. He wrote "A Little Stream," a novel about "two families, one very fair, one dark—separated from each other by a stream of water" ("Miss Jane and I" 28). It was rejected in 1949 or 1950 by a New York publisher, who "sent it back . . . in the original brown paper, tied with its original broken and knotted strings" (29). Gaines burned the only copy of the manuscript but continued working with the central idea of the story, which eventually became his first published novel, *Catherine Carmier* (1964). Upon its publication, Gaines had accomplished the goal that grew out of his departure from the plantation fifteen years earlier—to put on paper the lives of the black people in the small part of the South he knew from experience.

But when Gaines finally completed *Catherine Carmier,* he was no longer writing merely out of adolescent homesickness. After having served two years in the army, he had completed an undergraduate degree in English at San Francisco State College and studied creative writing in a graduate program at Stanford University. In 1962 he was considering a move to Mexico to concentrate on the book he wanted to write about Louisiana. Then in September of that year, James Meredith enrolled at the University of Mississippi, causing Gaines to make a significant change in plans: "I kept thinking and thinking about this brave, very brave man—and told myself that if James Meredith can go through all this—not only for himself, but for his race (and that included me as well)—then I, too, should go back to the source that I was trying to write about" ("Miss Jane and I" 31). So he returned to Louisiana, living in Baton Rouge for the first six months of 1963. There he not only wrote but drove back to the plantation near Oscar, about thirty miles away, to visit people he had known and talk with them about others who had died. This period of living once again in Louisiana and encountering what he remembered of it was vital in Gaines's growth as a writer. Six months after returning to California, he finished the manuscript over which he had been struggling for a decade and a half.

Catherine Carmier was not, however, to be the end of Gaines's goal to write about Louisiana, but rather the beginning. In each succeeding work, he has continued to draw imaginatively on his experiences as a child on River Lake Plantation. The passion he expressed in the following comment to Charles H. Rowell in a 1978 interview continues to characterize his commitment as a writer: "Maybe sometime in the future I will write a good book, or publish a good book, about California. But I doubt that I will be able to do it until I have gotten rid of this Louisiana thing that drives me, yet I hope I never will get rid of that Louisiana thing. I hope I'm able to write about Louisiana for the rest of my life" ("This Louisiana Thing" 40). Gaines was probably thinking about the three unpublished novels set in San Francisco that he wrote in a period of less than two years after *Catherine Carmier*, manuscripts he considers "three of the worst novels that have ever been written by a published writer" ("Miss Jane and I" 32). Since returning to Louisiana and his fictional St. Raphael Parish for *Of Love and Dust* (1967), he has never left home again in his fiction.

Gaines has published one collection of short stories, *Bloodline* (1968), and four other novels—*The Autobiography of Miss Jane Pittman* (1971), *In My Father's House* (1978), *A Gathering of Old Men* (1983), and *A Lesson Before Dying* (1993). "A Long Day in November," the opening story in *Bloodline*, was republished separately in 1971 as a children's story. Three short stories were in print several years before Gaines collected them in *Bloodline*. He also published early versions of portions of *Catherine Carmier, In My Father's House*, and *A Gathering* while at work on those novels. Four published stories remain unincorporated into a book. "The Turtles" (1956) and "Boy in the Double Breasted Suit" (1957) appeared in the San Francisco State College literary magazine, *Transfer*. "My Grandpa and the Haint" (1966) and "Chapter One of *The House and the Field, A Novel*" (1972) appeared in literary magazines. Gaines has published several autobiographical essays about his early life and his work as an author: "Miss Pittman's Background" (1975), "Miss Jane and I" (1978), "Auntie and the Black Experience in Louisiana" (1982), "Bloodline in Ink" (1989), and "A Very Big Order: Reconstructing Identity" (1990).

Over the course of his career, Gaines has received numerous awards. These include the Wallace Stegner Creative Writing Fellowship for graduate work at Stanford University, where he enrolled in 1958. In 1959 his short story "Comeback," which remains unpublished, won the Joseph Henry Jackson Literary Award. He has received a National Endowment for the Arts Study Award (1966), a Rockefeller Foundation Grant-in-Aid (1970), a Guggenheim Fellowship (1973–74), and a five-year MacArthur Fellowship (1993). *Miss Jane Pittman* earned him an award from the Black Academy of Arts and Letters (1972), and the American Academy and Institute of Arts and Letters has also presented one of its annual awards to him (1987). He has received honorary doctorates from Denison University (1980), Brown University (1984), Bard College (1985), Whittier College (1986), and Louisiana State University (1987). Since 1983 he has been writer-in-residence at the University of Southwestern Louisiana, teaching one semester a year and spending the other months at his second home in San Francisco.

Much personal information about Gaines is available in the interviews that have appeared frequently in the popular press and in scholarly journals. Interviewers typically elicit comments about his childhood and the aunt, Augusteen Jefferson, who raised him. Mary Ellen Doyle, in "Ernest Gaines' Materials: Place, People, Author," and Anne K. Simpson, in "The Early Life of Ernest Gaines," have drawn on biographical details in the published interviews to write illuminating accounts of his early life and his childhood home in Louisiana. Other scholars have also drawn on the interviews for background about how Gaines composes his works and for interpretive insights into his characters. It is interesting that scholars have shown a willingness to accept his right to speak authoritatively as a critic of his own work.

The most substantial of the interviews is the book-length *Porch Talk with Ernest Gaines: Conversations on the Writer's Craft* (1990), by Marcia Gaudet and Carl Wooton. The title recalls the taped sessions that the fictional history teacher conducted with Jane Pittman on the gallery of her house. The composition history of *Porch Talk* likewise suggests Gaines's novel. Just as the high school teacher talked with Miss Jane over a period of eight or nine months, Gaudet and Wooton conversed with Gaines at his home during an eight-month span. Then, like Gaines's fictional editor of the autobiography, they rearranged material covered in the sessions to make a unified whole rather than merely transcribe what their subject said. The book's particular strengths are found in Gaines's comments about folklore and ethnicity in his fiction and his recollections of the literary agents and editors with whom he has worked. A number of the illustrations in *Porch Talk* are photographs Gaines himself snapped at River Lake Plantation between 1963 and 1969. They were originally printed as "Home: A Photo-Essay" in a 1978 issue of *Callaloo* devoted to criticism of Gaines.

Interviewers typically ask Gaines which writers he admires. Invariably he recalls the early influence of the nineteenth-century Russian realists on his own craft. Among Americans, he pays homage to Mark Twain for his use of the vernacular and acknowledges a debt to Ernest Hemingway for teaching him about the technique of structuring paragraphs, sentences, and dialogue. Hemingway's use of repetition is likewise noteworthy for Gaines: "Hemingway can repeat the lighting of a cigarette, the length or shortness of the cigarette, or the ash hanging, to show how time moves. . . . These are the kinds of things I read carefully in his work" (Gaudet and Wooton 23). Yet Gaines feels that Hemingway's themes are equally important to him as an African American, as he explained to Rowell. To let students know how it was possible for him to be influenced by a white writer, Gaines explained that "when Hemingway, whose major theme was grace under pressure, was writing he was saying as much about the black man as he was about the white man, although very seldom were his black characters given any kind of sympathetic roles. Still his writings of that grace under pressure . . . made me see my own black people" ("This Louisiana Thing" 44). To Gaudet and Wooton he elaborated, "I see that Hemingway usually put his people in a moment where they must have grace under pressure, and I've often looked at black life not only as a moment, but more as something constant, everyday. This is what my characters must come through" (22).

As might be expected, William Faulkner has been an important author with whose reputation and accomplishments Gaines has had to contend since both men are interpreters of the South. He has acknowledged in particular Faulkner's handling of both dialect and humor as techniques from which he learned. Gaines denies, however, that Faulkner, unlike Hemingway, has had any larger influence on his themes or artistic vision: "I'd like to make this clear: Faulkner has influenced me in style only, not in philosophy" (Rowell, "This Louisiana Thing" 43).

Gaines states that black novelists did not influence his development as a writer. As a college student, he was not assigned their books and did not read them on his own, choosing instead to focus on the set curriculum since he felt "so far behind the average kid I had to go to school with, because I had not read anything" (Gaudet and Wooton 34). Now acquainted with works he did not know when he first started to write, Gaines states that "probably the only Black writer who has influenced my work is Zora Neale Hurston. But if I had read Jean Toomer's *Cane* before I developed my own way of working and writing, it probably would have influenced me as much as Faulkner, Hemingway, or Turgenev" (Carter 71).

Despite the lack of formative influences by African-American writers, he acknowledges a great debt to African-American musicians. He feels that he has learned "as much about writing about my people by listening to blues and jazz and spirituals as I have learned by reading novels" ("Miss Jane and I" 33). Despite his wide-ranging taste in music, the rural blues remain his favorite. "I listen to the great blues singers, especially the rural blues singers and how they in their own way describe the hard life out there. Maybe that's where the grimness comes from" (Saeta and Skinner 3). One particular example of why Gaines values the blues involves the great Mississippi River flood of 1927, an event about which Miss Jane Pittman speaks. He says that the "great blues singers like Bessie Smith, Josh White, [and] Leadbelly . . . described the black situation much better than the whites did" in newspaper accounts of the disaster. Furthermore, he observes, "when it came down to the more intimate things, I think the black blues singers gave us better descriptions even than the black writers did at that particular time" (Gaudet and

Wooton 19). Both "Three Men," collected in *Bloodline*, and *Of Love and Dust* derived, in part, from Gaines's meditating on events about which Lightnin' Hopkins sings in "Mr. Tim Moore's Farm" ("Miss Jane and I" 33).

While the rural blues have contributed to Gaines's way of viewing events in life, jazz has influenced some of his writing techniques. For example, he emulates the repetition he hears in jazz by frequently repeating words in dialogue. Gaines is also conscious that the skillful use of understatement in jazz compositions taught him more about this particular stylistic trait that he found also in Hemingway's fiction: "Certain musicians, like Lester Young—one of the greatest jazz saxophonists— could play around a note. For example, if he were playing 'Stardust,' he didn't have to go through the old beat-after-beat of 'Stardust.' He could give you a feeling of 'Stardust' by playing around the note" (Gaudet and Wooton 19).

The most current bibliography of Gaines's work and Gaines criticism was published by Mary Ellen Doyle in 1990. She provides a useful annotation of material that appeared between 1956, when he published his first short story, and 1988. In 1993 Rick Smith and Ruth Laney produced a video, *Ernest J. Gaines: Louisiana Stories,* that provides background material through interviews with Gaines, his relatives, residents of Oscar, and also prominent scholars. Other important additions to Doyle's bibliography include *Porch Talk* as well as the following two book-length studies, both issued in 1991.

In *A Gathering of Gaines: The Man and the Writer,* Anne K. Simpson offers no new critical interpretations of his fictions. The book is primarily a relatively indiscriminate reprinting of material from Gaines's letters, scrapbooks, unpublished speeches and notebooks, and the drafts of published works on deposit at Dupre Library at the University of Southwestern Louisiana. It also includes lengthy quotations from published criticism and interviews that are widely available. Despite the inconsequential nature of much that Simpson has selected from Gaines's papers, the assiduous scholar can find in her collection material that sheds light on Gaines's personality, vision, and craft. Among the odd bits Simpson records is, for example, that in 1989 the Freddie Thomas Foundation erected a drinking fountain in downtown Rochester, New York, in honor of Miss Jane Pittman. Gaines himself attended the dedication.

The most complete study of Gaines's fiction published to date is

Valerie Melissa Babb's *Ernest Gaines*. A volume in Twayne's United States Author Series, it excels in quality many of the other books in that series. There is a chapter on each novel through *A Gathering*. In an insightful final chapter on voice in African-American literature, Babb addresses the fact that Gaines has remained "dedicated to his personal vision of what a black writer should be and do" (135) and thus has not actively participated in the literary movements of his age. As Jack Hicks noted in his chapter on Gaines in an earlier book on contemporary fiction writers, "Gaines has allied himself with no coterie and has been promoted by no critical sponsor. He has maintained this aloofness in a time of heated debate about the role of black art and the proper stance of the black artist" (*Singer's Temple* 99). Babb observes that despite being criticized for "his seeming political neutrality," he writes with passion for "political and social equality. All his characters seek justice and recognition but do so on personal terms" (136). By commenting on the "political nuances" in Gaines's work, Babb suggests that scholars have not yet given him his due.

As Doyle's bibliography demonstrates, scholars have shown a great deal of interest in assessing Gaines as a Southern writer. Explication of his Southern setting has been important because the multiethnic culture of his locale differs markedly from most of the rest of the South, where racial tensions divide along white-black lines. Vying for status in fictional St. Raphael Parish are the different groups among whom Gaines lived as a boy: the Anglo and Creole whites, the Cajuns, the Creoles of color, and the blacks. The Cajuns are descended from the French Acadians, whom the British expelled from Nova Scotia in 1755. Upon arriving in Louisiana in the following decade, they settled in the swamps and prairies, where they remained largely isolated until the state began to develop its oil resources in the first part of this century. Some scholars see a resemblance between Gaines's Cajuns and Faulkner's Snopeses because of their willing adoption of modern farming methods and aggressive acquisition of lands sharecropped for generations by blacks. Yet, as Davis argues, Gaines's conception of Cajuns is related not to class but instead to issues of race and the "social dynamics affecting the lives, traditions, and aspirations of his black characters" ("Ernest J. Gaines" 137). Just as the Cajuns are an ethnic group unique to Southern literature set in Louisiana, the black Creoles in Gaines's fiction also belong exclusively to south Louisiana. They differ from the stereotypical tragic mulatto figure in much Southern literature. His Creoles are the descendants of antebellum free persons of color, who had both African and French Catholic ancestry, and they are part of a distinct Creole community. Many of the Creoles in Gaines's stories maintain their ancestors' commitment to isolating themselves from other blacks, using their Creole dialect and lighter skin color to secure a relatively higher status in the culture. This complex mixture of ethnic groups, whose lives and histories are in conflict with each other, has enabled Gaines to earn recognition for his unique treatment of themes he shares with other Southern writers.

Despite Gaines's devotion to putting his Louisiana on paper, the universal qualities of his fictional world are apparent. Rowell argues, for example, that the former slave quarters in which the action of his novels takes place is "a symbolic space" with an "epic dimension" ("Quarters" 749). The quarters is a microcosm like Faulkner's Yoknapatawpha, although Gaines does not reuse particular characters from one book to the next. As Rowell says, by focusing on events in the quarters, Gaines presents a place "symbolic of modern human experience in its questions about the individual, the family, the community, and the past." These are the very questions that link him to the Southern tradition at the same time that his answers separate him from the historically dominant white discourse about the region.

Gaines's most predominant theme comes out of his African-American heritage. It is the search for black manhood. *Miss Jane Pittman* is the only book in which his focus is not directly on the subject of the struggles of black men, but even there men's quest for status is the subject of some of Miss Jane's reminiscences. Gaines's dedication to exploring the predicament of black men in our culture may account, in part, for the lack of critical attention he has received at a time when scholars have produced numerous studies of his African-American female contemporaries and their novels about women's issues. Yet articles about Gaines's fiction demonstrate the subtlety with which he has explored the psychology of black men in confronting our discriminatory culture. In particular, he pays attention to the absence of a bond between fathers and sons that could sustain the younger generation in its confrontations with the world.

Among Gaines's noteworthy contributions to African-American literature is his concern for recreating the history of his race. His novels depict characters who find their identity within, not outside of, that particular history. The most memorable characters are the elderly Miss Jane Pittman and the old men of *A Gathering,* who talk about the legacy of oppression, capitulation, and resistance, keeping alive in the community the events of the past stretching all the way back to the days of slavery. Their stories, passed orally from one generation to the next, are part of African-American folk history, which stands in contrast to the white version of our national history. Through these characters, Gaines explores the complex relationships among race, memory, and identity. He refuses to ignore or sugar coat the facts of Southern history. Instead, he writes fictional narratives that force readers to remember the past, no matter the pain, in order to find their direction for the future.

Gaines's most important technical achievement is his rendition in fiction of the voice of the oral storyteller. Calling on the resources of African-American vernacular language, he has created a body of literature that continues the realist tradition rather than explores contemporary experimental forms. Gayl Jones notes Gaines's skill in creating not only the voice of a particular storyteller—Miss Jane, for example—but within it, the distinct voices of other characters whose stories the central narrator tells (164). Jones places Gaines among those African-American writers "concerned with the literary potentiality of their linguistic heritage" (163). His technical mastery of narrative voice explores possibilities for freeing African-American literature from European-American counterparts. The African-American roots of Gaines's voice thus parallel his recurring subject of black manhood, a thematic exploration of the African-American journey to independence.

This volume of studies of Gaines's fiction probes into the themes and techniques that scholars have identified as central to his achievement. Moreover, the authors hope to increase readers' familiarity with those works that scholars have generally neglected. To date, *Miss Jane Pittman* has received the most critical attention, and its popularity has drawn attention away from the other books. Furthermore, scholars have, on the whole, tended to write interpretations of individual works in isolation from the rest of his publications. The contributors to this volume, on the other hand, seek to enrich our understanding of individual pieces of fiction by reading them, wherever possible, in comparison to others Gaines has written. Although a few of the chapters are devoted to single books, most explore subjects that reappear in several texts. The authors of this volume also offer readers a variety of approaches to each book. The interpretations sometimes challenge each other as the contributors examine broad topics such as the pastoral mode, the depiction of women and the elderly, film adaptations, and humor.

The authors also take up the matter of assessing Gaines's place among American novelists. Almost every chapter offers comparisons of Gaines to other authors to clarify what is noteworthy in his works. Despite interviewers' expected questions to Gaines about his literary influences, scholars have not yet taken up the challenge of placing his writing in relation to that of others, not only those he has read but also those writing about similar cultural issues. More needs to be said about the relationship of Gaines's South to the "Souths" of Margaret Walker Alexander, William Faulkner, Zora Neale Hurston, and Richard Wright, for example. The contributors hope that by raising questions of intertextuality, they have made this volume one that will elicit further criticism on that point.

It is now thirty years since Gaines published his first novel. In conjunction with the publication of *A Lesson Before Dying* in the spring of 1993, that first book, *Catherine Carmier,* was reissued, making all of Gaines's books available in print. Through the essays in this collection, the authors hope, in part, to demonstrate the importance of approaching Gaines's fiction as a whole rather than commenting on parts of it in isolation. His substantial body of work challenges critics to respond with interpretations of it as a whole—to discern in Gaines's seven separate volumes an ongoing effort to inscribe Louisiana, to evaluate the patterns of inclusion and exclusion in his representation of its history and culture, and to measure his growth in those matters of technique and vision by which we judge writers.

Of Machines and Men:
Pastoralism in Gaines's Fiction

Frank W. Shelton

As Lucinda MacKethan has demonstrated in detail in her study of Southern pastoral literature, *The Dream of Arcady,* Southern writers have often been attracted to the literary mode of the pastoral. The conditions in the South that led to the development of the Southern version of the genre are familiar: "A seemingly simple kind of rural society finds itself being irrevocably set upon a more complex, urban course; it can be seen that in the process much that has always been held to be of spiritual value is being discarded or has already been lost, and in the resulting confusion the cultural aims of the society in question become divided between the pull toward progress and the grip of the past" (9). This dynamic can be applied to much of modern Southern literature. In its simplest form, the pastoral conveys a nostalgia for the past, for the rural, and for contact with the restorative powers of nature, which are contrasted with the more impersonal and more threatening forces of modern urbanism. Thus there can be the simplistic contrast of "good" rural experience and "bad" urban experience. Some Southern writers have not been above using some such formulation, for, as MacKethan has argued, Southern pastoralism is often characterized by the use of "the southern place as a golden agrarian world that is passing or past, always receding farther back into lost time" (4). Certainly the most important Southern writers do not uncritically accept such an idealization of the past or of nature. To their works can be applied Leo Marx's formulation of complex or "literary" pastorals, which, he

observes, "manage to qualify, or call into question, or bring irony to bear against the illusion of peace in a green pasture" (25). Southern black writers, of course, with their determination to emphasize that the Southern past involved slavery and racial discrimination, have found it impossible to associate innocence and purity with the pastoral ideal and have in fact found that ideal to be one of the barriers for many to a true understanding of Southern history. Their commitment to the idea that such elements of the past as racism must not be ignored, as did earlier Southern pastoral writers like Thomas Nelson Page, severely qualifies if not destroys altogether the aura of innocence and virtue the pastoral associates with the Southern past.

Yet many of the works of modern Southern black writers are deeply pastoral in impulse. In 1925 Alain Locke argued that the black writers had an advantage over their white counterparts: black writers could accomplish a return to closeness with nature "not by way of the forced and worn formula of Romanticism, but through the closeness of an imagination that has never broken kinship with nature" (52). The dichotomy between kinship with the Southern land and the oppression blacks experienced on that land informs the black Southern version of pastoral. Black writers have taken various positions with regard to this dichotomy, some completely rejecting pastoralism, others having a more complex attitude toward the mode. Ernest J. Gaines occupies a significant place in that black pastoral tradition. His contribution can be seen most clearly against the background of earlier black writers of the South. The turn-of-the-century writings of Charles Chesnutt provide a savagely ironic commentary on the plantation ideal as it was portrayed by Page and Joel Chandler Harris, but more illustrative of twentieth-century attitudes are the examples of Jean Toomer, Richard Wright and Zora Neale Hurston. In *Cane* Toomer dramatizes the tortured ambiguity of the pastoral ideal. Wright's work embodies an almost complete rejection of the validity of the pastoral, while Hurston's *Their Eyes Were Watching God* presents an overwhelmingly positive version of blacks at work on and in relation to the land. Among contemporary black Southern writers, Gaines provides the most complex and comprehensive adaptation of the pastoral mode to black fiction since Toomer. He vividly dramatizes the negative side of the pastoral, but part of his importance arises from the fact that, rather than completely dismiss the mode, as did Wright, he provides a version including all of its complexities. In his works, as in Toomer's, the Southern plantation is treated with irony and ambiguity. Gaines sees it as a force for entrapment and dehumanization that must be changed, yet paradoxically the plantation is at the same time a source of strength and continuity for his black characters, a point made especially clear in Gaines's contrast of Southern rural and urban experience. Particularly in *A Gathering of Old Men*, he treats pastoralism in its full complexity, but it is an important force in all his works to date, suggesting that this novel is a culmination of earlier work, not a departure from it.

The relationship between the artist and folk materials is especially important. In traditional pastoral works, such as those of Virgil, Spenser, Wordsworth, Keats, or Yeats, it is clear that the authors are self-conscious and educated in a culture and language very different from those of the simple rural folk about whom they write. Jerry Bryant observes, "The ballads of Keats and Yeats are 'art' rather than 'folk' ballads, and the pastorals of Virgil and Spenser reflect what educated, sophisticated men assume to be the simple expressions of country life rather than exact renderings of that life. Gaines bridges the gap between the folk artist and the cultured artist of formal education. He is both" (109). A more traditional pastoral artist, Toomer makes effective art in *Cane* from the inability of the cultured observer to bridge the gap between himself and rural, pastoral life; but Gaines, and perhaps to a lesser degree Hurston, are able to heal that split. Thus Gaines's works, while taking full account of all the evils of plantation life, are finally optimistic in a way that *Cane* is not.

Cane, which Gaines has said is his "favorite novel [*sic*] of any black writer" (Gaudet and Wooton 34), conveys Toomer's vision of the black people's sense of belonging to yet being alienated from the Southern land in the early twentieth century. The organization of the work into three sections clearly dramatizes this perspective. Part 1, set in rural Georgia, poetically captures the delight of a kind of life lived close to the soil, evoking the pine, the cane, the nurturing power of nature. Yet even in the first part ambiguity appears, for the way of life Toomer depicts is already passing. This change is presaged, for example, in the poem "Song of the Son:"

> In time, for though the sun is setting on
> A song-lit race of slaves, it has not set;

Though late, O soil, it is not too late yet
To catch thy plaintive soul, leaving, soon gone,
Leaving, to catch thy plaintive soul soon gone. (12)

Even in his reverence for the soil and a rural way of life, Toomer cannot ignore the fact that such a way of life is fading. In addition, he emphasizes another complicating factor—the presence of white racism and the accompanying violence and oppression. Part 2 is set in the urban areas of Washington and Chicago, cities where blacks moved to escape the oppression in the South. Those cities represent the mechanizing forces that are destroying the rural way of life, and the blacks who went there for greater opportunities become cut off from the land and lead sterile, meaningless lives. Part 3 brings the two forces together as Ralph Kabnis, an urban man, returns to Georgia. Toomer here dramatizes the issue of whether any reconciliation can be achieved between the urban and the rural. If one focuses simply on the character of Kabnis, it seems clear that no such accommodation can occur. For while Kabnis is very conscious of the emptiness of his own life and senses that sustenance can be found in rural Georgia life, he is unable (and unwilling) to open himself to it. Toomer describes him as "a promise of a soil-soaked beauty; uprooted, thinning out. Suspended a few feet above the soil whose touch would resurrect him" (96). Further, the racism and violence so prevalent in Part 1, especially in "Blood-Burning Moon," are emphasized again, and Kabnis is paralyzed by fear. His alienation from rural life results in spiritual emptiness, and there seems to be no possibility of resurrection for him. However, the book ends with a sunrise, the very symbol of resurrection: "Outside, the sun arises from its cradle in the tree-tops of the forest. Shadows of pines are dreams the sun shakes from its eyes. The sun arises. Gold-glowing child, it steps into the sky and sends a birth-song slanting down gray dust streets and sleepy windows of the southern town" (116). There has been much speculation concerning the meaning of this image, for it embodies a hope that the story itself seems not to validate. Whatever hope one finds exists in the aesthetic realm, in the artistry of the writing, not in the characters or their actions. In this regard Gaines represents a hopeful development from Toomer, for the resolution of *A Gathering* occurs on both levels—that of action and that of art. MacKethan accurately describes Toomer's dilemma in *Cane:* "How to resolve productively his sense of the richness of the black man's heritage in the South with his knowledge that the black man's fate was now inextricably linked to a modern world that was sterile and inhumane" (127). While Toomer was not able to solve the problem either in his art or his life, as Gaines has been able to do, Toomer's great achievement has been to make compelling and complex literature about the problem.

An examination of the pastoral work of the later Hurston and Wright will demonstrate how Toomer's comprehensive vision in *Cane* was divided in two, with each of the later writers emphasizing one of the two aspects Toomer brought together so effectively. In a fruitful comparison of the way that Hurston and Wright responded to the drama of modern times, Werner Sollors observes that "Hurston's and Wright's styles and attitudes toward their materials were dramatically different. Wright stresses the psychological and social dimensions of racial oppression and interracial conflict, whereas Hurston describes the *style* of folk, folkways, and foodways, and tries to capture specific characteristics of black language that she recorded in black communities" (129). Calling Wright's approach essentially sociological and Hurston's anthropological, Sollors provides a balanced appreciation of the works of both writers. On the other hand, in a recent attack on Hurston, Hazel V. Carby praises Wright at the expense of Hurston. She claims that "Hurston's representation of the folk is not only a discursive displacement of the historical and cultural transformation of migration [from the rural to the urban], but also is a creation of a folk who are outside of history" ("Politics" 77). Carby sees Hurston avoiding the history, change, and conflict that inform Wright's work. The purpose of this present essay is, like that of Sollors, to understand the works of the authors rather than to make any value judgment on their fiction.

In *Their Eyes* Hurston tends to downplay the debilitating side of rural life in her emphasis on the positive, nurturing aspects of black life in the South, while *Uncle Tom's Children*, Wright's most deeply pastoral work, does the opposite—stressing the negative while seeming to ignore the positive. This is not to argue that Toomer's work is better than theirs or that one of them is better than the other, but to suggest that between the publication of *Cane* and the works of Gaines and other present writers little attempt was made to provide a multifaceted picture of black rural life. One of the reasons *Their Eyes* is such a celebratory pastoral work is that Hurston almost entirely excludes the threatening white presence in the novel (the impact of white racism is seen only tangentially and only near the end of the novel). Yet characters are included who do offer a threat to the richness of pastoral life. One is Logan Killicks, Janie's first husband. Totally insensitive to her as a person, he wants Janie to work with him in the fields and to function as "the mule of the world." Hurston includes here some acknowledgment of the drudgery of rural work, but it is quickly dismissed from the novel when Janie runs off with the more appealing Joe Starks, a city man. He becomes mayor and principal landowner in the town of Eatonville. Although he removes Janie from the fields and offers her a more pleasant life, she is little more than an ornament to his store, and she remains cut off from the vitality of black life. Finally, Tea Cake Woods provides the kind of life which fulfills her. Rejecting town life, she sells the store and moves with him to the "muck," a rich agricultural area in the Everglades. She puts away her dresses and wears overalls; most revealingly of all, she works in the fields of her own will, to be near Tea Cake.

> So the very next morning Janie got ready to pick beans along with Tea Cake. There was a suppressed murmur when she picked up a basket and went to work. She was already getting to be a special case on the muck. It was generally assumed that she thought herself too good to work like the rest of the women and that Tea Cake "pomped her up tuh dat." But all day long the romping and playing they carried on behind the boss's back made her popular right away. It got the whole field to playing off and on. (127)

In the right circumstances work can become play. From a certain point of view Janie has lowered herself socially by moving from town to farm and from store to field, but she finds personal wholeness through work in the fields and through acceptance in the rural community surrounding those fields. *Their Eyes* celebrates the health and spirit of rural black folk, whose culture is inextricably linked with the land. Thus Hurston's novel builds on Toomer's evocation of the positive aspects of the pastoral while slighting the negative.

In *Uncle Tom's Children,* Wright's perspective practically reverses Hurston's. Though he does acknowledge the appeal of the land, the presence of white society completely destroys any possibility that blacks might receive sustenance from rural life. The book presents an unrelenting picture of the bleakness and barrenness of black life. The introductory essay in the volume, "The Ethics of Living Jim Crow," opens with a scene implying the terms by which the pastoral elements in the stories are to be read. Wright describes where his family lived in Arkansas: "Our house stood behind the railroad tracks. Its skimpy yard was paved with black cinders. Nothing green ever grew in that yard. The only touch of green we could see was far away, beyond the tracks, over where the white folks lived. But cinders were good enough for me and I never missed the green growing things" (3). Actually, he even liked the cinders because they were good weapons for the war games he played with his friends. But one day he realized their disadvantage when his gang got into a fight with the white boys. Not only did the whites use broken bottles, one of which hit him on the head, but "they hid behind trees, hedges, and the sloping embankments of their lawns," fortifications the blacks did not have. Wright ends the episode: "From that time on, the charm of my cinder yard was gone. The green trees, the trimmed hedges, the cropped lawns grew very meaningful, became a symbol. Even today when I think of white folks, the hard, sharp outlines of white houses surrounded by trees, lawns, and hedges are present somewhere in the background of my mind. Through the years they grew into an overreaching symbol of fear" (5). Though it occurs in a town rather than in the country, this experience is significant in that whites, not blacks, are associated with nature and growing things. Wright's exposure to violence and racism leads him psychologically to associate nature with whites and the fear they engender in him. The stories that follow the introductory essay take place in rural or small-town Mississippi, and they all suggest that, despite the fact that blacks long for a closeness to the soil, the presence of whites ruins rural life for them. "Big Boy Leaves Home" begins with several pages describing Big Boy and his friends playing at a swimming hole. It is off-limits to blacks, however, and the innocent peace and joy of the scene are destroyed by the appearance of a white couple. The white man is killed, and Big Boy must flee to the North, leaving behind all that had given meaning to his life. "Fire and Cloud" concerns a black lay preacher caught between radicals desiring to change race relations in the South and conservatives cautioning the people to go slowly out of fear of the repercussions from pushing for too much change. The heavy-handed brutality of the whites finally forces

Taylor to ally himself with the radicals, but early in the story he muses over his past life when things had seemed simple and clearcut.

> Yes, there had been something in those good old days when he had walked behind his plow, between the broad green earth and a blue sweep of sunlit sky; there had been in it all a surge of will, clean, full, joyful; the earth was his and he was the earth's; they were one. . . . Lawd, we could make them ol fields bloom ergin. We could make em feed us. Thas whut Gawd put em there fer. Plows could break and hoes could chop and hands could pick and arms could carry. . . . On and on that could happen and people could eat and feel as he had felt with the plow handles trembling in his hands, following old Bess, hearing the earth cracking and breaking because he wanted it to crack and break; because he willed it, because the earth was his. And they could sing as he had sung when he and May were first married; sing about picking cotton, fishing, hunting, about sun and rain. They could. . . . But whuts the usa thinkin erbout stuff like this? Its [*sic*] all gone now. (132)

Since the way of life Taylor remembers is itself contaminated by racism, to some degree his memory of the peace of his past is self-deluding. Yet the crucial point is that the actions of whites have destroyed the possibility for blacks of living in any kind of harmony with nature. Wright feels that blacks and whites *should* be able to live at peace with one another and with the land. As Sarah thinks in "Long Black Song," "Somehow, men, black men and white men, land and houses, green cornfields and grey skies, gladness and dreams, were all a part of that which made life good. Yes, somehow, they were linked, like the spokes in a spinning wheel." Yet violence destroys the unity. "Yes, killing of white men by black men and killing of black men by white men went on in spite of the hope of white bright days and the desire of dark black nights and the long gladness of green cornfields in summer and the deep dream of sleepy grey skies in winter. And when killing started it went on, like a river flowing" (126). Thus, while the pastoral dream of a life in harmony with nature and other people is alive in the consciousness of the characters, the violence rampant on the Southern landscape leads to the bleakness of Southern black existence.

Gaines began publishing his fiction in the 1960s, when the civil rights movement was in full force. At this time of change, Gaines began to make a comprehensive assessment of black life and history in the South.

His fiction redresses the balance in the pastoral by including both the negative aspects stressed in the fiction of Wright and the positive elements Hurston emphasized in *Their Eyes*.

Anyone familiar with Gaines's career is aware of his deep and abiding love for Louisiana. Early on, he spent most of his time in San Francisco, returning to Louisiana only for yearly visits; but since 1983 he has taught at the University of Southwestern Louisiana, returning to San Francisco for just part of the year. He clearly feels a profound connection with the Louisiana landscape. In a talk at Southern University in 1971, he described the primary reason he began writing fiction: "I wanted to smell that Louisiana earth, feel that Louisiana sun, sit under the shade of one of those Louisiana oaks, search for pecans in the Louisiana grass in one of those Louisiana yards next to one of those Louisiana bayous, not far from a Louisiana river" (Gaines, "Miss Jane and I" 28). Thus he commenced his career with a strong sense of place, and when asked whether he ever had difficulty writing about Louisiana while living in California, he responded: "If I wrote about the oil wells popping in Louisiana right now, maybe it'd be better if I were in Louisiana. But if I'm writing about something that happened forty years ago, I can face the wall in San Francisco and see it as well or better than I would if I sat in an apartment or a house in Louisiana and looked out at oil wells; they would distract me. Looking at the blank wall, I can see any kind of world I want to see there" (Doyle, "*MELUS* Interview" 62). The terms in which Gaines frames this answer suggest that he does not want to be distracted by manifestations of the present, the New South, for his interest is in the pastoral, agrarian world of the plantation past, which he can see most clearly—and perhaps only—in his imagination.

Gaines has described repeatedly how he came to write the kind of novels he has produced. When he became interested in writing, he read the work of anyone he could find who wrote about the earth and the peasantry. The names of nineteenth-century Russians, especially Turgenev and Tolstoy, as well as Americans Faulkner, Cather, and Steinbeck frequently appear in his conversation, but he rarely mentions earlier black writers. Finding no one who he felt wrote accurately about his own people and land, blacks from mid-twentieth-century Louisiana, he decided to fill the void himself. As a result, his fiction is saturated with the pastoral impulse, a reverence for nature, the land and the people who live on it. In fact, the health of the characters in Gaines's fiction can often be gauged by the degree to which they live in tune with the natural rhythms of the earth.

The dynamic of the pastoral form most typically involves a simple rural society beset by forces of change normally associated with urban society and its values, and Gaines's primary theme is the social and personal change resulting from this conflict. According to Gaines's version of Southern history, early in the twentieth century the traditional plantation way of life was transformed forever when the owners, weak in character themselves, began parceling out their land to the Cajuns, pushing the blacks who had previously sharecropped the land off the most fertile areas and finally off the land altogether. Originally poor whites, Gaines's Cajuns are rapacious and Snopes-like in their attempt to possess all the land for themselves. In the light of pastoralism, it is suggestive that Gaines associates them with the tractor, which has become for him the "machine in the garden." While Gaines certainly feels that social change is necessary, such mechanization of agriculture is portrayed as dehumanizing, and it does not bring with it improvement in the lot of his black characters. In fact, the whites' devotion to machines and technology is associated with the compulsion to own and manipulate and with an insensitivity to the natural rhythms of life. Miss Jane Pittman alludes to white society's need to control nature by building levees: "The damage from that high water was caused by man, because man wanted to control the rivers, and you cannot control water. The old people, the Indians, used to worship the rivers till the white people came here and conquered them and tried to conquer the rivers, too" (147). Miss Jane sees nature as sacred, going so far as to talk to a revered oak tree: "It's not necessary craziness when you talk to trees and rivers. . . . But when you talk to an oak tree that's been here all these years, and knows more than you'll ever know, it's not craziness; it's just the nobility you respect" (148). As Jack Hicks observes, "In Jane's mind, blacks and Indians have natural totems, sacred phenomena with which they can commune. For the earliest Americans, it was the river; for the blacks following them, the oak tree. But the white man—first seen with the arrival of the French—is fated to be the levee, the human version of the concrete spillways that possess the rivers and cut man off from the sources of life" (*Singer's Temple* 129). Such a desire to possess and control nature is sacrilegious and doomed to failure, but it is just such an impulse that characterizes the white frame of mind and results in the whites' alienation from the natural sources of human existence.

Whites are not the only characters associated with machines, urbanism, and the inorganic; a number of blacks are as well. In "Just Like a Tree," for instance, there is James, the city-bred son-in-law of Aunt Fe who plans to take her to a Northern city to live. He feels nothing but contempt for what he considers to be the backward ways of the country folk he meets. In the course of the story he gets drunk and loses consciousness. He is blind and completely insensitive to the communal experience which the story portrays. In "A Long Day in November," Eddie Howard neglects his family in favor of his automobile and the freedom it gives him to roam at night. He affirms his manhood and is accepted back into the community only when he burns that car, another manifestation of a technology which has invaded a rural setting. There is also the young man who accompanies Jimmy Aaron on his return to the plantation to attempt to organize the old blacks in *The Autobiography of Miss Jane Pittman*, a man who tries to dress appropriately for the quarters but who clearly looks out of place. Every time he opens his mouth, he reveals a lack of understanding of country people and rural ways. At one point he patronizingly extols the virtue of what he calls "good country lemonade" but most often uses, in Jane's contemptuous and dismissive term, "retrick" when he speaks (228, 230). Such characters as these are ridiculed because they do not understand and value rural life or people.

In *Catherine Carmier*, Gaines deals most extensively with a black character alienated from the rural ways. In this first novel, he seems to be working out his own sense of yearning toward rural Louisiana life while feeling cut off from it because of the years he has spent in San Francisco. Jackson Bradley's perspective here closely resembles Kabnis's in *Cane*. Educated, sophisticated, and rational, Jackson, upon his return to Louisiana from San Francisco, does not feel a part of the place where he grew up and the people who raised him. He suggestively uses natural images to describe his own sense of alienation and sterility. At one point he comments, "I'm like a leaf, Madame Bayonne, that's broken away from the tree. Drifting" (79). Later he looks out into a garden: "Just look at this place. Everything is drying up; everything is half dead. . . . Am I any better off? I'm in the same class . . . dry, dead" (102). Feeling no connection to the South, Jackson wants to take Catherine away from the region, but he can think of no place to take her. Thus the theme of the novel is isolation and paralysis, and the novel is a "declining pastoral," in the view of Valerie Babb (45–60).

Despite the fact that *In My Father's House* is set some ten or fifteen years later, during the civil rights movement, the condition of Philip Martin, the civil rights leader, is similar. Set in St. Adrienne, a suburb of Baton Rouge, this is Gaines's only novel to take place primarily in a town, and Martin's essential problem is his separation from his past and his rural roots. At one point, driven by an obscure need, he visits his godmother in the country but is unable to speak to her openly about his problems. Gaines vividly evokes the hellishness of urbanism both by his description of the life Martin's common-law wife and their children lead in San Francisco, which has helped to destroy them, and by Martin's night journey into the underworld of South Baton Rouge in search of the truth about his past. The association of characters with urbanism and technology reflects their alienation from the nurturing sources of life.

Yet another aspect of Gaines's treatment of the city, one which suggests the complexity of his vision, is evident in *Of Love and Dust*. In this work the most courageous and perhaps most admirable character is Marcus Payne, a city man from Baton Rouge, alien to the plantation to which he has been bonded instead of standing trial and serving a prison term for murder. He refuses to adjust to his new surroundings, going so far as to wear his city shoes and clothes when forced to work in the fields. Stubborn, totally self-centered, violent, and rebellious, he resists the forces of the rural past represented by the plantation and brings a more urban, contemporary perspective to the country setting. As Gaines does in portions of *Miss Jane Pittman* and *A Gathering,* he here suggests that rural existence has inculcated a deadly passivity by which blacks allow themselves to be exploited. The most complex and interesting character in *Of Love and Dust* is the narrator, Jim Kelly, who is positioned between the rural and urban. His woman earlier left him because he had neither the money nor the desire to live the fast life in New Orleans. But he works with tractors; in fact, he owes the trust whites place in him and his responsible position on the plantation to his knowledge of machinery. While he reveres the old blacks, the repositories of the memory of the black community, until Marcus arrives he seems more closely allied to the mechanistic forces of oppression. One of his jobs is to drive the tractor with which field workers, on foot, must keep up, thus forcing them to pitch corn "like two machines" (227). In essence he helps perpetuate the monotony and brutality of field labor and the racist system of which it is a part. Through the influence of Marcus, however, Jim too becomes more rebellious, leaving the plantation at the end and refusing to accept Marshall's letter of recommendation.

> "It's only a recommendation," he [Marshall] said. "Telling people that you're a good worker."
> After I had read the letter, I folded it neatly and put it back in the envelope. Then I laid the envelope on the desk.
> "You don't want it?" he said, getting red in the face.
> "No sir, I'll get by," I said. "Thanks very much." (278)

Jim has come to realize that work with machines leads to oppression and dehumanization, while the rebellion of the urban character Marcus leads to death.

Gaines does not romanticize rural life in his novels, as do numerous other (most often white) Southern pastoralists. He constantly emphasizes how backbreaking work in the fields is and how oppression can drain both body and spirit. The paralysis of spirit induced by slavery and racism is eloquently described by Philip Martin in *In My Father's House* when he tries to explain to his son why he abandoned him and his first family:

> I couldn't bit more leave that room, that woman I didn't care nothing in the world for, than I can right now carry this car here on my back. I was paralyzed. Paralyzed. Yes, I had a mouth, but I didn't have a voice. I had legs, but I couldn't move. I had arms, but I couldn't lift them up to you. It took a man to do these things, and I wasn't a man. I was just some other brutish animal who could cheat, steal, rob, kill—but not stand. Not be responsible. Not protect you or your mother. They had branded that in us from the time of slavery. That's what kept me on that bed. Not 'cause I didn't want to get up. I wanted to get up more than anything in the world. But I had to break the rules, rules we had lived by for so long, and I wasn't strong enough to break them then. (85–86)

Despite the fact that Martin has raised himself through his own efforts, he remains cut off from the sustaining elements of a rural community. Like Jackson Bradley, he is left paralyzed and confused at the end of the novel.

Not all of Gaines's characters, however, suffer that fate. Through a close relationship with the land and nature, which is the result of labor, and through the communal life the field workers lead, many of his rural black characters develop a sense of belonging which his more urban and perhaps more materially prosperous characters such as Martin lack. Miss Jane Pittman is not the only one of Gaines's characters associated with a tree; so is Aunt Fe in "Just Like a Tree." In that story Aunt Clo compares moving Aunt Fe up North to uprooting a tree from the ground. After much jerking, the tractor finally dislodges the tree. Aunt Clo declares, however, that "you never get the taproot. But, sir, I tell you what you do get. You get a big hole in the ground, sir; and you get another big hole in the air where the lovely branches been all these years. . . . Two holes, sir, you can't never fill no matter how hard you try" (236). Although Aunt Fe may at first appear to be a stereotypical black mammy who cannot live outside the idyllic world of the South, she possesses an admirable strength that derives from her relationship with nature; and when she is forced to move, both she and the community are bereft, having lost an important sustaining element.

In Ned's sermon at the river in *Miss Jane Pittman,* he also argues that the strength of his people comes through their work on and association with the land, a point Jimmy Aaron echoes when he returns to the plantation during the 1960s. Ned declares to his assembled congregation: "This earth is yours and don't let that man out there take it from you. It's yours because your people's bones lays in it; it's yours because their sweat and their blood done drenched this earth. . . . Your people's bones and their dust make this place yours more than anything else" (107). Despite using the word *yours,* Ned repudiates the white man's tendency to try to own the land: "You don't own this earth, you're just here for a little while, but while you're here don't let no man tell you the best is for him and you take the scrap. No, your people plowed this earth, your people chopped down the trees, your people built the roads and built the levees" (108). Through such labor, blacks have established a relationship with the land transcending legal ownership. Ned seems to be suggesting a distinction between legal ownership and a moral right to possession through labor. The white man's desire for legal ownership reveals his own alienation from and lack of understanding of the land and people. To Gaines, as to Ike McCaslin in Faulkner's deeply pastoral "The Bear," ownership of the land is a crime against nature, and ownership of people is a crime against humanity.

The character of Miss Jane Pittman is Gaines's profoundest portrayal of the moral strength a legally dispossessed people can develop in a pastoral setting. His next novel, *In My Father's House,* is his most bleak since *Catherine Carmier,* in part for the very reason that the protagonist has become a suburban man with no continuing connection to the land of his upbringing. In *A Gathering,* however, Gaines returns to the rural. The novel is his most contemporary in time setting, taking place in the late 1970s, and the landscape is certainly not attractive. The quarters appear empty; the land is dying; nothing seems left in the locale to nourish the human spirit. The Cajun Boutans and their tractors seem to dominate the landscape and the lives of the people, suggesting that the mechanized and indifferent New South has once and for all gained ascendance. Yet this apparently unpromising setting is the very context in which Gaines celebrates the heroism of his old men. Cowards their entire lives, they all defy the sheriff and the Boutans in an attempt to assume the blame for the murder of Beau Boutan. At the same time they assert their manhood in order to compensate for past cowardice, they also protest the destruction of the land and their way of life.

Several of the old men explain their actions in pastoral terms, specifically designating the tractor as the enemy. Johnny Paul, who provides the fullest explanation, does not deny the difficulty of their past lives.

> Sunup to sundown, hard, miserable work, but we managed to get it done. We stuck together, shared what little we had, and loved and respected each other. . . . I did it [killed Beau Boutan] for them back there under them trees. I did it 'cause that tractor is getting closer and closer to that grave- yard, and I was scared if I didn't do it, one day that tractor was go'n come in there and plow up them graves, getting rid of all proof that we ever was. Like now they trying to get rid of all proof that black people ever farmed this land with plows and mules—like if they had nothing from the starten but motor machines. (91–92)

Tucker next tells the story of his brother Silas, the last black man to try to sharecrop on the place and fight the Cajuns' tractors. In a John Henry-like contest pitting Silas and his plow against the white man's tractor, Silas won but was then beaten to death by enraged whites, while Tucker just watched. Then Yank, a former horse breaker, confesses to the murder of Beau because the tractors have eliminated the need for horses, thus leaving him directionless. All these men, and the people for whom they speak in the novel, mourn the loss of a pastoral way of life and attempt to defend its memory. The paradox, emphasized here and throughout the body of Gaines's work, is that this way of life is in central ways responsible for their cowardice. The difficulty of the labor, the reduced circumstances of their lives, and the very denial of their humanity involved in the tradition of discrimination with which they have lived have encouraged them to acquiesce and not rebel. At the same time, however, when they do rebel, it is in the name of that way of life which, while oppressive, has yet taught them that what is important is the strength of a people who band together.

That strength is additionally manifested in the character of Charlie, who actually killed Beau Boutan. He can be seen as an updating of Wright's Big Boy. While Charlie's initial impulse is to flee, as Big Boy did, and let someone else take the blame for him, he finally comes out of hiding to accept the responsibility for his actions and the consequences of them, thus earning the right to be called Mr. Biggs by the sheriff. The full complexity of Gaines's pastoral vision is evident in this novel. He shows that change has come, that in fact it had to come, and that in important ways it is a positive force. After all, the Boutans do not take the law into their own hands and try to lynch the blacks, as they had often done in the past. The presence of "Salt and Pepper" (Gil Boutan and his black teammate Calvin Harrison) in the same backfield on the LSU football team and their interdependence are further indications of that change. The South has changed as a result of the very self-assertion the black men manifest in the novel. Concurrently, however, something of great importance is being lost through the change, and the novel becomes an elegy for a disappearing rural way of life that the old men are trying to preserve in memory and that Gaines is trying to preserve in his fiction. Indeed, the extremely strong pastoral element in *A Gathering* may arise from Gaines's growing sense that the way of life he has devoted all his writing career to describing has almost entirely disappeared.

In considering why contemporary Southern writers do not seem as interested in the pastoral mode as earlier writers were, MacKethan makes the familiar point that the South is losing that land-based sense of community and tradition which has nurtured its residents and writers for so long. She observes, "The emphasis has shifted from the portrayal of characters within a compelling social system to an interest in what happens when people have no meaningful relation to a tradition or community, when traditions and communities in fact no longer provide any stimulus for the establishment of human bonds" (215). MacKethan makes the error here critics frequently make—identifying Southern literature wholly with white writers. Her observation certainly does apply to many recent writers, like Walker Percy and Bobbie Ann Mason and Harry Crews. It is, however, much less applicable to contemporary black writers like Gaines and Alice Walker, who are representative of the many black writers who have been looking with renewed interest to the traditions of black people for the very human bonds which sustain life.

In fact, Walker, who has long acknowledged her debt to and affection for Hurston and Toomer, exhibits a number of similarities to Gaines; together they illustrate the vitality of the pastoral mode for contemporary black writers. Early in her career, in an essay initially published in 1970, Walker praised the richness of her Southern background.

> There is a great deal of positive material I can draw from my "underprivileged" background. . . . In the cities it cannot be so clear to one that he is a creature of the earth, feeling the soil between the toes, smelling the dust thrown up by the rain, loving the earth so much that one longs to taste it and sometimes does. . . . No one could wish for a more advantageous heritage than that bequeathed to the black writer in the South: a compassion for the earth, a trust in humanity beyond our knowledge of evil, and an abiding love of justice. (20–21)

By no means does Walker romanticize rural black life in her fiction, for her black characters are often poor and violent. *The Third Life of Grange Copeland* makes manifest the destructiveness of the sharecropping system and, along with *The Color Purple,* vividly dramatizes the mistreatment of blacks by other blacks engendered by the Southern way of life. In fact, Albert, Celie's husband in *The Color Purple,* is particularly reminiscent of Logan Killicks of *Their Eyes.* Yet Grange Copeland must return South from the urban and impersonal North to work out his salvation, having found the North an even more dehumanizing place than his homeland. And while Celie does not travel widely, going no further than the city of Memphis, she too returns at the end of *The Color Purple* to be reunited with her sister Nettie in a rural community in the South. In light of the works of not only Walker and Gaines but such other recent black novelists as Toni Morrison, Sherley Anne Williams, and David Bradley, it seems clear that, for many current black writers

(Southern and non-Southern alike), unlike white Southern writers, the meaning of life is to be found through forging a personal connection with Southern history, a history that involves enslavement, prejudice, and racism but nevertheless strengthens individuals through offering them a relationship with the land and a place in a community of people nurtured by a pastoral environment.

In Gaines's world in particular, blacks must feel close to the soil both to establish past meaning and to survive in the present. His characters gain self-definition only through association with nature and membership in a community. The pastoral mode, with its emphasis on a rural life that is almost always in the past, is employed by writers to reflect upon the complexities of the present time and place in which they actually live. While progress has come to the South of Gaines's fiction—has in fact come because of the laudable efforts of some of his characters like Marcus Payne, Jane Pittman, Ned Pittman, and Philip Martin— Gaines suggests that if progress eventuates only in the mechanical domination and eventual destruction of the land, the all-important human dimension will be lost. The most successful of his characters are those who revere the land and the past way of life that was rooted in it yet find a way to live in the present. In *A Gathering* the rural community of the quarters is passing, but it remains vital in the memory of the old people themselves. It is perhaps a historical necessity that such places fade away, but all blacks, and all humans, will be poorer if memory of those communities is not preserved. Gaines's goal as a novelist is that of Toomer and Hurston: to commemorate in art the value of such a rural way of life. Unlike most contemporary white Southern writers but like a number of other black writers, he continues meaningfully to integrate past and present through his adaptation of the pastoral form.

Creole and Singaleese: Disruptive Caste in *Catherine Carmier* and *A Gathering of Old Men*

Joseph Griffin

In the work of Ernest J. Gaines the question of social status is a sine qua non: the hierarchical system within which the fiction is set, in which the dominant white race considers itself superior to the black, is itself a matter of social status. Gaines has a pervasive concern with the stratification of groups within white Louisiana society, specifically the subordination of Cajuns by the wealthy whites of French or Anglo-Saxon origin who own the land and maintain the racial code of the South. And his preoccupation with the question of social status and perceived superiority extends to his depiction of the African-American community as well. Sometimes this portrayal of status-conscious African Americans is humorous. In the short story "Just Like a Tree," collected in *Bloodline,* the northern city slicker and hip-talking character James has come south to rescue his wife's Aunt Fe during the troubles of the 1960s. At the farewell party for her he cannot abide the "primitive cats" among whom he finds himself and is bent on "show[ing] these country niggers how to have a good time" (230), but not long into the evening he has to be put to bed, laid low by an excess of his bottled Mr. Harper. Most often, however, Gaines uses African-American characters who assume a superiority over their fellows, and situations that arise from such portrayals, to more serious purpose.

In two novels, Gaines's first, *Catherine Carmier,* and the more recent, *A Gathering of Old Men,* the question of social status within the African-American community takes on a salient role in defining the problems of life in St. Raphael Parish, that little postage stamp of Louisiana ground of which Gaines may be said to be sole owner and proprietor.[1] In *Catherine Carmier,* the Creole man Raoul Carmier attempts to assert his superiority over the other African Americans living on Grover plantation by isolating himself completely from them and carrying on a one-man vendetta against his white oppressors. In *A Gathering,* the octogenarian Singaleese man Mathu has snubbed the other blacks both on and away from the Marshall plantation on the basis of pride in his pure African blood. The two characters pit themselves against other African Americans because they harbor feelings of superiority based on bloodline, which manifests itself in the color of their skin. But they ultimately see the fallacy of their attempts to maintain a class superiority that disrupts both the familial order and the larger social order as well.

Gaines's use of these two types of status-conscious African Americans is not limited to the two novels in question. Creole characters are omnipresent in the fiction, sometimes referred to as such and other times by the generic term *mulatto.* The term *Singaleese* comes up less frequently, though we may assume that at times the type does occur without being named. Fortunately, there are in *The Autobiography of Miss Jane Pittman* well defined examples of both Creole and Singaleese people, which help to fix their identity and social significance in the essentially rural Louisiana society of which Gaines writes. In *Miss Jane Pittman,* Creoles and Singaleese act as disruptive forces within the black community— as that community has been traditionally defined by the white establishment—in much the same way as they do in *Catherine Carmier* and *A Gathering,* although their presence and influence are not nearly so pervasive as in the latter two novels.

The term *Creole* is a "complex one," Valerie Babb reminds us: It "has been used as a classifier of many things, from race to culture, from language to cuisine. It has variously referred to diverse social, political, cultural, and economic groups as well. In Louisiana it has denoted whites of Spanish, French, or Italian descent who settled in Louisiana, as well as the descendants of European slaveholders and African slaves who upon manumission were known as *gens de couleur libre,* free people of color" (47). Gaines uses the term *Creole* to designate the latter group, "who emerged as a third class within a three-tiered society of free persons, free persons of color, and slaves," Babb continues.[2] In *Miss Jane Pittman,* in the seventh chapter, "The LeFabre Family," of book 3, Jane refers to the

Creoles of St. Raphael Parish, who live in a community called Creole Place, where they lead their own lives, independent of black and white alike, own their farms, and have their own Catholic church and school. Jane recalls that "no matter how white you was if you didn't have Creole background they didn't want you there" (159). Interlopers are referred to as "common niggers" (160) by Creole Place residents.[3]

The LeFabre family has come to Creole Place from New Orleans: Mary Agnes LeFabre, the schoolteacher at the Samson quarters—described as "one of them high yellow from New Orleans almost white" (168)—is the granddaughter of "one of those ladies for white men" (158), a product, in other words, of the placage institution, a part of antebellum New Orleans culture. Her motive for going to Samson to teach school is to try to make up for "what her own people had done her own people": when her grandfather LeFabre died he left his paramour and children "money and property—even slaves" (158). Mary Agnes's resolution and commitment are impressive, yet her life at Samson is marked by her typical Creole aloofness from the people among whom she works. She spends weekends in New Orleans away from the quarters since she has been barred from Creole Place; she discourages the interest of the males. And the harshness of Joe Simon's remarks about her at the time of her suspected rape by Tee Bob—"If he hadn't done it, somebody else had to do it. Playing like she Miss high-class" (179)—are testimony to how deeply the community resents her aloofness. For all her desire to help "her own people," she rejects them, unwilling and/or unable to acknowledge her racial and human kinship with them, and knowing full well that the Southern code will allow her no place in white society.

Singaleese (or Miss Jane's version of it, *Singalee*) is not nearly so frequently a racial designation as *Creole* in Gaines's fiction. Although there are no references to the etymology of the word in any of his novels, it seems clear that it is a local pronunciation of *Senegalese,* that is, a native of Senegal, the West African territory bordering on the Atlantic Ocean from which slaves were brought to America. Certainly there is no doubt as to what physical type of African American Gaines is referring when he applies the term. The Singaleese reference in *Miss Jane Pittman* is also in book 3, in the opening chapter, "Samson." Here Jane recalls a fieldworker: "Her name was Harriet Black, but she was so black (she was one of them Singalee people) and the people called her Black Harriet. She didn't have all her faculties, but still she was queen of the field. She was tall, straight, tough, and blue-black" (131). In the incident Jane describes, Harriet engages in a weed-picking race with Katie Nelson, "a little tight-butt woman from Bayonne" (131). Katie resents Harriet's speed and efficiency as a picker, her queenliness, her aloofness. And although Jane does not openly admit it (so tragic is the outcome of the race for Harriet), the other fieldworkers share Katie's resentment, encouraging her to better Harriet in the contest. Though Jane is and was appalled at the attack on Black Harriet by Tom Joe, the overseer, and though some of the other women throw themselves in the path of his blows, one senses the community's resentment for the tall, jet-black woman who works by herself and mutters and sings in the "Singalee tongue."

Neither the very brief Harriet Black episode nor the longer Mary Agnes LeFabre story assumes a pervasive role in the epic and kaleido-scopic narrative of Jane Pittman. But they serve as miniature versions of Gaines's extended examinations in *Catherine Carmier* and *A Gathering* of status-generated conflicts within the African-American community of St. Raphael Parish. In the former novel, the elder Carmier genera-tions, like Mary Agnes LeFabre, assume a superiority over their black neighbors based on their patrician New Orleans roots and the light color of their skin. In the latter, Mathu, like Black Harriet, separates himself from his fellows by virtue of the "blue-black" skin that identifies him as pure African. One has the sense, viewing the fiction in the context of these comparable characters, that Gaines has created not merely a number of satisfying novels but also a saga in the Faulknerian mold, a composite picture of a society spanning several generations, the parts of which enlighten the whole as they do each other.

When Robert, the grandfather of the title character of *Catherine Car-mier,* takes up residence with his family in the abandoned big house on the Grover plantation, we are not given any indication of the location of his former home, but we assume he has come from Creole Place or a similar community. In any case, he effectively makes his new home a place for Creoles only, and his son Raoul maintains that tradition. The descriptions of the Carmier home reflect its separation, both literally and figuratively. It is located on the fringe of the quarters, removed from them. To enter the Carmier property, one must cross a small bridge, then open and close the gate—a ritual its dwellers scrupulously follow. When Jackson Bradley looks out from his Aunt Charlotte's cabin across the road, "he could hardly see the house for the trees in the yard. . . . Regardless of how bright the sun was shining, the big trees . . . always kept the yard and the house in semidarkness" (30). Lillian, approaching her father's house, is aware of the "half-dozen or more trees—pecan and oak—[that] went from the fence to the house, from front to back. Gray Spanish moss hung from most of the trees all the way to the ground" (42). For Jackson the trees eventually take on the function of "sentinels" (190), guarding against the intrusion of the common blacks and hence frustrating his liaison with Catherine.

The ground rules for the relationship between the Carmiers and the black community in the quarters are established the day Robert moves his family into the house at the Grover plantation—and it is Robert who establishes them. When the bridge breaks in half and his wagon goes into the ditch, he refuses the help of willing hands, and it is soon learned in the quarters that the Carmiers "had little use for dark-skin people" (12). Not only does Raoul perpetuate this attitude of superiority at Grover, but also, as Lillian remarks, "it's the same thing his sisters are trying to prove in the city" (40). Lillian's contentions are shown to be true in the efforts of her Aunt Elvira in Bayonne to encourage a permanent relationship between Raoul and the Creole Bertha Tavaras and thus to supplant Della, his light-skinned but non-Creole wife.

It is well to note that the blacks at Grover maintain their separateness from the Carmiers as steadfastly as the Carmiers maintain theirs from the blacks. Seemingly entirely receptive of the Creole family on its arrival at Grover, they are put off at the initial rejection of their offer to help on moving day and antagonized by the male Carmiers' persisting attitude of aloofness and superiority. Raoul, who simply ignores everyone outside his family, is generally detested in the quarters. The gentle Catherine and her visiting sister, Lillian, are kept at a distance, the permanent resident Catherine especially isolated by the very fact of being Raoul's daughter. Jackson's boyhood friend, Brother, a typical quarters dweller, has very little to say to either of the young women. He speaks to them when he meets them on the road, but the conversations are brief and brusque. Even the gentle old Aunt Charlotte limits her talk with her neighbor Catherine to "speaking across the fence" (38), although it must be said that she does consider Catherine the superior of Lillian, about whom she engages in snide commentary with Mary Louise on the Creole woman's plan to go north so that she can pass as white (34). The peace between the two groups is an uneasy one, and the tension is rooted in the initial misanthropic gesture and persisting aloofness of Robert and Raoul Carmier respectively. Thus disharmony reigns at Grover among the beleaguered blacks unable to effect change and the one force among them that represents some practical measure of resistance to the status quo.

The absurdity of Raoul's aloof and superior attitude is underlined by its obsolescence. When Lillian proclaims that "Daddy's world is over with" (40), she is recognizing that her father and his sisters in Bayonne are anachronisms even among their own kind and indeed within the family itself. The uneasiness Catherine feels when she is with Jackson at Grover disappears when they are away from the plantation. At the roadhouse where they dance on their first date, no one expresses reservations at the presence of a "mixed" couple, even though the waitress recognizes Catherine from having seen her in the Creole church in Bayonne. Nor is their assignation the next evening in the room in Baton Rouge met with the least surprise by their hosts. The relationship Raoul attempts to thwart, both Lillian and her Bayonne cousin Jeanette aid and abet. At the church dance on the novel's final, crucial night, Jeanette "lures" away Catherine's Creole date, Paul Aguillard, so that Catherine and Jackson can be together. And at the Catholic church hall where the dance is held, not an eyebrow is raised at the presence of Jackson inside the Creole church.

Raoul's anachronistic sense of caste has a negative impact on the community in which he lives. There is something that even Jackson, his major antagonist, finds admirable about his bullish and single-handed assertions of equality with the white Grovers and his sense of superiority over the Cajuns. Nevertheless, he is a counterproductive force. Where a concerted, united initiative among the oppressed is needed, he antagonizes the black community and prevents any possibility of its reversing, or even denting, the status quo. Locked in a vision of social and racial superiority—and indeed his heroic gestures against the white people in a sense vindicate this vision—he will not submit to the place assigned him in the racial and social order established by the South. Rejecting the one race with whom he might find identity, and rejected by the other race, he is ultimately a figure whose heroism remains abortive, insular, and capable of no lasting affirmative impact.

In the narrower social unit of his own family, Raoul wreaks horrendous havoc. He rejected Marky, his wife's son by the non-Creole known as Bayou Water, because he could not abide his dark skin, and he is responsible for the child's "accidental" death. He has also rejected his wife and banished their younger daughter Lillian as an infant in reprisal for Della's indiscretion with Bayou Water. He has involved his older daughter Catherine in a nearly incestuous relationship—a relationship "with Electra overtones," as the critic Alvin Aubert describes it ("Tragic Mulatto" 71)—to fill the vacuum left by the absence of Della. And so blinded is he in his possessive attachment for Catherine that he gives not the slightest sign of acknowledging his grandson Nelson, the fruit of her affair with the Creole fieldworker named Bernard.

Gaines's handling of the character Nelson merits attention for a number of reasons. This child stands in sharp contrast to some of Gaines's other fictional children by the inconspicuousness of his portrayal. One thinks of Tite, Billy, and Willy in *Of Love and Dust;* Snookum in *A Gathering;* Sonny, James, and Chukkie in the various stories in *Bloodline:* all make their presence known, whether by their sensitivity, their mischievousness, their earnestness; Gaines never allows them to be nonentities. Although Nelson is only about two years old and the possibilities for exploiting his character are considerably fewer than with the other, older children, one senses that the lack of substance in Gaines's portrayal of Nelson is meant to be significant. He is often brought to his Carmier aunts for looking after; at times he is lovingly, if silently, cared for by Catherine or Della. No one talks to him or of him. He is simply there—all but absent from the novel, as he is from Raoul's life.

It is Madame Bayonne, Jackson's boyhood schoolteacher, who tells of Nelson's origins:

> Not too long ago—three years, I'd say—he [Raoul] hired a bunch of Creoles to help him get in his crop. Catherine fell in love with one of them and became pregnant. When the boy found out he came there for her. If that boy ever made a bigger mistake in his life, I'm sure he hasn't made two. The only thing that kept Raoul from killing him was Della and Catherine getting in the way long enough for him to get out of that yard. He went back to Baton Rouge and wrote for Catherine to follow him. He wrote and wrote and wrote, but she would not go. (119)

Not only has Raoul thwarted what seemed to be a mutually loving relationship between Catherine and Bernard and deprived Nelson of a father, he has rejected both son-in-law and grandson even though they are Creole. And so taken is he in his inordinate love for Catherine that he is blinded from recognizing the very succession he longs for so intensely. As he sits in his sister's house in Bayonne staring at his gold watch and chain, a gift on his twenty-first birthday that has been "passed down from father to son for the past three generations," he can only regret that "there was no one for him to pass it to" (208).

Gaines again takes up his critique of the Creole assumption of special status in *A Gathering*. Here Jacob Aguillard from Mulatto Place near the Marshall quarters is one of the ragtag collection of horseless Quixotes who gather to take a stand in defense of old Mathu. Matt, one of the other older men, remarks that "Jacob and his kind didn't have much to do with darker people, but he was here today" (39). And another of the old men, Cherry, undercuts Creole pretension by his sarcastic comments related to the shabby treatment Tessie, Jacob's sister, has received at the hands of her own people. Tessie, "one of them great big pretty mulatto gals who messed around with the white man and the black man," was run into the St. Charles River on Mardi Gras Day 1947 by the whites because she wouldn't "stay away from the niggers." But "her own people at the old Mulatto Place wouldn't even take her body home. They was against her living here in the first place round the darker people. I'm not dark myself, I'm light as them, but I'm not French, not quality. Them, they're quality, them, but they wouldn't even take her body home. Buried her with the kind she had lived with" (45). Of course, the designation of the Creoles as *mulattos* by various characters—who seldom use the term *Creole* to identity the "light," "French," "quality" African Americans—further undermines that group's claim to superiority. It is interesting to note also that the Creoles in this novel come from Mulatto Place (invariably referred to as "the old Mulatto Place") and not from Creole Place as in *Miss Jane Pittman*. Are Creole Place and Mulatto Place separate communities in St. Raphael Parish? Most probably not. Instead, it is likely that the change in name reflects the black community's repudiation of the Creole pretension to special status.

The Creoles, however, are not the major object of Gaines's considerations about assumed superiority within the African-American community in *A Gathering*. Rather, here it is the Singaleese, in the person of Mathu, whom he identifies as disruptive of the desired cohesiveness among the oppressed and ultimately even of a universal human unity. Because of this novel's particular structure and scope, it is not immediately evident that the question of Mathu's alleged class is at the heart of events, and this concern is not as pervasively and explicitly expressed as its parallel theme in *Catherine Carmier*. Yet Mathu is the central figure, and his dominance over and alienation from the community is the major theme around which all the actions and monologues turn. Mathu's centrality is evident early in the novel, but for various reasons—his own natural reticence, the "whodunit" nature of the novel, its monological structure—attention is focused elsewhere. As well, the present time of the novel (with the exception of Lou Dimes's final brief monologue, which covers the trial some days later of the miscreants in the shootout in Mathu's yard) encompasses only a few hours, the afternoon and evening of an early October Friday during the 1970s, and the tenseness of events as well as the often retrospective monologues of the old men divert attention away from Mathu.

It is Clatoo, the old men's leader, who labels Mathu as Singaleese and ascribes his aloofness to his bloodline: "He acted like he didn't care if we was even there. Mathu was one of them blue-black Singaleese niggers. Always bragged about not having no white man's blood in his veins. He looked down on all the rest of us who had some, and the more you had, the more he looked down on you" (51). His color is referred to elsewhere as well. The white woman, Merle, describes him as "black as pitch" (19); Snookum, with the literal-mindedness of the child, refers to him as "black black with a white beard" (6). Other characters single out Mathu's size and bearing. Rufe notes, "He wasn't quite as tall as Mapes [the sheriff, who is six feet three inches tall]. Built like a picket—no, more like a post" (84). In his color and stature, his aloofness and independence, Mathu recalls Harriet Black in *Miss Jane Pittman*.

During most of the afternoon, Mathu maintains his aloofness, despite the apparent fact that the other old men have come to his assistance. (By all appearances it is he who has killed the Cajun, Beau Boutan.) He studiously ignores his defenders; is the only old man, Lou Dimes notices, who doesn't stand in line to take Mapes's blows; and sits indifferently and silently as the others tell their tales of oppression. But the moving stories of the other blacks gradually wear away his defenses, and in the end he comes to see the wrongs he has endured that make him part of the community of suffering with his fellows: "I ain't nothing but a mean, bitter old man," he says. "No hero. Lord—no hero. A mean, bitter old man. Hating them out there on that river, hating y'all here in the quarters. Put myself above all—proud to be African. You know why proud to be African? 'Cause they won't let me be a citizen here in this country. Hate them 'cause they won't let me be a citizen, hated y'all 'cause you never tried. Just a mean-hearted old man. All I ever been, till this hour" (182).

Not the least reason for Mathu's guilt-ridden confession is that earlier in the day he has "pushed" into the hands of Charlie Biggs the gun with which Charlie has killed Boutan (191). Mathu has effectively put his godson Charlie's life in jeopardy and is responsible ultimately for his death. The childlike Charlie sees Mathu's handing over the gun as his godfather's effort to make him, finally, a man. The reader may very well perceive the gesture as having larger implications: having passed on to Charlie the task of disposing of Beau, Mathu has saved himself for the final showdown in his long-standing feud with Beau's father, Fix.

Charlie's own confession, made shortly after Mathu's, is the dramatic high point of the novel. It is, in effect, a repudiation, albeit an unconscious one, of Mathu's pretensions to superiority on the basis of color and bloodline. Charlie, godson of Mathu, jet-black, six feet seven inches tall, 275 pounds, probably Singaleese himself, extends Mathu's embarrassed and apologetic rejection of his old ways into a grand gesture of active dissent that cries out for emulation. This expression of his newly found courage in terms of becoming a "man" and his repeated use of the expression are noteworthy because they contain an implicit rejection of the notion of superiority based on class and color both within the black community and in the society at large.

Much is made in *A Gathering* of physical traits, especially skin color. Early in the novel, Clatoo, having established Mathu's pride in his Singaleese class, goes on to describe the old men he leads, with commentary on Mathu's attitudes towards them: "I was brown-skinned—my grandpa white, my grandma Indian and black, and both my parents black; so he didn't look down on me quite as much as he did some others, like Jacob, or Cherry, or the Lejeune brothers. With Clabber and Rooster, he just shook his head. Rooster was yellow, with nappy black hair, Clabber was milk white, with nappy white hair. Mathu just shook his head when he saw either one of them" (51). In the novel, the old men make frequent statements that betray their self-consciousness about their physical differences from Mathu, whose cause they have taken up. Chimley calls his bosom pal Matt a "fine-featured brown-skin man" (31). Matt remarks that Chimley is "blacker than me and Cherry, too, that's why we all called him Chimley" (39–40). Cherry refers to Clabber as "the albino from Jarreau . . . [whose] head and face from this distance was all one color—white white" (48). According to Matt, Cherry is "between red and yellow, with a lot of brown curly hair" (39). Rufe describes Johnny Paul as being "the color of Brown Mule chewing tobacco" (88) and Tucker as "a small, brown-skinned fellow" (93).

Mathu's view of the significance of skin color stands in contrast to the view of the novel's other African-American characters. His graduated assessment of his fellows on the basis of skin shade upholds his pride in his own pure black blood and repudiates the long-standing cultural preferences for light skin. The old men renounce all preference based on skin color, whether for black or for light, and manifest their attitude by including the Creole Aguillard and the albino Clabber as part of their number and by associating themselves in the defense of the jet-black Mathu. Clearly, Mathu's vision of superiority is being measured against a more egalitarian view. Mathu's conversion, when it does come, amounts to throwing off his exclusiveness and taking on a democratic inclusiveness, and his confession is couched in terms of acceptance of all his fellow African Americans. Significantly also, Mathu is now able to express implicitly the recognition that he has been patronized by Sheriff Mapes. Mathu says to the old men, "Till a few minutes ago, I felt the same way that man out there [Mapes] feel about y'all—you never would 'mount to anything. But I was wrong. And he's still wrong. 'Cause he ain't go'n ever face the fact. But now I know. And I thank y'all. And I look up to you. Every man in here. And this the proudest day of my life" (181). "I been changed," he continues, "I been changed. . . . I been changed by y'all. Rooster, Clabber, Dirty Red, Coot—you changed this hardhearted old man" (182).

Like Raoul Carmier, Mathu has maintained throughout his life an adamant position against white oppression. Chimley, who recounts the story of Mathu's beating Fix Boutan in a fistfight after he refused to return Fix's empty Coke bottle to the store, speaks for the old men and explains their allegiance to the Singaleese who has spurned them when he says, "Mathu was the only one we knowed had ever stood up" (31). But the old men's admiration is tempered by resentment of Mathu for his superior attitude, rendering their gathering in his defense as much a challenge of that attitude as an act of assistance. Some, such as Rooster, harbor personal resentments. "He never thought much of me," he says. "Used to call me Little Red Rooster all the time. People even said him and Beulah had fooled around some behind my back. I never asked him, I never asked her—I was too scared. But I wasn't scared now. He knowed I wasn't scared now" (181). And as a group the old men must surely resent Mathu's fraternizing with the brutal and racist sheriff, Mapes, who himself patronizes Mathu. "I admire the nigger," Mapes tells Lou Dimes. "He's a better man than most I've met, black or white" (74). Rufe gives an account of the friendship between Mathu and Mapes: "Mapes liked Mathu. They had hunted together. Wildcats, alligators, deers. They had fished together. And Mapes had had a few drinks with Mathu at Mathu's house. He liked Mathu" (84). As Raoul Carmier's heroic stand is diminished by his monstrous conduct, so is Mathu's by those gestures that are in tension with the very qualities that elicit admiration: his willingness to associate with a man who sees him as a "nigger," his casual manipulation of his simple-minded godson, his general disregard of persons.

The critique made in both *Catherine Carmier* and *A Gathering* is directed at self-perceived superiority based on class within the African-American community. The repercussions of this alleged superiority in the elder Carmiers and in Mathu become emblematic of the destruction such perception of superiority has wrought in the society as a whole. In *Catherine Carmier* this extended critique remains implicit. In *A Gathering* it surfaces in Charlie Biggs's announcing his conversion in terms of attaining manhood, that manhood from which he has previously felt disqualified because of his race and which he insists now be recognized by his being addressed by his family name. The same manhood is asserted for the old men in Gaines's choice of title for his novel and in his labelling the various monologues with the full Christian and family names of the speakers.[4] The manhood the old men are confident of having attained transcends color and race. Not so, however, Mapes's concept of manhood, for it is necessary that he preface his elevation of Mathu to that status with the words "I admire the nigger." Among the whites in the novel, it is Gil Boutan who most closely expresses the concept of egalitarian manhood that the blacks demand. Gil, the brother of the murdered Beau, is an LSU football star, the white half of the racially mixed backfield tandem known as Salt and Pepper. Convinced of the necessity and efficacy of racial integration, he has been sensitized to the evils of black victimization by whites as a result of his own experience as a Cajun living in a society dominated by a higher white class.

For two novels written twenty years apart, and so different in tone and narrative perspective, *Catherine Carmier* and *A Gathering* show striking similarities, not the least of which is the way in which broad societal and narrower familial tensions are assuaged with the capitulations of Raoul Carmier and Mathu from their adamant stances of superiority. Jackson's defeat of Raoul in the ultimate violent fistfight scene prepares the way, potentially at least, for Catherine's taking up a normal sexual union with Jackson, as well as for a reparation of the rift in Raoul's own marriage. Mathu's more spontaneous acceptance of his fellows is seen as being of a piece with the release of the ties between him and his "foster" daughter Candy, an occurrence that enables Candy to pursue unthwarted her relationship with Lou Dimes. That Mathu's surrender eases the way for a successful relationship between two whites only reinforces the notion that Gaines's vision is focused on the inevitable interconnectedness of all the inhabitants of St. Raphael Parish.

In the work of African-American fictionists, the theme of disharmony among African Americans is a common one. In *Catherine Carmier, A Gathering,* and to a lesser extent in *Miss Jane Pittman,* the choice of focus for the dramatization of tensions within the community, the pitting of characters who have no pretensions to class superiority against Creole and Singaleese characters who do, gives these novels something of the flavor of a rustic, though not unsophisticated, fiction of manners. Whereas in Ellison's *Invisible Man,* for example, tensions within the community often turn on matters of political leadership, or in the fiction of Alice Walker or Gayl Jones, on matters of sexual conflict, in Gaines's books they take on a decidedly social cast, especially in the novels being discussed here. By identifying and isolating two social groups, seizing upon one character who is a major representative of each group, and dramatizing the interaction of these two characters with the mainstream of black people in his chosen locale, Gaines is able to bring much insight to the human predicament and to articulate it in a literary art of high order.

As a Louisiana native, Gaines is heir to the extensive actual and recorded history of the Creoles, the Louisiana people who prided themselves in light color, material accomplishments, and culture and maintained a separation from other African Americans who were either enslaved or the children of slaves. Pride in light skin and white facial features related to the Creoles' identification with the dominant race from whose upper social strata they were descended. But Gaines undercuts the Creole pride of color. In the first place, the sense of their "whiteness" is unilateral, and even the possibility that they are able to go north to "pass for white" forces them out of their homeland, the place in which they conceive their special status to have been achieved. Gaines undercuts their pride in their material accomplishments and culture as well. Raoul Carmier successfully works the land with his small family, but at tremendous cost to all. The majority of Gaines's Creole characters are the very antithesis of culture—that is, of cultivated manners and behavior, of sophisticated speech, of education. In *Miss Jane Pittman* the natives of Creole Place virtually lynch intruders at their fete; in *A Gathering*, Mulatto Place inhabitants have murdered one of their own women and refused to allow her burial in their cemetery. Most of all, Gaines questions the fundamental premise of Creole superiority at its origins when he points out, through Mary Agnes LeFabre, that they have enslaved their own people. It is worth noting that those Creoles who cling to the image of their exclusiveness are least in possession of the group's alleged virtues, while those who are humane, gentle, and even sophisticated—the Carmier daughters, for example—have no use for Creole separateness.

The Singaleese in Gaines's fiction, on the other hand, do not represent a people of such high profile in Louisiana history as the Creoles; our sense of what Mathu and Black Harriet represent derives from the fiction itself. The most telling sign of Mathu's attitude of racial superiority is his snubbing of other African Americans generally and his relegating them to lower positions according to the lightness of their skin. The lighter the skin, the more the black blood is diluted, in Mathu's simplistic view of things. Given that he considers mixed blood a sign of weakness and inferiority, it is not surprising that his only friendly contacts are with people of pure white blood, his foster daughter Candy and Sheriff Mapes; such contacts reinforce his notion of his own superiority. The fact is, though, that Mapes does not consider Mathu his equal, even if he does see a certain quality and stature in him. It is Rufe who tells us that "Mapes had had a few drinks with Mathu at Mathu's house"; certainly Mapes had not invited Mathu to his house. Mathu's sense of superiority over his African-American fellows is being deflated here, just as his feeling of moral superiority is deflated by his gesture of handing the slow-witted Charlie the gun with which he kills Beau Boutan.

Both Raoul Carmier and Mathu isolate themselves from the racial group which would have most readily accepted them by virtue of their assumed superiority. By acting independently to achieve their single-minded goal of equality with their traditional masters, they come close to being fanatical. They are milder versions of those characters in Gaines's fiction who in their desire to destroy the great white monster of prejudice indulge in a kind of Ahabian monomania and drive themselves to the very edge, perhaps over the edge, of insanity: "Bloodline's" Copper, also known as General Christian Laurent, who imagines himself the head of an army of revenge; and Billy, the twenty-four-year-old Vietnam veteran from *In My Father's House,* who claims to be training disadvantaged people in guerilla tactics toward an eventual overthrow of the white establishment. Though they escape the extremes of Copper and Billy, Raoul and Mathu are rendered ineffectual in their isolation. Acting on their own, they deprive themselves of the benefits of broader perspectives and concerted action. Both are admired for their courageous stands, Raoul by Jackson Bradley and Mathu by the assembled old men who have been the victims of his intolerance. But they are so hardened in the conviction of their high status that they cannot bring themselves to the point of collaborating with those whom they consider their inferiors. It is one of Gaines's major points that if Raoul and Mathu share a certain moral stature, a courage and perseverance in their pursuit of acceptance, these qualities derive from what they are, not from color and not from a privileged caste status. Indeed, much of Gaines's critique is based on the fragility of insistence on special status.

The insistence on the democracy of color among African Americans, on the absurdity and inefficacy of privileged status based on skin shade and bloodline, is a salient element in *Catherine Carmier* and *A Gathering.* The implicit thrust of such an insistence is to brand interracial prejudice with the same iron, of course, and Gaines's critique applies to the entire society as well as to its parts. In *Catherine Carmier,* the question of racial equality in the broadest sense is addressed explicitly, though not in the context of the Creole-black dynamic. In *A Gathering,* Gil Boutan's resistance to his debasement as a Cajun in a white society and his significant gestures questioning the notion of white supremacy bring to the fore the theme of racial equality in its most comprehensive sense. His words to Candy as he surveys both his brother's corpse and the men gathered to protect the killer refer literally to his victimization as a Cajun: "You never did like Beau. You never liked any of us. Looking at us as if we're a breed below you. But we're not, Candy. We're all made of the same bone, the same blood, the same skin" (122). Given the cross section of St. Raphael society in whose presence these words are spoken and the racial sensitivity of the speaker, they cannot but have a broader reference.

Notes

1. The ways in which Gaines's use of fictional place is similar to Faulkner's has been noted by Fabre. See also Rowell, "Quarters."

2. Commentators often distinguish between "Creoles of color" and white Spanish or French Creoles. See, for example, Davis, "Headlands"; Mills; and Woods. I follow Gaines's habit of using the term *Creole* to designate Creole of color.

3. For a discussion of Creole isolation, see Aubert, "Tragic Mulatto," which touches on the question of the Creole attitude of superiority acting as a divisive force within the black community. Babb deals in detail with the question of Creole separation and caste (45–60).

4. For a discussion of the significance of names in the novel, see J. Griffin, "Calling."

Bloodlines and Patriarchs: *Of Love and Dust* and Its Revisions of Faulkner

David Lionel Smith

In the climactic scene of the novel *Of Love and Dust,* the young black man Marcus fights with Sidney Bonbon, a Cajun plantation overseer, in Bonbon's front yard. Bonbon has returned home just in time to catch Marcus attempting to elope with Mrs. Bonbon. Their battle ends quickly when Bonbon seizes a scythe blade and chops Marcus to death. This grim reaper tableau echoes one of William Faulkner's most famous scenes. In *Absalom, Absalom!* Wash Jones, a poor white, avenges an insult to his granddaughter by killing the patriarch Thomas Sutpen with a scythe. These scenes are very similar yet very different. Wash Jones and Sidney Bonbon might be viewed as analogous figures, but Marcus and Sutpen are exact opposites. For Wash to kill the unrepentant child molester, whom he reveres, seems ironic yet just. For the adulterous overseer to kill the reckless but heroic Negro, whom he has tormented throughout the novel, seems all too inevitable and not at all just, even to the callous Bonbon. Gaines's echo of Faulkner produces complex reverberations.

Gaines echoes Faulkner in various ways, yet he never seems merely to imitate Faulkner, because in every instance, his echoes are combined with deliberate, purposeful dissonances. In some cases Gaines models entire books upon works by Faulkner. For example, Faulkner's *Go Down, Moses* is clearly the paradigm for Gaines's collection of stories, *Bloodline,* and both collections take their titles from one of the in-
46 cluded stories. Like Faulkner's *As I Lay Dying,* Gaines's *A Gathering*

of Old Men comprises numerous short sections, each told from the perspective of a particular character. In other instances, Gaines uses symbols that Faulkner used, though not necessarily with the same meaning. Thus, wild horses appear in Faulkner's "Spotted Ponies" as forces of uncontrollable but benign nature. In *The Autobiography of Miss Jane Pittman,* wild horses are ominous harbingers of mortality. Joe Pittman gains status and fame as a horse breaker, but horses also cost him his life.

Thematic interests are what these writers most often have in common. *Miss Jane Pittman,* like *Absalom, Absalom!,* explores the construction of historical narrative as a communal activity. Gaines shares Faulkner's interest in the complexity of relationships between black and white Southerners, especially where love and friendship clash with rigid social prescriptions of racial roles. Both examine interracial love affairs. The passionate sexual relationship of Marcus and Louise in *Of Love and Dust* resembles the stormy encounters of Joe Christmas and Joanna Burden in Faulkner's *Light in August.* Finally, both authors are fascinated and troubled with the uneasy dialectic between social stability and historical change.[1]

Faulkner is important to Gaines not just because he is the greatest writer of the South, but even more, because Faulkner addressed so trenchantly the issues of race, history, and community that so deeply preoccupy Gaines. Consequently, in order to be taken seriously, Gaines has been obligated to acknowledge the precedents established by Faulkner and to locate his own work relative to them. Michel Fabre identified this issue more than a decade ago: "Faulkner's shadow, more than ever since his death, hovers over every American novelist who writes about the South. This is perhaps more true for the black novelist because Faulkner spoke of his people with so much depth at times and often with so much compassion that his racial myths are the most indestructible. . . . The excellence of the Faulknerian style makes anyone who takes up his challenge look like an imitator. . . . Of all the new black novelists, Ernest Gaines alone really takes up Faulkner's challenge" (110). One may quibble with Fabre's assessment of Faulkner's black characters, but he accurately identifies the monumental status of Faulkner's work and its challenge to subsequent writers. He is also quite right in identifying Gaines as the contemporary author whose work reflects the most explicit relationship to Faulkner. Gaines himself has often acknowledged this relationship. In a 1978 interview with Charles Rowell, for instance, he remarked: "Faulkner has influenced me, as I think he has influenced most Southern writers. But I'd like to make this clear: Faulkner has influenced me in style only, not in philosophy" ("This Louisiana Thing" 43). This distinction between style and content, while neat, is somewhat disingenuous, since earlier in the same interview Gaines acknowledged his agreement with Faulkner that "the past ain't dead; it ain't even passed" (42). Nevertheless, the more salient point is that Gaines explicitly asserts the importance of his complex and critical engagement with Faulkner's work. This essay examines certain aspects of that engagement. It focuses on *Absalom, Absalom!* and *Of Love and Dust,* considering first some specific revisions of Faulkner by Gaines and returning in the end to the larger implications of the philosophical differences between the two.

Despite their many similarities, Gaines and Faulkner differ fundamentally in their views of history. Faulkner's view is perhaps best summarized in a familiar passage from *Absalom, Absalom!*: "Maybe nothing ever happens once and is finished. Maybe happen is never once but like ripples maybe on water after the pebble sinks, the ripples moving on, spreading, the pool attached by a narrow umbilical water-cord to the next pool which the first pool feeds, has fed, did feed, . . . that pebble's watery echo whose fall it did not even see moves across its surface too at the original ripple-space, to the old ineradicable rhythm" (210). This vision of endless repetition stresses the inescapable power of the past. Gaines's historical vision seems to me best represented not by any single passage but rather by a characteristic situation: an individual making a difficult personal choice that will have dramatic impact on the future of both the person and the community. Marcus decides to seduce Louise Bonbon. Miss Jane Pittman decides to join a demonstration. The father in "A Long Day in November" decides to save his marriage by burning his car. By contrast, Faulkner's characters seem not so much to decide as to act by compulsion. They look constantly backward, overwhelmed by past events and trapped by their tragic inability to make meaningful change. Gaines's characters are also deeply bound by the past, yet they recognize that change is possible if one is willing to pay the price. Gaines's emphasis on personal choice seems to reflect the folk wisdom of an oppressed people still struggling with the heavy shadow of slavery, just as Faulkner's tragic fatalism embodies the guilt of a slaveholding class. This is the difference in philosophical perspective that Gaines's revisions of Faulkner seek to highlight.

Let us return for a moment to the pair of scythe killings. In *Absalom, Absalom!* the killing of Thomas Sutpen by Wash Jones is apt for many reasons. Most obviously, Wash acts as the avenger of his wronged granddaughter. Upon noting that Milly's newborn child is a girl and not the son he had hoped to father, Sutpen remarks, "Well, Milly, too bad you're not a mare like Penelope. Then I could give you a decent stall in the stable" (151). As he strolls arrogantly out the front door, intending to leave his paternal responsibility forever behind him, Sutpen instead meets the outraged, scythe-wielding Jones in the yard. Jones's skewering of Sutpen is in fact more than merely a grandfather's vengeance. He has tolerated the grizzled Sutpen's courtship and seduction of this fifteen-year-old in the misguided conviction that "whatever your hands tech, whether hit's a regiment or men or a ignorant gal or just a hound dog, that you will make it right" (228). For Wash, Sutpen is a superhuman figure: "If God Himself was to come down and ride the natural earth, that's what He would aim to look like" (226). Thus, Sutpen's cruel dismissal of Milly represents the betrayal of both Wash's explicit consent and implicit faith. Sutpen stands exposed in his fatal, all-too-human hubris, and Wash's scythe blade calls the false God to account.

At a deeper level, Wash symbolizes Sutpen's original self: the poor white who was turned away from the patrician's front door by a condescending black servant. That humiliating encounter provokes Sutpen's lifelong quest for wealth and social status. This being the case, his forcing Wash into an analogously humiliating position is revealingly ironic. Wash represents the poor white trash origins that Sutpen flees but cannot escape. Herein resides his tragedy. His own repressed self rises up to destroy him. Such a death is perfectly in keeping with the tragic designs of the novel. The heroic figure struggles to transcend his own human limitations and inevitably fails. Wash Jones, in his final guise as grim reaper, imposes that ultimate justice of human mortality.

The killing of Sutpen by Wash Jones represents, then, both human justice and a literary fulfillment of the novel's tragic designs. By contrast, the scythe-slaying of Marcus by the overseer Bonbon in Gaines's *Of Love and Dust* sounds a profoundly troubling echo. The setting and action are virtually identical, except for certain details that Gaines reverses for ironic effect. In Gaines's novel, Marcus, the underdog, is the attacker, and Bonbon, his tormentor, warns him to desist. In *Absalom, Absalom!* the enraged Wash Jones assaults Sutpen, his social superior. One effect of Gaines's reversal here is to provide Bonbon a legitimate claim of self-defense. The alleged criminal, Marcus, who is innocent of any real crime, is struck down, while the predatory Bonbon triumphs once again. Thus, injustice is compounded, not avenged.

Other factors intensify the reader's sense that injustice triumphs with the killing of Marcus. Sutpen clearly deserves no sympathy. He precipitates his own demise when he rejects and insults the girl who has just borne his child. By contrast, Marcus meets his death as he attempts to rescue Louise Bonbon from her life as a despised prisoner in Sidney Bonbon's house. While Marcus's attempted elopement is adulterous, it is also an act of devotion, the first unselfish act he has performed in the entire novel. When Marcus has the opportunity earlier in the day to leave the plantation freely, without placing himself at further risk, he opts instead to keep his promise to Louise. Where Sutpen's death results from his failure of compassion, Marcus dies in the name of love. Bonbon kills Marcus only to defend himself, not to protect his home or the wife whom he has long ceased to love. Indeed, this killing liberates Bonbon to devote his exclusive attention to his black mistress.

In both novels, the women who are the pretexts for these duels suffer devastating consequences. Wash Jones cuts the throats of Milly and her newborn daughter, while Louise goes mad upon seeing Marcus slain and ends up in an asylum. Milly's death seems inconsequential, because Faulkner has portrayed her only as an abstract object of attention, devoid of consciousness, who speaks only a few words before she perishes. Louise, on the other hand, is a major figure in Gaines's novel. She evolves from a pale, girl-like apparition behind her picket fence to a woman rejuvenated and emboldened by an overwhelming, improbable love. Gaines depicts her struggle to understand what is happening to her. Her confusion resonates in the poignantly naive and revealing question she asks her black maid: "Margaret, do you think a white girl could love a nigger? . . . I mean a nig-gro" (184). The pathos of this limited, semiarticulate young woman, awakened to a consciousness of human possibilities and dreams of freedom by her dangerous affair with a black man, makes her compelling.

At the end, Gaines's narrator describes Louise's encounter with the bloodied corpse of her lover in a spare, indirect manner that contrasts sharply with Faulkner's grandiloquence. Indeed, while Faulkner's narrative emphasizes the verbal representation of imagined scenes, Gaines offers a depiction that seems virtually a camera shot: "Louise's right hand was up to her mouth—no, not the hand, the tip of her fingers. . . . She brought her right hand slowly from her mouth and touched his face. . . . 'You hurt, Marky-poo?' she said softly. 'You hurt?' " (272). The absurdity of her blackface disguise, which she has put on in anticipation of their elopement, vanishes in the fragile incredulity of her gesture. A few pages later, the narrator, Jim, provides our last information regarding Louise: "The same night of the fight, some people had taken Louise to a hospital in New Orleans. Not long after that, they took her to Jackson—the insane asylum" (278). This laconic report is poignant because Gaines has brought his reader to understand both the fragility of this woman and the intensity of her love. Unlike Milly Jones, she has weight and particularity for the reader.

Milly is merely the last victim of Sutpen's callousness, but Louise has a history, feelings, and aspirations. While Milly's death is interesting only in relation to Sutpen's tragic hubris, the destruction of Louise carries its own pathos. This contrast reflects Gaines's conscious design and one of his fundamental differences from Faulkner. In *Absalom, Absalom!* Sutpen is the central obsession of all the major characters: his contemporaries are consumed with the hopeless desire to establish intimacy with him, and his posterity are equally driven by the compulsion to understand his acts and his legacy. Even the deeds of his descendants are explained as reactions to or manifestations of Sutpen's deeds. Though the lives of characters in *Of Love and Dust* are closely interrelated, no one is merely a pawn.

This contrast represents a subtle but significant difference between Faulkner and Gaines. In Faulkner's world, characters are trapped within a history that they cannot hope to change. They compulsively reiterate narratives of past events, but those narrative acts yield, at best, only entertainment or perhaps fatalistic understanding of their own places in an unalterable pattern of events. Gaines uses historical narrative as a vehicle for understanding the complex interplay between continuity and change, the maintenance of community and the destruction of community. For Gaines, the possibility of significant change provides the grounds for hope, even as it simultaneously promises to undermine cherished comforts. This difference between Faulkner and Gaines is more than a disparity of emphasis. Gaines's view makes possible an orientation toward the future, albeit a future fraught with uncertainty. For Faulkner, the future is at best a foregone conclusion. These contrasting implications are reflected in the conclusions of the two novels.

At the end of *Absalom, Absalom!* Shreve articulates a nightmare of racial degradation: "I think that in time the Jim Bonds are going to conquer the western hemisphere. Of course it wont quite be in our time . . . But it will still be Jim Bond; and so in a few thousand years, I who regard you will also have sprung from the loins of African kings. Now I want you to tell me just one thing more. Why do you hate the South?" (302–3). This flight of racist fantasy inflates the Sutpen family curse into a curse upon the entire white race, which Shreve predicts will devolve into negroid idiocy. Unable to dispute this prophecy that the future will merely echo the past, Quentin pathetically asserts, over and over, echoing himself: "I dont hate it. I dont. I dont! I dont hate it!" (303). Though his denials are abject, at least they intensify rhetorically, in contrast to the novel's general vision of historical entropy. Regardless, inevitability trivializes hope.

Of Love and Dust has a very different conclusion, as the narrator, Jim, bids farewell to Aunt Margaret: "I picked up the suitcases and the handbag and walked away. When I looked over my shoulder, I saw her going back home" (281). This passage suggests a vision of history comprising both continuity and change. As the novel ends, these two characters consider possibilities, and each makes a choice. Margaret returns home to her organic community with all its familiar limitations and comforts, while Jim departs in the opposite direction toward an unknown future. No monolithic "fate" presides over this world. Consequently, multiple possibilities remain open, though freedom is sharply constrained by the high costs attached to certain choices. Marcus, for instance, has paid the dearest price.

The openings of the two novels offer even more dramatic contrasts regarding stasis and change. *Absalom, Absalom!* opens with the stultifying images of a "hot weary dead September afternoon" in "a dim hot airless room . . . with yellow slashes full of dust motes which Quentin thought of as being flecks of the dead old dried paint itself blown inward from the scaling blinds as wind might have blown them" (3). This passage embodies stasis and introspection, a triumph of the sterile dust settling on the room. The only hints of vitality are the sound of Rosa Coldfield's outraged voice and the suggestion that her voice may call forth ghosts "out of the biding and dreamy and victorious dust" (4). This dust symbolizes Rosa's obsession with long-dead things and the absence of movement or change. The stillness of this room is reiterated by the stillness of Quentin's dormitory room in the closing pages, while the movement from hot Mississippi September to frigid Massachusetts winter represents an even greater slippage into morbidity.

Of Love and Dust opens with a very different image of dust: "From my gallery I could see that dust coming down the quarter, coming fast, and I thought to myself, 'Who in the world would be driving like that?' I got up to go inside until the dust had all settled" (3). In contrast to Faulkner's use of dust to depict a static, involuted world, Gaines uses it to signal disruption, a portent of the impact Marcus will have on this ingrown plantation. *Absalom, Absalom!* begins indoors, emphasizing stillness, while *Of Love and Dust* begins outdoors. The passage quoted above bristles with motion. These explicit contrasts represent conscious choices by Gaines to challenge Faulkner's representations. The echoes of Faulkner that resound throughout this novel are deceptive. In *Absalom, Absalom!* the past exerts a corrosive power over the present, and history plays itself out in deteriorating repetitions. Change, though painful and costly, slowly undermines the repressive status quo in *Of Love and Dust,* making possible new conceptions and forms of social relations.

We cannot read Gaines's response to Faulkner as a simple displacement or parody or reversal. Instead, I would argue, Gaines uses these powerful echoes to indicate his simultaneous agreements and disagreements with Faulkner. Gaines accepts the importance of most of the issues posed by Faulkner's texts, but he differs on fundamental points of interpretation. For example, making a young black man the tragic hero entails an implicit criticism of the South's dominant order. In Faulkner's world, even a powerful black man like Lucas McCaslin owes his strength to a white patriarch. Gaines disrupts such genealogies. More important, the death of Sutpen changes nothing. It simply underscores a pattern of repetition and failure: a view of history as the degenerative reiteration of an unchanging pattern over time. By contrast, the death of Marcus changes everything. It ruptures the community and disrupts social relations, sending some characters into exile and altering everyone's consciousness of social possibility. To understand the difference between these two historical visions, we must consider the fates of the two murderers. Wash Jones commits suicide; Sidney Bonbon leaves Louisiana—probably with his Negro mistress. Despite Gaines's insistence on the terrible cost of social change, he shows that change does happen, and he presents the future, guardedly, as a realm of possibility.[2]

Gaines responds much more simply and overtly to Faulkner in his story "Bloodline." In it a young mulatto named Copper returns home to confront his white uncle and to reclaim his birthright. Like an updated Charles Bon, he demands acknowledgment. Like Rider from "Pantaloon in Black," he exhibits superhuman physical prowess as he easily dispatches the men sent to capture him. Like Samuel Worsham Beauchamp in "Go Down, Moses," he has grown hard and cynical from his experiences in the world beyond the plantation. But unlike Faulkner's defiant Negroes, who are all killed by white men, Copper proves unconquerable. He declares at the story's end: "We'll be back, Uncle. And I'll take my share. . . . Your days are over, Uncle. . . . It's my time now. And I won't let a thing in the world get in my way" (*Bloodline* 217). Even the word "Uncle" becomes ironic, as the young Negro applies it to an older white man, neatly reversing the traditional condescending use of this term in the South.

Superficially, the conclusion of "Bloodline" is more satisfying than Faulkner's tragic endings and the conclusion to *Of Love and Dust*, but it is also less persuasive. Clearly, Gaines intends "Bloodline" as a whimsical departure from the realism prevalent in the collection's other stories, just as "Pantaloon in Black" contrasts the dominant style in *Go Down, Moses*. Furthermore, this defiant conclusion aptly reflects the increasingly militant spirit of civil rights activism, which was emergent as Gaines wrote this story. Nonetheless, the painful conclusion to *Of Love and Dust* seems more true to experience. Ironically, just as critics have argued that "Pantaloon in Black" weakens the structural integrity of *Go Down, Moses*, one might also say that the story "Bloodline," with its painless comedy, compromises the book *Bloodline*.

At the beginning of his interview with Gaines, Charles Rowell asked him why he had not published any fiction set in California. Gaines made a surprising response: "I suppose I have written four or five novels about California, but they are not very good books. They have not been published. They will not be published during my lifetime, if I have anything to do with it. Maybe sometime in the future I will write a good book . . . about California. But I doubt that I will be able to do it until I have gotten rid of this Louisiana thing that drives me, yet I hope I never will get rid of that Louisiana thing. I hope I'm able to write about Louisiana for the rest of my life" ("This Louisiana Thing" 40). This comment suggests the degree to which Gaines's imagination is rooted in a particular landscape and sense of community: his own postage stamp of Earth. Such a comment might imply a writer with a nostalgic relationship to his subject matter; but in fact, Gaines's work maintains a forward-looking spirit that deftly evades the regressions and naively restorationist impulses of nostalgia.

Miss Jane Pittman and *A Gathering*, which overtly embody this concern with traditional communities in transition, focus explicitly on historical experiences and dramatic events that change the nature of social relationships within communities. *Of Love and Dust*, however, provides the most subtle meditation on the dynamics of continuity and change. The profundity of this novel manifests itself in the painful conclusion and particularly in the troubling ironies of the scythe-killing of Marcus. This tragic conclusion undercuts any impulse toward nostalgia that might otherwise accrue to a narrative about rural life in the past. Unlike the death of Thomas Sutpen, which represents the just dispatch of a hero gone degenerate, the death of Marcus Payne thwarts the development of a selfish adolescent into heroic manhood. Thus Gaines forces us to confront the cruel injustice of the Southern status quo and invalidates any impulse we might have to romanticize it.

The ultimate challenge that Gaines poses to readers in his depiction of Marcus's death is to understand the complex interplay of continuity and change. I have already noted that this scene represents simultaneously the triumph of the status quo in the sense that the overseer Sidney Bonbon kills the upstart Marcus, and the emergence of social change in the sense that Marcus's sacrifice inspires Jim and requires both Bonbon and Jim to seek new lives. We need also to consider two related issues: why the black community itself is resistant to change and why the positive results of Marcus's heroism can emerge only indirectly. To understand these points takes us to the heart of Gaines's argument with Faulkner.

First, despite the subordinate positions of the black people on the Hebert plantation and the wrongs they continue to suffer, they have deep investments in the status quo. In a fundamental sense, "status quo" is a cognate for "community," as they know community. Specifically, it means membership in a social order that is so old, so in-grown, and so thoroughly routinized that it has come to seem natural, organic. In an organic community all of the social roles, institutions, and activities are fixed through long-standing tradition. Thus, organic community frees its members from troubling uncertainties and difficult choices. Everything is always already decided for them, and if they conform by behaving as expected, they are rewarded with all the comforts of fellowship. Furthermore, they can even enjoy a sense of absolute knowledge, within their context. The characters Ma and Pa Bully, for example, sit on their porch and immediately recognize individual voices in the choir of the nearby church. They even recognize Marcus as someone who will soon be dead. Margaret, too, sees the future. "Y'all ain't going nowhere," she tells Louise (239). Unfortunately, the future for Margaret is merely the unchanging logic of the world as she knows it. Her folk wisdom cannot conceive of change. The necessary cost of membership in organic community is that one must accept its liabilities as well as its benefits. The permanent acceptance of racial and class subordination, the sexual exploitation of women, economic impoverishment, and rigidly proscribed social options are among the entailments of this particular Southern organic community. Its comforts are purchased at a high price.

Gaines makes this point most directly with the traditional "house servant" figures of Bishop and Margaret. Bishop, the butler for Marshall Hebert, feels a debt to his ancestors to maintain the prevailing order, symbolized by the plantation's big house, precisely as it has always been. Marcus bewilders and terrifies Bishop with his aggressive, insubordinate demands to enter through the front door of the plantation's big house and to speak with Hebert, whom he refuses to address as "Mr." Both gestures express his rebellion against the prescriptions of submissive Negro etiquette. As Bishop declares incredulously: "He just pushed his foot in there. . . . The house his great-grandparents built. The house slavery built. He pushed his foot in that door" (215). Jim explains that "Bishop wanted me to understand that any black person who would stick his foot in a door that slavery built would do almost anything" (216). Bishop is so consumed with the duties he has inherited that he lacks any critical perspective regarding what he is actually defending. His failure to turn aside Marcus, the symbol of emergent social change, devastates Bishop. Jim leaves us with a pathetic image of him, slumped on the floor and reduced to abject prayer: "He was asking the old people who had died to forgive him for letting them down" (237).

Similarly, Aunt Margaret despises Marcus and the challenge he poses to her orderly life as housekeeper and babysitter. Unlike Bishop, she feels contempt toward her white employers. Sidney and Louise Bonbon are just poor white trash to her. Her devotion is toward the child, Tite, whom she tends. Thus, she opposes the romance of Marcus and Louise partly because of the threat it poses to the welfare of the child. Margaret also has, however, a profoundly fatalistic attitude. When Louise naively asserts that she and Marcus just want to be happy, Margaret remarks: "Some people can't be happy together, Miss Louise. . . . It's not made for them to be happy" (243). This comment represents both the resignation and the wisdom of a person who understands how the system works. This wisdom, which facilitates survival, also perpetuates the status quo. Margaret's satisfaction in and commitment to her role as guardian allow her to find contentment within the prescribed limits of her social role but also prevent her from conceiving or even approving any action that might change her role.

Gaines's inclusion and serious portrayal of these characters is neither gratuitous nor disparaging. They both represent familiar and traditional values within the black community. Furthermore, Gaines recognizes that such conservative values are crucial in maintaining community, just as the selfishness and aggressiveness of Marcus threaten to destroy the community. This difficult paradox has not been sufficiently understood, especially by liberal and progressive thinkers. Change alters and may undermine community. People like Margaret are willing to live with familiar evils precisely because they understand that the worst and best aspects of their lives are all bound subtly together in the fabric of community. To cut one strand may result in unravelling the whole. The benefit of eliminating what they despise may not be worth the cost of losing what they cherish.

This consideration is especially relevant given the time of the book's composition. Published in 1967 as the civil rights movement faded, to be superseded by the black power movement, this book looks back to the historical moment just before the civil rights movement began to thrust its foot inside the door of the house built by slavery. It reflects upon the difficulties implicit in efforts to precipitate change in rural Southern communities—the sort of communities in which voter registration drives operated in the early 1960s. We know as a matter of historical fact that civil rights activists met considerable resistance, for different reasons, from both white and black people. Aside from the obvious white racism and black fear, compelling reasons for resistance included the uncertain costs and equally uncertain benefits of social change.

We know from Gaines's subsequent work, such as *Miss Jane Pittman* and *A Gathering*, that he has taken an enduring interest in this conflict between traditional community and the struggle for progressive change.[3] Unfortunately, too many critics have missed the larger social implications in *Of Love and Dust*. In any case, the echo of Faulkner in the scythe-killing of Marcus should be understood with these factors in mind. Marcus must die because his victory over Bonbon would imply a kind of effective black heroism that would not have been plausible in the Louisiana of 1947. For Marcus to triumph would conclude this narrative with a historical lie. Yet ironically, Marcus's sacrifice makes it possible and necessary for Sidney Bonbon to leave the South; and Jim and Margaret speculate that Bonbon has gone north with Pauline, the black woman he loves. This irony, that Marcus and Louise lose everything while Bonbon and Pauline are set free, is in keeping with the uncertain nature of social movements. Those who take the risks and make the sacrifices may not be the beneficiaries.

These ironic reversals in Gaines's appropriations of Faulkner's fiction reflect a subtle understanding of social processes. Similarly, the high cost in blood and broken lives for very uncertain future benefits reflects Gaines's honest acknowledgment, even before the assassination of Martin Luther King, Jr., of a bitter lesson taught by the civil rights movement. Once again, however, the difference between the two authors is decisive. In *Absalom, Absalom!* the deaths have absolute finality, while in *Of Love and Dust* deaths lead to new possibilities for others. Though unsettling, Gaines's vision in this novel is more true than the glib optimism of "Bloodline." By turning Faulkner's images in contrary directions, Gaines demonstrates possibilities of historical understanding that Faulkner's ideological perspective precluded.

Still, one might argue that Gaines could have made these points without relying on Faulkner. One might regard Gaines's intensive use of Faulkner as an indication of Gaines's own inadequacy—the anxious, futile struggles of a literary son to escape the overwhelming influence of his patriarch. This would make Gaines rather like one of Faulkner's own characters. One might also see him as engaged in parody, "signifyin(g)," or some other such attempt at one-upmanship. Both perspectives, however, would have the likely effect of perpetuating a hierarchical concept of discursive relations by granting a monumental status to the earlier text.[4] Such a view would make Gaines not only temporally but logically and ontologically secondary to Faulkner. In general, the problem of how to address the work of writers who labor in the shadows of great artists without subordinating the former or disparaging the latter deserves broader attention by literary theorists. To achieve this end, we need an egalitarian hermeneutic, which would insist upon locating both authors as respondents to and participants in an on-going cultural discourse. This hermeneutic would allow for chronological ordering but would also facilitate an emphasis on the discursive engagement between texts. By focusing on the egalitarian criterion of cogency rather than the hierarchical notion of relative greatness, such an approach would constitute a hermeneutic without patriarchs.

To draw this inference is not to suggest that Gaines's work explicitly makes these or any claims about interpretive theory. Rather, the point is that his work reminds us of the deep interdependence of African Americans and European Americans, especially in the South. Obviously, there is no necessary correlation between social realities and forms of literary criticism. Still, insofar as Gaines's work provides an intellectual example, it seems to urge us to develop broadly inclusive forms of literary study, which will allow us to understand literary works not just as self-contained artifacts, but more important, as elements in an American cultural discourse. Gaines uses Faulkner just as Faulkner uses European mythology. He recognizes that Faulkner's sense of tragedy and fatality represents deep truths about Southern history, but he also recognizes that these are not the only truths. Gaines does not attempt to discredit or displace Faulkner's work nor to imitate or endorse it. Rather, he uses Faulkner as a point of reference in his own effort to understand the experience of Southern communities. Where they differ fundamentally, however, is in their philosophical perspective regarding social change.

This last point brings to mind one of Walter Benjamin's pithy statements about historical study in "Theses on the Philosophy of History": "The tradition of the oppressed teaches us that the 'state of emergency' in which we live is not the exception but the rule. We must attain to a conception of history that is in keeping with this insight. Then we shall clearly realize that it is our task to bring about a real state of emergency" (259). In the first instance, the "state of emergency" refers to triumphant fascism; in the latter instance, it envisions a revolution that will overthrow fascism. Though Benjamin's context is different, his point is relevant to our understanding of Gaines. In *Of Love and Dust* the plantation folk recognize the crisis precipitated by Marcus, but they fail to understand how it reflects and reveals the constraints in their accustomed way of life. In effect, their way of life is a perpetual "state of emergency." Only Marcus has the daring to try to break free. Though his elopement fails, his attempt ruptures the system, leaving open a crack in the door through which others might escape. Gaines, the novelist-historian, offers this insight to his readers.

By insisting on the possibility of real change, Gaines voices the dream of black people for a better future; but by taking seriously the cynicism and tragic sense of Faulkner, he reminds us how painful and difficult all serious change must be. This struggle requires endurance, dignity, and toughness. Gaines captures this point in the conclusion to his story "The Sky Is Gray." The narrator, a small boy, and his mother walk out into a storm. He observes: "The sleet's coming down heavy, heavy now, and I turn up my coat collar to keep my neck warm. My mama tells me turn it right back down. 'You not a bum,' she says. 'You a man' " (*Bloodline* 117). This storm symbolizes the suffering and hardship that characterize the boy's life. His mother's point is that dignity is more important than comfort. Without such a conviction, one is not likely ever to challenge a status quo that strips away manhood and womanhood as the price for admission to the comforts of community. Gaines calls our attention to the significance of such small gestures.

Benjamin's "Theses on the Philosophy of History" offers another apt observation that extends the previous point:

> The class struggle, which is always present to a historian influenced by Marx, is a fight for the crude and material things without which no refined and spiritual things could exist. Nevertheless, it is not in the form of the spoils which fall to the victor that the latter make their presence felt in the class struggle. They manifest themselves in this struggle as courage, humor, cunning, and fortitude. They have retroactive force and will constantly call in question every victory, past and present, of the rulers. As flowers turn toward the sun, by dint of a secret heliotropism, the past strives to

turn toward that sun which is rising in the sky of history. A historical materialist must be aware of this most inconspicuous of all transformations. (256–57)

Though Gaines is not a Marxist, Benjamin's comments are pertinent to his work because of Benjamin's explicit concern with the perspective of an oppressed class. As a historian, Gaines is Benjaminian. He emphasizes the qualities of courage, humor, cunning, and fortitude as expressions of his characters' unvanquished spirits. Faulkner praises the same qualities, but always in the context of enduring under tragic circumstances. Gaines, on the other hand, is more interested in those gestures that challenge the victories of the rulers. This is what makes *Of Love and Dust* so fascinating. Like Benjamin's flower, it strives to turn toward that sun which is rising in the sky of history.

Notes

1. My reading of Faulkner has been strongly influenced by King's *A Southern Renaissance*. For the most detailed discussion of Gaines's relationship to Faulkner see Fabre. Gaines himself comments frequently on Faulkner in Gaudet and Wooton.

2. Bryant notes that Gaines originally planned a different ending for this novel, allowing Marcus and Louise to escape ("Gaines" 855). It is difficult to imagine how Gaines could have erred so blatantly, since both the logic of this narrative and the Faulknerian precedents demand a tragic ending. Ironically, the death of Marcus makes hope for change meaningful, while the triumph of Marcus would have been so anomalous that no social generalization could have been drawn from it.

3. Of the various articles addressing the politics of these two novels, none has been more discerning about the complex interplay of cultural and political values than Callahan, "Image-Making."

4. I have in mind, first, the literary theories derived from Freudian psychoanalysis, elaborated in works such as Harold Bloom's *The Anxiety of Influence;* and second, the theory of African-American literature developed by Henry Louis Gates, Jr. in *The Signifying Monkey*. Neither critic has addressed these specific texts. I am suggesting, however, that their theoretical approaches would not be conducive to the broadly contextual reading of Gaines that I advocate.

The Pulse of *Bloodline*

Robert M. Luscher

While often treated as a miscellaneous collection of stories, Ernest J. Gaines's *Bloodline* can be more fully appreciated when analyzed as a short story sequence: a volume of short fiction in which various unities and modes of coherence meld autonomous stories into a work whose whole becomes greater than the sum of its parts as readers sequentially process and organize its components.[1] This genre's roots may be traced back to Chaucer and Boccaccio—before the short story was a formally defined genre—yet many of the form's early manifestations as well as its two seminal works, Sherwood Anderson's *Winesburg, Ohio* and James Joyce's *Dubliners,* attempt to provide a composite picture of a locale that might not be possible within the spatial confines of the plot of a novel. Using setting rather than plot or character as the central element, regional-based collections such as *Bloodline* exhibit a remarkable unity, one in which the locale transcends the role of background and ultimately exerts ideological and aesthetic control over the work's contents.

Place—which Eudora Welty calls the "lesser angel" (116) of the novel —can supplant the more traditional causal and temporal narrative spine of the novel to provide short story sequences with an alternative mode of equilibrium and sense of direction. Even without incorporating other devices to lend coherence, regional writers with strong feelings for the shaping effect of environment can create volumes whose stories seem cut of the same cloth rather than merely patched together. Although the stories in such collections may vary in focus and emphasis, they work together to map out a region's physical and emotional geography.

62   An author may also organize a short story sequence by recurrent

themes, a common narrator or characters, reiterated character types, or repeated symbols and motifs, but it is the unity of setting that provides the collection with a literal common ground that these other spatial modes of textual organization may easily complement. Technical and structural devices (such as titles, headnotes, maps, frames, section division, juxtaposition, or a loose temporal framework) can also lend regional-based volumes a greater degree of formal wholeness. Hamlin Garland's *Main-Travelled Roads,* Sarah Orne Jewett's *The Country of the Pointed Firs,* and Charles Chesnutt's *The Conjure Woman* exemplify the piecemeal fashion in which late-nineteenth-century writers in the American local color tradition constructed unified pictures of particular locales. Such works illustrated formal possibilities later emulated and augmented by twentieth-century short story writers such as Anderson, Toomer, Steinbeck, Faulkner, Welty, Updike, and Gaines. Contemporary writers are adopting the form with greater frequency, often to illustrate the fragmentation or multiplicity of a region or community, although at the same time the result may affirm connections that transcend the sense of separateness promoted by the volume's division into stories.

Bloodline's place in this generic tradition has yet to be recognized fully.[2] It clearly stands in a direct line of descent from the form's paradigmatic representatives, Anderson's *Winesburg* and Joyce's *Dubliners,* both of which Gaines has professed intimate acquaintance with (Rowell, "This Louisiana Thing" 44), although he does not acknowledge either as a formal model. *Bloodline* resembles Joyce's work more than Anderson's, as it lacks the consistent, sometimes intrusive narrative voice and the central protagonist who figures so strongly in complementing *Winesburg*'s village setting. In *Bloodline*'s emphasis on the paralytic effect of environment and the creation of a composite regional figure out of different protagonists, it bears a strong resemblance to *Dubliners* in both theme and structure: the progression of Joyce's characters from youth to adolescence and then to mature life and finally public life loosely reflects the shifting male characters in *Bloodline* as they move from youth in the quarters into the struggle for civil rights.[3]

A number of works by writers from different traditions might be seen as forerunners to *Bloodline*. As a student at San Francisco State, Gaines began to "read about anybody who would write about the earth" (Laney 5). Among those writers who published short story sequences, Turgenev and Steinbeck head the list, although Gaines was more interested in the milieux than in the form of their works. Nonetheless, Turgenev's intimate depiction of rural peasant life in *A Sportsman's Sketches,* which Gaines has praised for its clarity and beauty, offers a composite regional portrait made up of numerous smaller works. Gaines does not mention any particular works by Steinbeck, but in *The Pastures of Heaven, Tortilla Flat,* and even *The Red Pony,* a number of autonomous tales are unified into a sequential narrative occurring in the same locale.[4] Gaines was also an avid reader of Hemingway, whose "writings of that grace under pressure . . . made me see my own black people" (Rowell, "This Louisiana Thing" 44) and whose *In Our Time* employs a complex alternating structure of stories and vignettes to sketch the evolution of a central protagonist whose experiences are counterpointed by those of other characters. Finally, Gaines has acknowledged that, among Southern writers, Faulkner's influence is strongest, yet he has taken pains to emphasize that the debt is predominantly in style rather than philosophy. Still, in expressing his fondness for the structure of *Bloodline,* he has compared the result of "getting all these [stories] together to make a novel" with Faulkner's *Go Down, Moses* (Gaudet and Wooton 34).

While Gaines primarily studied white writers in college, he has singled out Jean Toomer's *Cane* (which he read around 1960—after he had begun writing *Bloodline*'s first stories) as "one book by a black writer that would have had as much influence on me as any other book" in both subject and structure. "What he does in those short chapters are things that I wish I could do today, those little short chapters, those little songs, the poetry between the chapters" (Gaudet and Wooton 34). Although *Bloodline* consists of much longer stories and has a more deliberate movement from beginning to end, *Cane*'s first two sections— one focused on rural Georgia women and the other on urban blacks— offer a model of thematic development through regional-based portraits. In addition, the long concluding story, "Kabnis," creates a coda-like structure that stresses the value of the rural community's roots in much the same way that "Just Like a Tree" does in *Bloodline.*

Gaines's admiration of *Cane,* with its variations on themes structured in a fashion emulating jazz, suggests that non-literary sources from the African-American tradition should not be ignored in the list of potential influences on *Bloodline*'s form. From listening to jazz (and reading Hemingway), Gaines has noted, he learned the virtue of "not hitting the nail on the head, but playing around it" (Gaudet and Wooton 20). As in a short story sequence, repetition and variation are favored over a straightforward development. In the "cut" technique used in some black music, Keith E. Byerman notes, the aesthetic structure, which abruptly skips back to previously heard beginnings, "marks a difference from the European notions of progress and resolution. . . . It envisions instead a world of organic process in which repetition and change are the only constants" (*Fingering* 7). If one substitutes the word *novelistic* for *European* above, the description of the pattern aptly fits a work such as *Bloodline,* whose stories reiterate common themes concerning the tension between rootedness and change through progressive variations. Finally, the call-and-response pattern that Byerman argues exists in much black verbal art contains parallels to the multiple voices that comprise *Bloodline.* Each voice is answered by the subsequent one of the next story, which returns to consistent themes and motifs; in addition, the volume concludes with echoes of previous voices by the multiple narrators of "Just Like a Tree."

Such traditions form the background for other short story sequences by black writers that precede Gaines's work. Todd Duncan (85) is the only commentator on *Bloodline* who cites other volumes that are part of an existing African-American tradition in the genre: Charles Chesnutt's *The Conjure Woman* (1899) and Richard Wright's *Uncle Tom's Children* (1938). While lacking *The Conjure Woman*'s narrative frame and metafictional dimension, *Bloodline* shares its genesis in the oral tradition. Gaines's fiction attempts to capture the storyteller's voice heard so often in his youth: "I come from a long line of storytellers. I come from a plantation where people told stories by the fireplace at night. People told stories on the ditch bank. . . . I think in my immediate family there were tremendous storytellers or liars" (Laney 3).⁵ Like Chesnutt's work, *Bloodline* also takes a critical stance—though a much more explicit one—toward the contemporary remnants of the plantation system.

Although Gaines did not read *Uncle Tom's Children* until later in his career, Wright's series of portraits thematically anticipates Gaines's treatment of the tension between the black male's struggle for self-realization and the community he is in danger of leaving behind. Wright's men fight against oppression, but their individual efforts are portrayed as ineffectual unless they work together against injustice. Other African-American works that might be seen as precursors to *Bloodline* include Langston Hughes's four volumes of Simple stories (published between 1950 and 1965) and James Baldwin's *Going to Meet the Man* (1965). While Hughes's tales feature a common narrator and an urban setting, Baldwin arranges stories of black males in order of his protagonist's increasing age to sketch social change during roughly the same era as *Bloodline*. Only with Toomer's volume can one draw a direct line of influence to *Bloodline*, but Gaines's book should ultimately be linked with these representatives of the genre by black writers and seen as the precursor of such works as Alice Walker's *In Love and Trouble: Stories of Black Women* (1973) and Gloria Naylor's *The Women of Brewster Place* (1982).

Beyond physical setting, *Bloodline* is unified by a number of themes that develop concurrently as the volume progresses: the definition of black manhood through conflict with white social institutions, the role of women and the community in relation to social progress, the failure of traditional religion, and the importance of visionary characters in defining the nature of change. These recurrent themes are sufficient to provide the volume with substantial intertextual unity, but the existence of a definite sequence of male protagonists provides a solid unifying framework. The following analysis, although schematic, foregrounds the stories' intertextuality within the volume and the complementarity of the themes in the individual narratives.

Composition History

Only three of the five stories that comprise *Bloodline* were published previously. "A Long Day in November," which Gaines started and then reworked while enrolled at San Francisco State and Stanford in the late 1950s and early 1960s, is not only the first story in the sequence but also the first to be written; Gaines published an abbreviated version in 1964. The volume's second story, "The Sky Is Gray," appeared in August 1963. According to John F. Callahan, the final story, "Just Like a Tree," also published in 1963, was the second one written ("Hearing" 107).[6] The third and fourth stories—"Three Men" and "Bloodline"— appear for the first time in the collection.

Using Forrest L. Ingram's three distinct types of short story sequences —composed, arranged, and completed (17)—one might argue that Gaines was subconsciously composing the sequence, returning to the locale with different perspectives until there seemed sufficient material to present a comprehensive treatment of his themes. Ascertaining that such a holistic vision preceded the work's genesis, however, makes the volume no more unified or coherent, since it is the reader's pattern-making faculties that must ultimately formulate the volume's wholeness.

Nonetheless, as Gaines has remarked, the stories have been "definitely arranged" in an order that not only takes into account the narrators' increasing ages but also seeks to portray a curve of "constant growth from the first to the last story" (O'Brien 91). This arrangement (discussed below in more depth) highlights the male protagonists' growth in sensibility from the sheltered limitations of a childhood in the quarters to readiness as an adult, who has grown beyond the community but still not forsaken it, to confront a region in transition. Furthermore, the selection of "Just Like a Tree" as the final story provides the volume with a definite sense of closure.

In addition to expanding "A Long Day in November" to near-novella length, Gaines appears to have filled in the frame with stories featuring characters whose moral and ethical development fits between those of the young boy passively absorbing the environment around him in "A Long Day in November" and the departing activist Emmanuel in "Just Like a Tree." Ultimately, however, the composition history serves only to highlight certain structural features the reader discovers during the sequential experience of negotiating the text, which involves positing interconnections, recognizing juxtapositions, and overcoming perceived gaps.

Title

A short story sequence's title "adumbrates a cryptic meaning which the reader must decipher" (Kennedy 14). Adopted from the penultimate story, the volume's title foregrounds the continuity that runs through the stories—not just a family bloodline but a racial one that relates the generations of residents segregated in the quarters and in the black sections of towns such as Bayonne. While the black bloodline is often perceived as monolithic, the stories themselves highlight the variety of skin colors and the complex and crossing lines of kinship that ultimately mingle in one continuous stream. As Duncan notes, the title "applies not only to a specific story or to blood kin; it is a metaphor standing for Gaines's entire network of implied kinship" emerging from a common ethos (100). That kinship is ultimately based on place and on a shared historical suffering that knits individuals together in families and as a community— much like the book itself. Thus the title becomes an appropriate organic metaphor for the volume's unity, especially the sequential dimension that depicts the progress from the older generations to the next. However, the metaphor might also signal the presence of the affinities that kinship carries, alerting readers to the presence of reiterated characteristics, motifs, and themes. Thus the stories, like the characters within them, merge into a single bloodline, moving forward in time with a continuity that weaves diverse lives together.

By assigning to the volume as a whole the title of the story that most markedly emphasizes social inequities and that features the most developed radical sensibility, Gaines emphasizes the need to move forward as the old order is disappearing. In contrast, naming the volume after the final story, "Just Like a Tree," would have stressed the Faulknerian endurance of the generation of old aunts and the value of rootedness in the vanishing community. While both dimensions are crucial to an understanding of Gaines's vision, the relative balance of the two is altered by his emphasizing the penultimate story and the progressive, sequential dimension. Furthermore, *Bloodline* as a title carries connotations of blood spilled—past and future—in the struggle for change and subtly echoes the spatial image in the title story of "blood weeds" beside the road to the quarters.

Structure, Pattern, and Arrangement

Gaines does not precede the stories with a prologue, authorial note, map, or framing device. Instead, readers enter directly into the characters' environment in the initial story and experience the sights, sounds, and smells with an immediacy granted by a young child's perception. With each subsequent story, the vision becomes more sophisticated and the ethical problems more acute. The physical limitations of the quarters and the interpretive limitations of childhood ultimately give way to a more complex vision of experience, structurally represented by the multiple voices that comprise the final story. More than a random amalgamation of stories, *Bloodline* is arranged so that it builds out from the quarters to the town of Bayonne, then returns, via a decaying plantation, to the quarters. This movement not only expands the reader's sense of the locale but also reaffirms the importance of the vanishing community, especially for the composite male character seeking to realize his independence outside its limits.

The general pattern of increasing age and greater sophistication of vision serves as a prototype for the progressive expansion of the reader's own consciousness through the sequence. Six-year-old Eddie's world of sight, sound, and sensation in "A Long Day in November" is related in terms of an ego still seeking a protective niche in a stable family. Eight-year-old James registers an increasing consciousness of the inequities of the cold world that he must face outside the quarters in "The Sky Is Gray." In "Three Men" nineteen-year-old Procter Lewis comes to understand, under his fellow inmate's tutelage, the societal forces that have delimited his behavior. The narrator of "Bloodline," seventy-year-old Felix, offers a dispassionate view of the struggle for ascendancy between the old and new; by not presenting the story through the voice of the rebellious mulatto, Copper, Gaines allows the reader a glimpse inside the mind of a male representative of the generation raised before serious challenges to the South's old order emerged. The final story's polyphony of voices—incorporating young and old, male and female, black and white—demands a much more complex integration of perspectives that points toward the multiplicity of experience and the ongoing nature of social change.

Within the context of *Bloodline,* each story depicts a stage of growth, as progressively older black males come to terms not only with the forces within the black community but also with the wider Southern society that has historically delimited it. In essence, the five main characters become a composite protagonist; indeed, in Gaines's sketch of the volume's structure, he talks about the characters in the first three stories as if they were the same person.[7] Duncan argues that the stories collectively gain "cumulative importance and power" by depicting the latter stages of Erikson's eight epigenetic phases of personality development (86). While such a schema may represent an implicit ideal, the volume's form undercuts the possibility of such a climactic progression by emphasizing the discontinuity inherent in the black male's life cycle. Despite the common bloodline, the composite protagonist in fact suggests an identity not totally integrated and the necessity for bridging experiential gaps that inhibit the growth process.

Even given the presence of discontinuity, the chronological arrangement of the stories naturally lends itself to the merging of the protagonists' struggles into a loose evolutionary process, and Gaines's choice of first-person narration subtly augments this process. Until the reader discovers differently, the *I* of one story, given no antecedent, might very well be the character from the previous one. Additionally, since each character reaches a threshold or stasis by the end of his story, the reader tends to expect that the older character who appears in the next will advance further as he meets increasingly more profound challenges. Gaines's comments on Tee Bob (*The Autobiography of Miss Jane Pittman*) and Jackson (*Catherine Carmier*) express faith that when characters achieve only a partial escape from the past, others may carry on: "This is the kind of thing I am doing in all of my work. These characters make an attempt toward change, and some other character might continue where they left off. But to break away from the past, from one philosophy to another, is a burden that one person cannot endure alone. Someone else must pick up and go from there" (O'Brien 84). This message clearly emerges from "Three Men," and *Bloodline*'s discontinuous form reinforces the black community's need to support and nurture change, even as the volume's contents reveal its disintegration. The story sequence form is ideal for Gaines to affirm that one character may pick up at the threshold reached by the previous one, while at the same time he recognizes the limitations of each particular life. Those attempting to break from a repressive past thus seem less isolated figures.

Place: The Quarters, Bayonne, and St. Raphael Parish

That events in the five stories occur in the same place invites the reader to draw them together—to take their literal common ground and build them into a world of accumulative detail and internal consistency. Like every contemporary Southern writer, Gaines labors in the looming shadow of Faulkner, whose repeated returns to Yoknapatawpha County created a teeming fictional population and a realm of near-mythic proportion. While Faulkner occasionally journeyed outside of this terrain,

Gaines has focused exclusively on his own particular "postage stamp of native soil" located in and around Bayonne—the fictional equivalent of New Roads, Louisiana—seeking to understand what he has called "this Louisiana thing that drives me" (Rowell, "This Louisiana Thing" 40). He depicts a world united by a historical tradition that involves a sense of community, a legacy of oppression, and an ethos of struggle. Charles H. Rowell's description of the quarters as "enclosed communities whose limited space forces each inhabitant into the private lives of others" ("Quarters" 739) could describe the sequence as a whole: an enclosed community whose limited space (confined within the covers of a volume) thrusts together the lives of separate individuals. Like the cabins whose doorways and front porches face the dusty roads leading to the fields, the stories share a common symbolic geography that dictates the nature of the protagonists' struggles and forms the enduring reality of place.

The palpable sense of place is strongest in the early stories, related by narrators whose primary experience of the world is sensual rather than intellectual. Bitter cold dominates the first two stories; in subsequent stories, images of weathered houses, open fires, dust, cane fields, blood weeds, oppressive heat, rain, and mud all reinforce the prominence of the elemental and the constant struggle for survival. The segregated facilities in Bayonne complement the harshness of the weather in the second story, presenting a world that James's mother shows him is fraught with subtle proscriptions and that demands calculated and creative strategies for survival. The obvious taboos involve crossing those physical boundaries that divide the town into separate but unequal districts, where services such as dentistry are decidedly discriminatory and the warmth of the white merchant's store cannot be enjoyed without a ruse such as shopping for ax handles. The rain in the final story recalls the misery of the sleet in "The Sky Is Gray," in which the weather serves as a metaphor for the cold white world that James must face with dignity in the segregated town and that Procter Lewis must face with courage in jail in "Three Men." The penultimate story, "Bloodline," sketches a plantation in decline, although while inspecting its fields, Copper envisions a revival of its former economic vigor. In the background, however, looms the inevitable Cajun ascendancy, which would lead to wholesale destruction of the quarters and its way of life.

"I suppose as children we loved the quarters," Gaines has stated. "I mean we loved it more than the people who owned it loved it, but we were limited" (Gaudet and Wooton 75). These limitations are evident in the volume's first narrator, to whom the enclosed community is the world; his father, in contrast, seeks escape from the confines of an environment in which he will never rise above the status of a laborer or tenant farmer. While the central male characters in each story strive to transcend their surroundings, the female characters are generally better able to endure isolation and economic deprivation on a daily basis. As a community, the quarters constitutes a historically determined entity whose poverty and segregation perpetuate the antebellum social order. Although such conditions foster a desire for escape, they nevertheless provide the roots of strength and tradition. In one sense, the quarters is analogous to the Old South in Faulkner: an ambiguous conservatism preserves there both an outmoded and stultifying social code as well as the eternal verities of the human heart.

Segregation and the remnants of the plantation system constrict the existence of those in the quarters, yet while some of the parish's white characters clearly perpetuate the old order, others seem determined to make a gesture that bespeaks their difference. The old woman in Bayonne, for instance, takes pains to aid James and his mother, although Octavia stubbornly insists on refusing charity until she casts the drama in terms of an exchange. Paul, one of the white police officers in "Three Men," is more sympathetic than his sadistic partner T.J. and reminds Procter of a white man who used to cross the color line to play baseball with him and his friends. Despite Paul's gentler character, he still enforces the expected show of deference by blacks toward whites. Finally, only two paths remain open to Procter in his clash with the white world: T.J.'s simmering hatred and physical abuse or the perpetual servitude that will result if he accepts the offer he expects from Roger Medlow to bond him out of jail to work on the plantation.

Frank Laurent in "Bloodline" provides a more in-depth characterization of the white planter, albeit a fading one without Medlow's sway. Weakened by two heart attacks, he envisions himself as the last line of defense against Cajun ascendancy. Even though Laurent may not question the need to change from the ways of the waning white order, he fears and blocks the new order. Although he allows the descendants of the plantation's slaves and sharecroppers to live rent-free on the land (perhaps in partial atonement for his ancestors' injustice), his laissez-faire paternalism may ultimately be as responsible for keeping the blacks' condition static as Medlow's manipulation of the system. Neither responsible for creating the social codes nor distant enough from his upbringing to change them, Laurent steers a middle course in an attempt to keep his world together and to retain his accustomed "dignity." With the older generation of blacks, he maintains some semblance of genteel decorum, though he still expects their deference. Yet Felix's compliance stems largely from personal respect, not from an acceptance of the old code. No longer submissive, Felix has carved out a unique relationship in which he holds his ground and speaks his mind, indulging in sarcasm and refusing to affirm his employer's illusions. Felix shares Procter Lewis's surface compliance and Octavia's subterfuge, but the gradual erosion of the system in the rural areas allows him greater success in extending his liberties and redefining his role. Frank Laurent may be weak, but he is more humane than his brutal but effectual brother Walter (whose nature Copper seems to have inherited); Frank finally admits his kinship with Copper, even as he resolves to fight the claim.

In "Just Like a Tree," Anne-Marie Duvall exhibits the courage to leave her comfortable hearth fire for an alien one to make a gesture that, though largely symbolic, affirms her emotional attachment to Aunt Fe across the physical and social obstacles that have grown more formidable with maturation and marriage. Less substantive than the food James and Octavia receive in "The Sky Is Gray," this gesture symbolizes buried emotional depths reflected in her attempt to bridge the racial gulf and follow the ancestral injunction to "look after" Aunt Fe. Certain limitations in her understanding are evident: she accepts the quarters' distant location as "ordained before" and yearns for a false innocence in her fantasy about being "a little nigger gal" who "could pick pecans and eat them under the big old dead tree" (241). She is unable to see behind the stereotyped vision of the "laughing black" and understand that the humorous facade of those gathered in Aunt Fe's cabin masks a deeper suffering. Her failure to comprehend the underlying causes of discontent becomes painfully evident when she speculates that the black agitators may want money to buy a car (a thought that contrasts with Eddie's struggle in the opening story to get rid of his car in order to regain his wife). She weeps only because of Aunt Fe's personal connection with her past and cannot fathom the deeper problems that animate racial unrest. As the volume's final representative of the white world,

Duvall offers a glimmer of hope, tempering Frank Laurent's paternalism with true compassion, but her remarks highlight the gulf that still exists between the two races in St. Raphael parish.

The Composite Protagonist

"All men have hopes, and all men brutalize other things near them, at home, when they cannot fulfill those hopes. I read Joyce's Dublin stories, and I see the same sort of thing," Gaines has observed (Gaudet and Wooton 44). Each story in *Bloodline* primarily concerns the growth of a young black male whose hopes of achieving manhood are in danger of being brutalized. Read in sequence, the experiences of each story's male protagonist comprise a composite narrative of "a larger odyssey toward human dignity" (Babb 16). Initially, the environment of the quarters—with its potential to stifle, subvert, or misdirect the development of manhood—delimits the characters' possibilities for complete maturity. Nevertheless, Gaines makes it clear that continuity with the historical community embodied in the quarters must not be sacrificed in the struggle for self-realization.

In "A Long Day in November," the young narrator, Sonny, receives part of his education in manhood by witnessing his father Eddie's tribulations. Sonny's main concerns in a world ordered by routine and dominated by sensation are elemental: warmth, comfort, elimination. Though he is clearly a long way from manhood, his chances of succeeding in school and escaping from the cycle hinge on Eddie's presence as a positive role model who can mediate successfully between external forces and his own quest for manhood. While Jerry H. Bryant's description of Eddie as "a whiner and a handwringer" ("Gaines" 856) is apt, he is doubly compromised in the struggle for independence by the community's expectations and by the limited alternatives available for defining manhood. Eddie measures his prowess by how much cane he can cut and how good a provider he is. Chafing under the limitations of the traditional communal definition of manhood, he has, however, become preoccupied with his car, a source of the mobility and power traditionally denied to the black male in the quarters.

Eddie finally transcends this obsession and assumes the status of manhood in the community's eyes, but some doubts about his relative success remain. Although burning the car is a sacrifice that represents capitulation, this dramatic action nonetheless raises his esteem in the community, as Gran'mon declares: "He's a man after all" (71). He demonstrates the power to control his own destiny by destroying something he wants in order to retain something he needs, yet Amy dictates the end of the episode: she will not let him pay for towing the car by salvaging its fuel pump, and later she compels him to beat her. Through the lessons of sacrifice and love orchestrated by females, Eddie overcomes a simplistic definition of manhood based on symbolic power.

In "The Sky Is Gray," the father figure's absence exacerbates the world's harshness and forces Octavia to tutor her eldest son James in manhood. When he exhibits qualms about killing two redbirds, she beats him until he accedes to her will and learns to stifle his sympathies for the family's welfare. Better able to endure adversity than Sonny, James suffers his toothache in silence to save the family money. Yet his trip to the dentist in town, with the crossings of the color line it necessitates, ultimately teaches him more about manhood than does enduring physical pain. His mother's final words—"You not a bum. . . . You a man" (117)—show that he will no longer be allowed the latitude of childhood; he cannot turn up his collar against the sleet but must endure it with dignity. James, as Craig Werner notes, "has bought his manhood at the cost of his youth" (37); given that he is not that much older than Sonny, the cost is dramatized further by the story's place early in the sequence.

Munford's lesson to his fellow inmate in "Three Men" is that "face don't make a man—black or white. Face don't make him and fucking don't make him and fighting don't make him—neither killing" (138). Just as channeling one's energies into fixing and driving cars serves no constructive purpose in the first story, exhibiting machismo through sex and violence only steers the black male away from challenges that shape a strong, self-actualized person. Becoming a man involves hard moral choices that will break the cycle of dependency on the white world; a man with physical strength and sexual potency can still be caged, Procter finally realizes. Forced to make a difficult choice between self-preservation and self-willed adversity, he learns to separate animal urges from ethical behavior. His resolve to resist his white oppressors is couched in terms that remind readers of Sonny asleep in his bed at the end of the first story: "I didn't want have to pull cover over my head every time a white man did something to a black boy—I wanted to stand" (152). Unlike Sonny, Procter is ready to forsake the warmth of the figurative security blanket that would blind him to the injustice he knows exists.

Munford, like Octavia, deliberately repudiates the expression of emotion, and it is up to Procter to mediate between the two extremes of divergent manhood that the violent Munford and the more empathetic but passive homosexual Hattie Brown embody. At the same time Procter rejects Hattie, he changes his opinion about the qualities Hattie embodies, as is evident not only in his role as a physical comforter but also in his new attitude about crying. Initially, Procter believes that survival in prison demands suppressing tears of loneliness, yet when he realizes what his resolution to refuse Medlow's help entails, he cries, temporarily overcome by frustration over injustice and by doubts whether others will follow him in resisting. Unlike Eddie's public weeping, Procter's catharsis transcends self-pity. It also sensitizes him to the plight of the recently beaten youngster put into the cell with him after Munford is released. Placed at the center of the collection, "Three Men" is the most optimistic story of the five: Procter, in discovering the route to authentic manhood—not exaggerated machismo—recovers a portion of his humanity as well as a measure of control over his own life.

Copper Laurent, in "Bloodline," is a more tragic figure whose wider experience and mixed blood produce a more heightened consciousness. Recounting his ten years of experience in the world to Frank Laurent, he summarizes in Kurtz-like fashion what he has witnessed: "The suffering, the suffering, the suffering" (213). He has traveled widely, observing in many cities that "men like my father. Men like Walter Laurent" are responsible for the suffering and "they hide behind the law. The law they created themselves." Like Munford, he has also been in prison and encountered firsthand the brutality inflicted on blacks by white jailers. These experiences have driven him close to the edge of insanity, and he appears to have less desire than Munford to educate others of his race in resistance, even though he speaks of raising an army of followers. In order to assert his manhood, he stands firm in his resolve to enter the plantation house by the front door, breaking the pattern of subservience as well as obtaining recognition both as a Laurent and as a man.

Duncan calls Copper the volume's "culminating figure of young adulthood" (95), yet despite his determination and physical strength, he is clearly an ambivalent model. Able to express his ideas cogently and re-solved to leave the plantation on his own terms, he earns the admiration of Felix, whose concluding description emphasizes Copper's steadfast-ness. This quality nevertheless suggests his inflexibility and fanaticism, and his adamant militancy—so clearly ahead of its time—translates itself into a blind cruelty against those of his own race. His act of tying up fellow blacks with trace chains when they try to capture him, while possibly ironic, recapitulates his white fathers' crime of slavery. Despite the visionary capacity Copper has derived from suffering, he has trouble seeing what is actually in front of him and treating others with compas-sion. While he may represent an older version of Procter, he lacks those nascent virtues of the heart that appear at the end of "Three Men," as his refusal to cry over the world's suffering demonstrates. Yet for all Copper's deficiencies, he maintains an attachment to the land he is deter-mined either to possess or to bathe in blood. He stands as a forerunner of a generation of social activists and embodies a promise that the inertia of his own day will be overcome. Ironically, however, his reclaiming his birthright involves the reemergence of the callous masculine sensibility that initiated injustice.

Emmanuel, the young activist in "Just Like a Tree," has, unlike Copper, grown as an organic part of the community from which he must depart. Lacking Copper's delusions of grandeur, he participates in a small movement of nonviolent resistance. Although sketched only briefly, Emmanuel represents the culmination of the new manhood. Through telling the story of his grandfather's lynching and mutilation, Aunt Fe has fostered his consciousness of the wrongs blacks have suf-fered down through the years. In striking contrast to Copper, Emmanuel begins with a consciousness of grief and suffering and rejects violence because of the potential repercussions against those who remain in the quarters.

Failed Religion and Wider Visions

Gaines presents his visionary characters against the background of orga-nized religion's failure to play its traditional role of providing social and political leadership. Gaines has expressed skepticism about the effec-tiveness of Christianity to heal the breach between generations of males:

"I don't know that the Christian religion will bring fathers and sons together again" (Rowell, "This Louisiana Thing" 40). Furthermore, it failed to invigorate the movement for social change—at least during the era depicted in *Bloodline,* when "the Church was only concerned with sending someone to heaven [rather] than with creating social changes," as Gaines has said (O'Brien 92). Not Christianity per se but rather the static, conservative forms that maintain the status quo come under attack in *Bloodline.*

In the opening story, religion is the first avenue to which Eddie turns in a crisis, yet Reverend Simmons's counsel proves ineffectual. He urges Eddie to "be strong" and "kneel down sometime" with his family (43–44), but his all-purpose platitudes reveal no understanding of the situation. The conservative forces of religion are ultimately allied with matriarchs such as Gran'mon, who attempts to promote a sexual liaison between Amy and Freddie Jackson that Simmons fails to censure. Within the family, Amy is the impetus behind maintaining vestiges of religious observance, making Sonny kneel before his father for evening prayers. Ironically, when Sonny blesses those who have had a role in the reconciliation, the minister is conspicuously absent from the list.

Although the white woman's nonpatronizing Christian charity brightens the second story's otherwise gray sky, other characters exhibit Christian passivity. James's aunt closes discussion about his father's being drafted by stating, "All we can do is us job, and leave everything else in His hand" (108). The preacher in the dentist's office, whose weight and gold chain indicate indulgence and prosperity, urges the women not to question the Lord's mysterious ways and to maintain faith in the face of suffering, yet the student's logic easily overcomes these shallow injunctions. Furthermore, the preacher's inexcusable violence against the young agnostic indicates clearly which of the two has the Christlike ability to turn the other cheek.

As has Munford Bazille in "Three Men," Copper has abandoned religion in frustration after repeated clashes with injustice: "I used to pray once. . . . But the same God I was praying to was created by the same ones I was praying against. And Gods only listen to the people who create them" (214). More effectual, he believes, would be claiming his share of earthly property and attempting to share it with other disenfranchised blacks. Munford delivers the most stirring denunciation of organized religion in the entire volume in a crude fable that sketches how its emasculating effects begin unobserved when the preacher christens a baby boy: "At the same time he's doing that mumbo-jumbo stuff, he's low'ing his mouth to your little nipper to suck out your manhood" (140). Subsequent religious encroachment, he asserts, eventually perverts the sexuality of or bestializes black males.

Munford's words are counterpointed by Hattie's singing a spiritual in "a high-pitched voice like a woman" (143), thus suggesting that religious faith has become predominantly a feminine rather than masculine mode of coping with adversity. Although he is not visibly affected by the hymn, Procter nonetheless later urges the young boy who is placed in the cell to pray for him when the white guards take him for "interrogation": "And I don't want you praying like a woman, I want you to pray like a man. You don't even have to get on your knees; you can lay on your bunk and pray" (153). As Procter's lack of concern about an appropriate posture for praying indicates, he seeks only an expression of faith in *something,* not necessarily a standard religious creed. His hope that the next generation's proponents of change can renew the faith he has lost echoes sentiments expressed by the young agnostic in the preceding story.

Although the first four stories present a generally negative view of religion's role in reinforcing prevailing social conditions, the final story takes its title from an old Negro spiritual that alludes to the endurance and rootedness bred by deep and abiding religious faith: "Made my home in glory; I shall not be moved. / Just like a tree that's planted 'side the water." Emmanuel's recollection of the times he has walked to church with Aunt Fe illustrates that religion has the potential of binding the community together across generations. Her spiritual certainty, while inaccessible to many of the next generation's young males, is depicted as an admirable source of strength; she dies after praying, certain of her ascent to her heavenly reward. The portrait of Aunt Fe readjusts the negativity suggested in the first four stories but certainly does not erase it. Traditional religious faith remains the domain of an older generation, and its conservative nature can serve to hinder change.

While there is some hope that future generations might renew this faith once the current irresolution and injustice pass, the more tangible promise for immediate change is invested in *Bloodline*'s visionary characters. Whether by design or by accident, each story features a character whose clarity of vision sets him or her apart from the others. By virtue of intuition, reasoned reflection, or a heightened sense of history, each possesses an ability to see beyond the present in ways that others cannot. While some may serve as catalysts for personal or social change, others merely counterpoint reality with an ideal, uncorrupted vision. Their function may be to steer the protagonist to a clearer conception of his role in the black rural community, to challenge the complacency of Christianity, to break the cycle of dependence on paternal whites and foster self-reliance, to challenge the decayed plantation system and its right of succession, or to acclaim the role and value of the past when change finally becomes imminent.

Although such characters may at times seem authorial mouthpieces who utter "truths" that other characters are unwilling to accept because of self-interest or unwillingness to change, some are undercut by mild irony or revealed by juxtaposition to be able to see only part of the situation with clarity. Taken singly, each visionary character provides some recognition of potential remedies for the historical plight of Southern blacks; yet only when their visions are taken together—with all the inherent contradictions between past and present, head and heart, male and female, security and change—does a fuller answer to the complex question of change become clear.

Madame Toussaint, the conjure woman in "A Long Day in November," understands the price that Eddie must pay for domestic peace. Duncan remarks that she embodies "a connection to intuition and to dimly remembered traditions on the Mother Continent" (87). Despite her mystic aura, this shrewd businesswoman's insight into Eddie's predicament may simply derive from her superior knowledge of the community and of human nature. She understands the sexual politics of domestic tensions engendered by life in the quarters, where the black male's alternatives for exercising manhood are few and the married woman retreats into making her home serve as an emotional shelter from poverty.

The conjure woman's first advice to Eddie, though somewhat oblique, lays out a less painful alternative than the second: it is easier to "give it up" than to set fire to the car, but Madame Toussaint seems to realize that the situation has worsened and will require more dramatic measures. As Walter McDonald notes, her advice urges sacrifice and love as the ultimate requirements of true manhood (47)—qualities that subsequent stories also affirm. Her prescription arises out of sympathy for the plight of black women, victimized by husbands so obsessed with their own restlessness that they lose sight of their spouses' needs. "You men done messed up the outside world so bad that they feel lost and out of place in it," she observes. "Her house is her world. Only there she can do what she want. . . . Y'all never know how a woman feels, because you never ask how she feels" (61). Despite Madame Toussaint's astute diagnosis of the communication problem, assigning blame to men for the outside world's condition may be only partially valid, as later stories that depict the social situation in more detail illustrate. Madame Toussaint's final scene, in which she subdues her ominous dog, may highlight her isolation and strangeness, but it also foregrounds female dominance in this story of manhood gone awry and subsequently reintegrated into the quarters community.

While Madame Toussaint's association with the African past and her present-day community are the sources of her vision, the young student in the dentist's office in "The Sky Is Gray" derives his from books and education. His words offer a prescription for change from the "cold logic" of an agnostic who sees God as an abstraction foisted upon blacks to keep them ignorant and disenfranchised. His logic is opposed by the preacher's faith in the dictates of the heart. This dichotomy is re-iterated in the title story, in which excesses of both are shown to be deficient. The student's knowledge of language's arbitrariness offers an escape from its stultifying connotations and gives him new power of assignment. Freed from the prison house of language, he moves closer to overcoming other conventions that limit his possibilities. His logic, however, leads to a somewhat precarious relativism and to isolation from those whose visions he might help clarify. To the initially sympathetic woman, he replies that he does not believe in God "because the wind is pink" (100), a statement that serves to isolate him further because she cannot comprehend his logic.

Yet if the wind can be pink and the grass can be black, as he contends, then perhaps James's sky need not be gray. While the student may have no immediate effect on his adult auditors, James accepts him as a role model because of his clothes and books. James attempts to give his mother a book to read from the office tables and also exhibits a rudimentary understanding of the student's ideas about color words when he observes that the woman's outfit consists of "a green sweater under a black sweater" (101). John Callahan argues that "behind James,

Gaines's stance toward the radical skepticism of this young man seems comically equivocal" ("Hearing" 97). Nonetheless, beyond his vision's shortcomings and alienating influence, it contains a truth that may ultimately assist in reordering reality. The student must exist in a transitional world where old definitions cease to apply and new ones have not been formulated. Ultimately, his habit of questioning, no matter how strange his statements may seem to the community, will do more for progress than the survival ethic that merely helps those in the quarters endure the cycle of poverty.

In "Three Men" Munford is more successful in directly influencing an immediate personal change with his vision. He shares the student's distrust of organized religion, but his main role is to reveal how the white power structure encourages blacks to fight among themselves, thus rechanneling the violence and rage bred by socioeconomic oppression. For this cycle to end, men such as Procter must shun the easy way out and stop allowing paternal whites to free them from jail. As Jack Hicks observes, however, Gaines depicts Munford "with a distanced irony reserved for his black rebels" ("To Make" 14). Urging Procter to resist is Munford's only way of subverting the system, which has trapped him in a cycle of powerlessness, cynicism, and violence. In addition, the stoic Munford's cruelty to their homosexual cellmate illustrates his lack of compassion. Procter must assimilate Munford's vision and also synthesize it with Hattie's ethic of compassion. Although Munford is not a complete model, he astutely perceives that the black man has allowed Southern whites to cast him as their negative image because "with us around, they can see us and know what they ain't" (137–38). True escape requires a self-recreation in a new image.

Copper's experiences in prison link him to previous characters, but he is much closer to the edge of madness than they are. He has witnessed social inequality on a larger scale than the inequality he experienced on the plantation and has returned staggered by the knowledge. Duncan calls him "one of life's shell-shocked seers" (94). Copper now envisions himself as a "General," leading shadow troops of the disenfranchised to claim the land and the rights due them. "The earth for everybody. Just like the sun for everybody. Just like the stars for everybody" (161), he remarks, but he bases his claim to the land on his Laurent heritage, not on his status as a human being. Because Copper's gaze consistently focuses on some distant point rather than on those with whom he is speaking, Felix compares him to a sleepwalker. Perhaps, however, nothing in the surrounding reality matches the particulars of his vision. Perpetually lost in abstraction, Copper has a habit of touching his left temple before he drifts off, signaling that his head may be overworked; like Munford, he has a deficient heart. Although more committed to active striving for social justice than any of the other visionaries, Copper seems the least able to relate his vision of impending revolution to the nearer human realities. His shadow army lacks any connection with the surrounding black community, whose men he spurns as tools of the white order. His frustrated quest turns into an obsession for justice that leaves behind those like Felix who have waited patiently for change. Nonetheless, Copper is sufficiently astute to know that with his vision currently unrealizable, he must settle for obtaining Frank's recognition of their kinship rather than leading his imaginary legions to reclaim the land.

Finally, "Just Like a Tree" contains two complementary visions that, rather than looking forward as Copper does, attempt to see the present within the context of the historical past. In Etienne's section, the young activist Emmanuel is portrayed as the natural result of the deeply rooted human envy and greed that begat slavery and perpetuated a cycle of violence that will lead to Aunt Fe's displacement. In the long view, both he and Aunt Fe are destined to be "turned over" by the winds of historical change. Accompanying Etienne's acknowledgment of human smallness is a positive recognition of the place of these two within the bloodline's shared history of suffering and their contributions to social change. Aunt Clo's metaphoric description of an attempt to uproot an old tree complements this linear vision. Recognizing the void that Aunt Fe's departure will create, she nevertheless affirms the persistence of the "taproot" that the elderly woman and other members of her generation have anchored in the soil. While Etienne places Emmanuel within the horizontal sweep of history, Clo looks down the vertical axis into the seeming void of a vanished community and perceives evidence of endurance.

The concluding story's form—a progressive montage of ten different voices—reminds the reader that multiple perspectives yield a more comprehensive vision of experience. Such a way of seeing is necessary in order to get beyond dominant cultural myths and break the oppressive cycles that stand in the way of widening the horizons of blacks, both in the quarters and beyond. Since these visions occur in a sequence, it is tempting to perceive them as a hierarchy, arranged from simple to complex, ever widening in scope. Yet *Bloodline*'s form challenges the reader to develop continuity among these visions, whose individual strengths and weaknesses—and whose variety of focus—suggest that they might be seen more productively as complementary, sweeping down the vertical axis of Aunt Clo's rooted, communal past as well as across the horizontal axis of time that Etíenne's vision encompasses. In the context of the dissolution of an old way of life, clarity of vision along both axes is essential not only for progressing socially but also for preserving and renovating tradition. The work itself does not integrate the perspectives of its visionary characters, but it does suggest the need for a complex and comprehensive vision of social progress, ever evolving toward a viable combination of memory, imagination, and action.

Closure

Gaines's choice of "Just Like a Tree" as the final story is extremely appropriate on both the formal and thematic levels. The first few lines of the spiritual in the headnote reiterate the resolve shown in the previous story by Copper, who demonstrates that he "shall not be moved" by either Frank's injunctions or the men sent after him. In addition, the bad weather in the beginning makes it seem to Chuckkie's mother "like this whole world coming apart" (224). Thus "Just Like a Tree" carries forward the previous story's theme of the dying old order, but by focusing on the black community rather than on the white plantation house. Aunt Fe's initial consent to move from her birthplace reiterates the theme of sacrifice—an ethic in which the men of the previous stories have been schooled. Yet her strong will echoes the complementary note of fierce independence that animates their struggles.

Like the volume itself, "Just Like a Tree" is a composite of voices and thus serves as a microcosm of the book as a whole in its merging of different perspectives on the same scene. Moussorgsky's *Pictures at an Exhibition*, Gaines has remarked, served as one prototype for this structure (Callahan, "Hearing" 112). Admittedly, each section of the story is not independent: with the shift to each subsequent speaker, the plot follows a linear progression through time up to Emmanuel's departure and Aunt Fe's death. The narrative voices are ordered so as to begin with Chuckkie, a young boy, and end with the oldest character, Aunt Lou, in a manner similar to that which the voices in the preceding stories progress from Sonny to Felix. Thus the final story reschools the reader in the process of integrating the multiple voices, yet it reminds him or her that these voices exist in unresolved tension. The overall arrangement of the stories in *Bloodline* gives some sense of an increasing social consciousness, but the final story depicts the value of the communal past and the need to preserve the vivifying essence embodied in Aunt Fe, who appears "to affirm all and negate nothing" (Byerman, *Fingering* 86). Paradoxically, while the volume's curve of growth and increasing independence suggests the likelihood of social change, the sequential element that moves the stories forward in time is balanced by another force: the abiding nature of place imbued with a history that lends continuity to character and overcomes disjunction. Ending the volume with "Just Like a Tree" emphasizes the rootedness in place that feeds Emmanuel's courage and also introduces a feminine power that nurtures but does not stultify. As embodied in Aunt Fe, the feminine ethic is rooted in the community but stresses complementarity with the male struggle for self-realization. The bloodline that will dominate the future runs, finally, across gender lines. Flowing from Aunt Fe to Emmanuel, it carries the memory of past injustice and emerges in the nonviolent resistance Aunt Fe symbolically condones. Her immobility and endurance are transmuted into the revolutionary spirit that will invigorate a new order.

"Just Like a Tree" takes on a different character when it is considered in light of the development of themes in the preceding stories. Werner observes that "out of context, it seems to express Gaines's helplessness before the contradictions which force him to admire the system which enslaved his ancestors. . . . In context, it marks a resolution of Gaines's realistic and symbolic perceptions; it rejects the southern system, despite its noble elements" (36). Had the book concluded with "Bloodline," the call for a cataclysmic change from the sterile old order would have made such a rejection more absolute, yet Copper's unrequited and somewhat fanatical idealism would lack realistic grounding and foster doubt about the possibility of resolving the gap between the real and ideal. In "Just Like a Tree," although the radical youth departs from the quarters, the conclusion is more hopeful since the masculine element receives its strength from the enduring African-American communal tradition. Exactly what Emmanuel will *do* is no more concrete than Copper's promise to return, yet he will preserve a noble spirit of resistance cultivated under the old order. However, as William Burke notes, while the future may appear to bode well for male dignity, consoling maternalism will be absent (544).

Given the context provided by *Bloodline*'s setting and themes, the short story sequence form becomes a structural analogue for the two seemingly contradictory historical impulses that Gaines's stories depict. The generic autonomy of the stories emphasizes the historical separation—from each other and from the community—that is part of the black male heritage. At the same time, the volume's sequential and associative dimensions join the lives of its distinct characters and organize them into a sequence that sketches—albeit loosely and provisionally— a coherent vision of progress that recognizes the tension between continuity and change.

Like other short story sequences, *Bloodline* demands that the reader begin to understand the larger story emerging from the inherent connections between lives united by a common setting that dictates shared struggles. Gaines illustrates that these seemingly disjunct lives partake of a single bloodline—one that may be connected in a meaningful sequence that not only reaffirms a vanishing and ambiguous community but also reasserts the importance of the nascent spirit of social change emerging at the same time the community becomes weaker. Gaines has remarked that "there are certain things that, yes, I do want retained, I want kept. However, we have not reached a point in our lives of knowing how to keep this and make changes, too" (Gaudet and Wooton 49). Yet this short story sequence appears to embody that possibility, encapsulating the communal legacy and ultimately connecting it to a progressive spirit.

Form and theme thus converge neatly, as the formal paradox of each story's simultaneous independence and interdependence reflects not only each maturing individual's movement away from the past toward self-realization and manhood but also his unseverable relationship with the larger community and its "feminine" virtues of compassion and endurance. Because the volume's disjunction and heterogeneity coexist with overarching unities derived from the common locale and the arrangement of the five stories, the reader is spurred to trace and connect the repeated motifs that promote the loose overall coherence in this community of stories. Paradoxically, in doing so, the reader recreates and thus preserves a historical community that is in the process of dissolution as time and social change transform it. The deep structure generated from the repeated themes and scenarios that bind the stories thus becomes the bloodline linking the diverse struggles over time. While the progressive, sequential dimension of *Bloodline* affirms the value of progress and change that will be the fruit of independence from the historical roots of oppression, the spatial unity established over the course of the volume affirms the respect for the communal past that must not be abandoned. For Gaines, the form of the short story sequence helps capture this dynamic tension between opposite impulses and ultimately serves as a formal reflection of his hope that the pulse of place will continue to animate the new order.

Notes

1. The debate continues over the more appropriate name for this form. Both Ingram and Mann employ the term *cycle.* Kennedy follows suit in a recent special issue of *Journal of the Short Story in English,* although he remarks that the more general term *short story collection* might suffice. Other names for the form have also been proposed, ranging from *rovelle* to *short story composite.* Nevertheless, I prefer the label *short story sequence* because of its affinity with the poetic sequence and the dominant sequential dimension of the reading experience.

2. A number of critics have commented on one or more of *Bloodline*'s various unities. Mann includes a listing for *Bloodline* in her annotated bibliography. Bryant ("Gaines") and Hicks ("To Make") examine the role of history in delimiting the individual struggles. Burke, McDonald, and Shelton ("Ambiguous") focus on the central importance of the theme of manhood. Byerman (*Fingering*) traces the narrators' quests for "the presence that must always be deferred" (74) in his study of the black folk aesthetic. Callahan ("Hearing") discusses the importance of voice in creating a unified landscape. Duncan argues that the volume depicts stages in Erikson's model of the human life cycle. Roberts ("Individual") examines a theme that runs throughout the volume but looks only at its presence in the first two stories. Werner's study of Gaines's debt to Joyce contains the best discussion of the volume's closure. Babb provides the most comprehensive explication of the volume as "a connected whole, a bildungsroman depicting a quest toward manhood and stressing the importance of family and community in the making of dignity" (15).

3. For a more extended discussion of the Joycean influence on Gaines, see Werner 34–40.

4. "When I did not find my people in the Southern writers, I started reading books about the peasantry of other places," Gaines has stated. "I read the John Steinbeck people of the Selinas [*sic*] Valley, the Chicanos as well as the poor whites" (O'Brien 83).

5. For Gaines's most extended remarks on the oral tradition, see Gaudet and Wooten 7–21.

6. "A Long Day in November," *Texas Quarterly* 7 (1964): 190–224; "The Sky Is Gray," *Negro Digest* 12 (Aug. 1963): 72–96; "Just Like a Tree," *Sewanne Review* 71 (1963): 542–48.

7. See O'Brien 91.

The Autobiography of Miss Jane Pittman as a Fictional Edited Autobiography

Mary Ellen Doyle

"A Short Biography of Miss Jane Pittman" or "The Collected Tales of Miss Jane Pittman." The former title is the one Ernest J. Gaines first gave his novel; the other, a title suggested for the first three books of the novel (Gaines, "Miss Jane and I" 37; Callahan, *Grain* 205). Why was Gaines wise in finally titling his work *The Autobiography*, although it is a novel? Given his plot, he required a simulation of that genre; given his protagonist, he could hardly expect to get it. But endowed with his own creativity and craft, he was able to invent a character—an editor—and through him, seize the artistic opportunities and solve the special problems of the unusual subgenre that would meet his needs.

Critical theorists of autobiography have been especially busy the last fifty years. They agree that autobiography is more diffuse than memoir because it embraces a long stretch of the autobiographer's life, usually including some significant childhood events. It has some of life's random quality yet also exhibits selectivity according to a pattern imposed by the purpose for writing. Above all, the form involves a public, conscious self-presentation and interpretation, perhaps self-creation and even unconscious self-revelation.[1] The freedom and variety allowed by the autobiographical form have made it attractive to novelists creating a protagonist whose story can best be self-told. Yet not every novel with a first-person protagonist-narrator can properly be called fictional autobiography. The crucial variants are those of the form being imitated: a **89** long stretch of the character's life, which can be presumed to continue beyond the end of the novel; seemingly random events loosely patterned by the protagonist's purpose, which may be minimally focused; a certain degree of self-awareness and a self-definition, either explicit or implied by the author standing behind the character.

To illustrate from American literature, *Adventures of Huckleberry Finn, The Color Purple, The Autobiography of an Ex-Colored Man,* and *The Autobiography of Miss Jane Pittman* are all first-person narratives of some length, but only the last two can be called fictional autobiography. *Huckleberry Finn,* despite its picaresque quality, is too narrowly focused on Huck's adolescent confrontation with social evil; his fictional life lasts only a short time; he himself is barely aware of its implications; and when the novel ends, he is as fictionally finished as any happy-ever-after protagonist. In *The Color Purple,* Celie's knocked-about life continues many more years than Huck's, but only near the end does she seem very aware of its wider meaning, and the epistolary form indicates her private purpose as well as creates the impression of the text's having been written very soon after the events. The nameless "writer" of *The Autobiography of an Ex-Colored Man,* on the other hand, tells his story from the earliest memory of his white father to a time after his white wife's death, and he has clearly selected just that time span. His life is far from over, but the crucial choice has been made, and his reasons for the decision and the emotional consequences of it have been made known. His purpose in telling has been accomplished. He knows his own ambivalence, yet not as clearly as Johnson, the author, knows and has made the reader know. Jane Pittman's long and varied life, by contrast, is loosely patterned by the development of her personality and her movement through changing locales and eras. As her story progresses, she seems to grow in modest awareness of its communal nature and significance, and her fictional denouement is literally another step forward in a march that must end only because she is too old to go much farther.

Gaines's novel, however, reveals one problematic difference from "real" autobiography. In the latter, narrators can and do tell or write their own story, even in "told to" accounts such as *The Autobiography of Malcolm X.* Malcolm was so busy, harassed, and emotionally reluctant to talk that it took his collaborator, Alex Haley, to elicit and edit the story. Still, Malcolm was intensely aware of the implications of his experience, and he remained in control of the contents and even the form of the book. But what if the real form cannot be even simulated? What if the protagonist of a novel could not plausibly tell his or her own story in anything like book form or even see any reason to tell it at all?

One solution to such problems, used as early as the eighteenth century, has been to invent an editor, a person supposed to have received the tale from the protagonist, given it appropriate literary form, and then published it. This person may be a thin mask for the author himself (as in Defoe's *Moll Flanders*) or a distinct character with a created history, personality, and motivation (as in *Miss Jane Pittman*). Either way, the editor inevitably has a stance toward the protagonist and the tale, which is revealed in the exercise of such editorial prerogatives as selecting and arranging episodes, recasting language and style, and commenting explicitly within the text. The author's view, then, is revealed through both the protagonist and the editor.

The story of Jane Pittman inevitably required the form of fictional edited autobiography. In narrating it, Gaines encountered obstacles that might have seemed insurmountable. He wanted to cover a century of Miss Jane's life and that of her people, to make her a distinct individual with her own thoughts and feelings who could yet embody their common experience. That time span would require a seemingly loose yet cunningly crafted narrative. Unless he was to use the omniscient mode (which he says he does not like to do), he would have to simulate either biographical reminiscence or autobiography.[2] The latter form probably seemed out of the question. How could Miss Jane write her own story? She is illiterate and, at 110 years of age, inevitably confused sometimes in telling about the century she remembers. Moreover, she sees no purpose for the account; according to her, there is "no story to tell" (v).

Given such obstacles, in writing initial drafts of the book, Gaines leaned on a custom in the black plantation community and wrote the story from the multiple points of view of old people who gathered after Miss Jane's funeral to talk about her. But he found they would naturally ramble too much and know too little, especially of her thoughts. He needed a "straight line" amid the anecdotes and opinions and could get it, he thought, only through Miss Jane's own narration; she was much the best storyteller anyway (Gaines, "Miss Jane and I" 36–37). When he found that she, too, rambled, he invented the editor, a young black history teacher, who, in 1962–63, tape-recorded Miss Jane's life story over months of interviews with her and with other folk of long memory. Some months later, at her funeral, this editor talked with many people she had mentioned, who more or less—mostly more—corroborated what she had said. Then he selected, ordered, and shaped the account, using only Miss Jane's voice regardless of the actual source of information, and wrote an introduction stating exactly what he had done and why.

In Gaines's own testimony in a personal interview, this editor "solved all my problems." Content and form can both be credibly accounted for (albeit with slight strain in an instance or two) by the function of the editor, who could employ two main resources: the rich oral traditions of rural Southern blacks, especially older ones, and his own editorial prerogatives. All events are those Miss Jane could have experienced directly or vicariously; she or someone else could remember and tell them. The editor could retain her voice and views while giving all that material the shape necessary to make the book he wanted, a better book of history than his students' texts.

Among rural black folk, conversation and storytelling have long been the basic ways of gathering news, entertaining, and remembering history. On porches or before fires, the young listen to the old; friends exchange stories at any time. Into this oral world, Gaines easily fit his young teacher with a tape recorder who, by questions and comments, elicits all he wants to know about personal and communal history.

Miss Jane cannot write, but she can talk! She cannot talk too long without fatigue and cannot take events in a straight line from 1862 to 1962, but the fictional pretense of taping and editing allows for gathering materials in any order during numerous sessions.[3] It makes a plausible way to overcome her limits of memory, clarity, and endurance through the assistance of the other folk who, out of curiosity, would traditionally gather wherever talk was being shared. These folk, old but not as old as she, can provide information she lacks, remember what she forgets, keep going when she gets tired or confused, and correct her errors (or give the editor a choice among versions). They can also stimulate one another's memories with comments beginning "You remember . . ." or "Don't forget . . ." or "That brings to mind. . . ." The whole story as written could not have come from Miss Jane alone. Given the black oral tradition, it would not and need not. Rather, the entire community contributes and thus becomes the guarantor of the truth of her history, to both the young interviewer and his readers.[4]

Oral tradition accounts also for the preservation of so many memories and for Miss Jane's knowing so much that neither she nor the folk at the taping sessions had witnessed. Stories were repeated many times until fixed in many minds, and the grapevine stretched through the quarters, from one plantation to another and one generation to another. Thus she can tell of slaves' escape attempts through the bayous (71) or the history of the LeFabre family back to Mary Agnes's grandmother and the Creole balls (158–59), and she can assert that there are "people here at Samson right now who can back me up" (159).

Miss Jane narrates many events she has not witnessed directly. In only a very few instances, such as the dismissal of Timmy (146), would she have had to be present or to eavesdrop in an improbable way in order to know what she tells. In all other cases, especially those relating to the tragic suicide of Tee Bob Samson, Gaines has skillfully provided witnesses who told her the events: Albert Walker and Cleon Simon saw the fight between Timmy and Tom Joe (145); Etienne, Tee Bob's first sight of Mary Agnes (163); Ethel Hawkins, Tee Bob's first visit to the school (165–66) and his locking himself in the library (181); Clamp Brown, the meeting of Tee Bob and Mary Agnes at the bus stop (166–67); Jules Raynard and Jimmy Caya, their conversations with Tee Bob (Miss Jane eavesdrops on Jimmy's report, as well she might) (181, 191); and Clamp, Ida, and Joe Simon, the discovery of Mary Agnes and her talk with Jules Raynard and Sheriff Guidry (177–80, 191–92). From these witnesses at the scene, everyone in the quarters would learn the whole story of Tee Bob. Other events, similarly reported, occur within the quarters: Miss Lilly's protest to Oscar Haynes about his "smoking" his sons (154–56), Joe Hardy's dealings with Francine Bouie (156–57), Sappho and Claudee's adventure with the Creoles (159–61), and Jimmy's first sexual adventures with Eva Strut (208–11). In reporting these to the editor, Miss Jane could say that Ida said that Clamp said that he saw . . . and so on. Or many folk could tell the tale for her, allowing her to agree or not (vi–vii). The editor would transcribe it more or less as she told it or conflate her version with that of Pap, Mary, or the others to whom Miss Jane turned when her memory was weak.

The thorniest problem in arguing for the accuracy of this autobiographical narrative is accounting for Miss Jane's remembering in detail events sixty to a hundred years in the past. Unquestionably, she would have recounted her own main experiences, perhaps hundreds of times by 1962, thus carving them in her memory and making herself a living archive. How many times, for instance, might she have retold her trek toward Ohio, Ned's youth and departure, his return and death, Joe Pittman's breaking free of Colonel Dye, Miss Jane's own visit to the hoodoo woman, and Albert Cluveau's death—all replete with detail? She went to Samson's in her late fifties, with those memories of Ned and Joe still sharp, and she would have told them often to the people who now, at the taping sessions, could jog her memory, say what she'd said before, and fill in the gaps as she tried to tell the editor. Living in the parish for all his eighty years (vi), Pap must have been in his twenties at the time of Ned's sermon. Consequently, he could assist Miss Jane in recalling both general circumstances and specific details, which he, as much as she, might have recounted often over many years. Most of us have known very old people for whom the far past is more vivid and detailed than the latest hour; repetition must be at least partly responsible.

Finally, Miss Jane recounts both single events and the atmosphere of broad historic periods, matters that had been so often and so widely discussed as to become the stuff of enduring plantation legend. Her mother's altercation with the overseer (28) and the shooting of Ned (114–16) would be such events.[5] The Confederates' boasts of a one-day war to save their Biblically ordained way of life (5) would have been ironically embellished by house servants and repeated for years afterward. The accounts of the floods (147–50) and of Huey Long's career and assassination (151–53) clearly result from many people's reminiscing aloud over many years. Now they sit with Miss Jane and the young teacher-editor; she listens to them, agrees or disagrees, recreates her own version, and inserts her own philosophical comments in the traditional oral mode. And he takes this mass of material and edits it into something readable and publishable.

Oral tradition alone would obviously not solve all of Gaines's problems in creating Miss Jane's narrative voice. Stories the folk could provide in plenty, and one could easily recreate their storytelling; but the problem of selection and order remained. This he could overcome only by the prerogatives of his created editor.

The teacher-editor says he wanted Miss Jane's life story to help him explain history to his students (v). Once she has consented to give it to him and the folk have agreed to cooperate, he has the right to edit according to his purpose. Gaines says that Miss Jane is *not* a "capsule

history of black people of the rural South during the last hundred years";
she is herself, Miss Jane ("Miss Jane and I" 37). Yet he likens her to many
old women who have seen and remember much, and he has been said to
view history as the character of people, especially the "little people." [6]
Certainly that concept of history is what his teacher-editor illustrates by
selection and style.

His principle of selection is to use what pertains to Miss Jane's own
life, what she told or could have told from her own experience or hearing. However much others may have contributed at the tapings, the editor never interpolates their unrelated personal experiences or his or their
interpretations of historical events to supplement Miss Jane's. The era
of Reconstruction, for instance, is evoked in her recollections of sending
Ned to the "little school on the place" taught by "a young colored man
from the North," of "colored politicians" who would "hold meetings
with Bone" and then "gather us at the school" to listen to speeches about
the "Fedjal Gov'ment" and the "Freedom Beero," of typical arguments
and a fight at a political rally, and of beatings and harassment by the
"secret groups" (66–68). The causes and effects of the end of Reconstruction (a history teacher's concern) are suggested, from Miss Jane's
point of view, in Bone's explanation of why "he didn't own the place no
more," the appearance of Colonel Dye in his "Secesh uniform," and the
closing of the school (69–70). Thus history is what happened to people
Miss Jane knew. "Truth to Miss Jane is what she remembers. Truth to
me," as Gaines says, "is what people like Miss Jane remember" ("Miss
Jane and I" 37). And so also is historical truth to the editor.

The writing of a "history" of any sort, however, demands that the
selected memories be put in some order. For his students, the editor preferred the chronology of Miss Jane's life in relation to American history.
The childhood section from the massacre of the fleeing ex-slaves to her
settling at Bone's has no links to specific historical events. The episodes
and encounters did not necessarily occur in the exact order given; we
might suppose that Miss Jane simply narrated them as they came to
mind and that the editor created sequence by such markers as "that evening" and "the next day." Later personal events, however, are ordered
by datable public events: Ned's return the "next summer" after the end
of the Spanish-American War; his death "a year later, almost to the day"
(98); the death of Cluveau "just before the high water there of '12"
(124); Jimmy's departure "the same year they passed that law in Wash-

ington" [she is referring to the *Brown vs. Board of Education* Supreme Court decision in 1954] (217). Miss Jane or Pap or someone else might have made these links spontaneously; Gaines says that Pap was modeled on Walter Zeno, an old man on his home plantation who could not remember exact dates, distances, or numbers but narrated many far-back events by association with the "last big storm" or the "time so and so drowned in a certain bayou" ("Miss Pittman's Background" 23). On the other hand, the interviewer might have deliberately elicited the historical connections. In any case, he has used them so skillfully that Miss Jane's, Ned's, and Jimmy's principal life events can all be dated, and the reader perceives them as truly a part of the flow of American history.

Chronological order is most apparent in the sectional divisions, which are the work of the editor (see Callahan, *Grain* 201–2, 205). The four "Books" are four "ages" of Miss Jane: childhood, maturity, seniority, old age. They also illustrate those significant differences in her function at each age, which would have interested the history teacher, a younger black male. In the first two sections, Miss Jane is directly active, the brave black woman forced into early maturity and leadership but, at her best, learning to encourage the maturity and free choice of her men. As she ages, she becomes more an observer of episodes in which she has little or no direct part but which continue to shape the wisdom she passes on to such young folk as Jimmy—and the editor. Finally, in her old, old age, she becomes again an activist and leader. Having helped to form Jimmy, she is the first to decide to demonstrate with him, and her courage brings out the people.[7]

When more complex arrangements of material occur within each of the four sections, we may well remember Gaines, the craftsman, creating both Miss Jane and the editor, simulating both the natural, convoluted storytelling of an old woman and the ordering work of her historian. Within individual episodes, for instance, some startling variations in chronological order occur. At the tragic climax of Tee Bob's infatuation with Mary Agnes, Miss Jane is not in the quarters. She is working in Samson's house and witnesses only what occurs there. The rest she hears later from Jules Raynard and especially Ida. The narration of the whole story, however, mixes the orders of occurrence and of her awareness. Beginning with Tee Bob's conversation with Jimmy Caya, the story proceeds in chronological order until the high point of suspense, when Mary Agnes tries to leave the cabin (172–77). Then the narrative abruptly switches to the experiences of Clamp, Joe Simon, and Ida after Tee Bob runs out (177–80). Next come the events Miss Jane saw and heard herself surrounding the suicide at the house (180–91). At this point she apparently eavesdrops on Jimmy Caya as he is telling about his last conversation with Tee Bob earlier that day (172–74). Next comes Mary Agnes's account to Raynard and Guidry, overheard by Ida, of what transpired inside the cabin (191–92). The narrative ends with Raynard's taking Miss Jane back to the quarters and giving her his version of that event and of the suicide in the locked library (193–96). However much Raynard's account may be "specalatin," the reader by now has seen him enough to share Miss Jane's view of him as "a good man," dependable for psychological and moral insight, and so may be willing to accept his version at least as much as she does.

But why are the events of this tragedy narrated in such an intricate order? For at least three discernible reasons: for clarity, as some sense of the chronology of the earlier events spares the reader useless confusion; for suspense at the moment of maximum tension and moral choice for Tee Bob; and for realism, as a reflection of the bits-and-pieces process in which the people acquired knowledge of events and recounted them on the tape. For the most part, however, the arrangement reenacts the unraveling of acts and motives required of those who want justice (the quarters residents and Raynard) in the face of those impelled by fear, vengeance, or the "old rules" (Caya, Robert Samson, Guidry). Thus the focus of the tale is not on tragic love so much as on justice, on the rules that allow all who accept them to kill those who don't, and on Raynard's final words to Miss Jane late that night—"Poor us."

Selection and arrangement imply deliberate omission of materials, and here especially an editor can intensify an accurate focus of character or can falsify. What might Miss Jane's editor have chosen to omit, and why? Granting that any answers are necessarily "specalatin," they gain credibility from what we know: that the taped interview sessions went on for "eight or nine months," that the editor tried "not to write everything, but in essence everything that was said" (vii), and that he is a history teacher and a man.

Over so many months, with so many folks talking, we may suppose much was said about common daily labor and daily events; these the editor reduced to their essence and placed in the background of the narrative. Except for the story of the horse breaker Joe Pittman, work is mentioned casually, briefly: "We was in the field chopping cotton" (10); Bone asks about the work Miss Jane has done—"I told him" (59). Twelve years of Reconstruction at Bone's are capsulized in five pages focused on the black teacher and politicians (65–69); the years under Colonel Dye center first on Ned and then on Joe Pittman. Miss Jane spends ten years at Clyde's, all of them working inside the house. But except for her encounter with Molly, she says nothing of her labor there; the story is about Joe Pittman and his work with horses. It is Ned's and Joe's work that seems to matter, and if that seems a biased focus by a male editor, it may be. It may also, however, express the vital importance these two men had in Miss Jane's life and in her overall recollections of the past. Moreover, it may express the editor's simple awareness that field and kitchen labor were common knowledge to his intended audience—the schoolchildren—whereas the work and status of a teacher, political leader, and "Chief" cowboy would be signals of possibility, dignity, and aspiration for them.

Other omissions about features of daily life may be variously accounted for. Two could well be Miss Jane's rather than the editor's. From her childhood, she probably would call up only those episodes that were startling, frightening, or otherwise sufficiently significant to a child to fix them in her memory so that retellings over the years established them as legends. The editor might well keep all such early material and simply reconstruct scenes and dialogue. Similarly, the tone and brevity of the paragraph allotted to the three years with Felton Burkes (98)—less than is given to the strangers she meets in book 1—seem a sign of her indifference to him rather than editorial excision of the tape transcripts.

Book 3, "The Plantation," does contain more about the fieldwork, religion, and life-style in the Samson quarters, also about outside events of the natural and political world as these affected Miss Jane and her people. Still, of the forty-five people named, only eight have active roles, and none is prominent. The longest story is that of white Tee Bob and Creole Mary Agnes. Even more significant is the total focus of book 4, "The Quarters," on Jimmy, beginning with his birth in 1938 and ending with his death in 1962. A lot more must have happened in "The Quarters" in twenty-four years, even to Jimmy, than what is told. Who omitted so much and why? The real "who," of course is Ernest Gaines, who consciously structured his novel around the four principal men in Miss Jane's life (Gaines, personal interview). Within the context of the novel, however, one may "specalate" that Miss Jane talked a great deal about Tee Bob and Jimmy and their shocking, violent deaths and that the history teacher chose to minimize and dim the background scenes in order to highlight them and their representational function. Indeed, all four books, though differently focused in content, suggest omissions of the common and daily business of life in order to accentuate certain motifs: identity, manhood, leadership, relationships of black men to the women and the families that love them, the "rules" of race relations, and, above all, endurance, courage, and the importance of moving on even when one stays, even when one dies.

The emphasis on the forward movement of people and history accounts for several omissions clearly made for dramatic impact. Several chapters end at a dramatic moment, even in the middle of a conversation, such as the one Miss Jane has with Vivian, who will stay by her threatened husband (106), and the one she has with Ned, who will stay to die (112). The finest instance is the ending of the novel, almost certainly not where a reminiscing old lady would have stopped her story. The editor would surely have obtained a full account of the demonstration in Bayonne and the aftermath of the confrontation between Robert Samson and his defiant tenants. It is therefore the editor's choice to make the blunt and dramatic finish: "Me and Robert looked at each other there a long time, then I went by him" (246). The drama renders and emphasizes its meaning: when Miss Jane has led the people past the modern symbol of "ownership" and oppression, her essential task is done. Only by inference from the introduction does the reader realize that the people did overcome, that this time Robert was unable to evict the troublemakers; they are all still on Samson's plantation, telling this story, as noted by John Callahan (*Grain* 213).

After selecting and ordering, the editor would have to make his work realistic and yet readable by reconstructing Miss Jane's language. Since she rambled and digressed, he must improve her coherence yet retain her diction and cadence. And he must fill out the approximations of dialogue she remembered aloud. Although most of Miss Jane's digressions were corrected by chronological reordering, the editor could and did retain some of her ramblings to preserve the style of oral history being passed on in its natural context and the personally meaningful associations of apparently disconnected events. Miss Jane's narratives weave together three distinct time periods: present storytelling, past story-action, and even-before-that memory. Telling the past story-action ("the people started leaving" after Reconstruction) reminds her of some prior event, and she's off on an old folk-history segment (the slaves trying to escape through the bayous); then she returns to the story time (official discussion of the reasons for the post-Reconstruction black exodus), clearly with her mature present understanding (71–72). In a similar way, the introduction of Mary Agnes LeFabre leads to the history of her grandmother and thus to the comment from present wisdom that Mary Agnes was "trying to make up for the past—and that you cannot do" (158). In many cases, Miss Jane's memory simply carries her from a deadly serious point (the indignity and inconvenience of segregated facilities) to purely comic recollection (Unc Gilly's large overalls that he couldn't return and the "looney" guard chasing Bertha round the courthouse) (231–32). The editor apparently retained these digressions to illustrate how "laughing to keep from crying" sustained the people in this history.

The editor says he retained three particular features of Miss Jane's language: her diction, rhythms, and repetitions (vii). Although he does not say so, in transcribing audiotapes, he also had to decide how to represent her pronunciation by spelling and how much dialect to use. He needed to avoid two errors: the crude representations of dialect that have exaggerated and degraded black speech in much Southern white literature over the years, and the sustained use of dialect in long passages where it might confuse or distract readers. The editor seems to have the experience of listening in the quarters that could help him avoid the former error if he also had skill or assistance in rendering dialect. The second error was avoided by a sensitive balance, in the narration, of standard English interspersed with colloquial diction and rhythms and by a reversal of those proportions in the dialogue. Of course, the literal fact is that Gaines himself made Miss Jane's voice distinctive, probably not by consciously deciding to create such balance or avoid exaggeration but simply by having listened mentally to the voices of ex-slaves in the WPA narratives and aurally to those of his aunt and her visitors on the gallery: "I worked her voice, plus the ex-slaves' voices, over and over until I got the one I liked. It took a while but it was no problem. I could look at my walls and remember" (Carter 71; see also Callahan, *Grain* 19–21, 190–92). He simply transferred his own skills to his editor. The result is that in the published text Miss Jane's "language contributes to rather than detracts from the force of her personality" (Jones 165). Dialect is chiefly represented by phonetic spelling and contractions ("Secesh," "rarrying to go," "clamb no tree," "y'all," "go'n," "kinda"), by grammatical irregularities ("knowed," "gived," "memories was," "don't like no old rabbit nohow"), and by colloquial diction ("one of them laws" for "policeman"). To capture Miss Jane's rhythms, sentence structures are abbreviated, fragmented, interrupted by reminiscent phrases, or extended by colloquial questions: "I ain't going no South" (49); "I told Yoko, I said. . . . Yoko, dead and gone now, said. . . ." (219); "That was one more day, you hear me?" (222). Her repetitions may convey the drama of grief as Vivian sits "just looking at the body. . . . Just looking at the body. . . . — just looking at the body" (117). Or they may convey humor, as when she lectures on a proper diet and life-style: "It's good for you—fish. Fish and work. . . . plain steady work. . . . Steady work and eating plenty fish. . . . Greens good, too. Fish and greens and good steady work" (102). Miss Jane would have used even more such rhythmic repetitions than the editor kept. He had to decide what to retain and where, and his judgment has created a book of history we can "hear" from an elderly, untrained historian whose experience we can share.

To infer how the editor reconstructed Miss Jane's conversations, one must first ask how she would have reported or recreated them. More crucial for credibility, how could she have remembered them, especially those of her childhood? Book 1 consists almost entirely of her encounters while wandering in central Louisiana and is therefore rich in dialogue. These she would recall and repeat in terms of their essential meaning for her: geographical reality impinging on her hopes. The prime instance is that of the man with the map: Miss Jane might well have remembered that he had one; talked "all this lat and longi stuff" (48); and named the many states, cities, and rivers on her route. She might even have acquired a little understanding of geography since then to supplement her memories. From that much, the editor would add numbers and names and so create the whole comic-ironic scene.

Crucial adult conversations, such as that with the hoodoo woman (93–96), offer fewer problems. Miss Jane might well have recalled them much better because of having repeated them often and closer in time to the original events, and she could repeat them during the taped interviews in "I said . . . she said" form. Or she might still be adept at the folk art of creating dialogue and dramatizing scenes during storytelling. Recent dialogues, such as the argument in church with Just Thomas, she could recreate in some detail to show how she relished making points (225–26).

In all cases, it remains the editor's prerogative to fill in words or delete the interruptions that might have occurred on the gallery and thus to intensify and focus Miss Jane's stories and to give order and exact form to her dialogue. In these reconstructions, perhaps more than in any other element, he creates the text, and it could not conceivably or credibly exist without him. Yet he is not wholly free to develop or compose; ethical bounds forbid his giving Miss Jane a personality or history of his own making. An editor is not a novelist. The literary irony is that by creating an apparently ethical editor, Gaines has masked the very techniques he, the novelist, has used.

Yet a final question remains: to what degree can this text, the "autobiography" of Miss Jane Pittman, aged and female, credibly exist *with* this editor, much younger and male? This question has been largely answered by implication in the previous discussion of his techniques, yet the disparity of age and gender as an influence on his choices merits closer examination. Is this a man's book, a masculine manipulation of Miss Jane's viewpoint? Although he loves and respects Miss Jane, does he also understand her enough to render those experiences particularly defined by gender—the interests and feelings she shares with other women and her friendships or antagonisms for them? He does seem to have omitted much material of that sort. Numerous women actively enter Miss Jane's story as her friends, coworkers, or acquaintances: Molly, Madame Gautier, Vivian, Mary Agnes LeFabre, Verda, Lena Washington, Amma Dean Samson, Adeline Cluveau, and others who are sources of her information. Yet the book contains very few scenes of the small events or conversations in which women alone share their emotions, hopes, and values. The principal ones are Miss Jane's visit to the hoodoo woman and the daily gatherings of old women at Samson's. The conversations at these moments, however, focus on Joe Pittman and Jimmy. Young men are prominent at all stages of Miss Jane's life; no woman has an importance approaching that of Ned, Joe, or Jimmy. Are the omissions Miss Jane's or the editor's?

Other black men, of course, are not always portrayed as fully and sympathetically as those three are. The editor is sufficiently objective to note several examples of significant weaknesses or absences of black men. Clamp and Joe Simon are terrified to report the apparent rape of Mary Agnes and want to foist the task on a child (179–80); Felton Burkes deserts Miss Jane after three years (98); and Jimmy's father similarly decamps (199–200). The first desertion "didn't bother me none," Miss Jane says, because no man could replace Joe Pittman (98). She is much more disturbed, however, by the desertion of Jimmy's father and puts it in the historical context of the black family; in having children, he "done what they told him a hundred years before to do, and he had forgot it just like a hundred years ago they had told him to forget" (200). That "excuse" has a rather masculine tone; what did "they" tell women to do? If the link were made by Miss Jane herself, the history teacher would undoubtedly have picked it up, or he might have originated it editorially as an explanation for his students and a sort of apology for a phenomenon with which they are painfully familiar. The related sexual exploitation of women by both white and black men and the responsibilities thrust on older women for raising children are also made clear in Jimmy's life, but not so explicitly discussed as in the story of Mary Agnes LeFabre. It seems either that Miss Jane left alone what she knew too well and did not need to explain, or the editor left alone what he could not enter by direct sympathetic knowledge.

The novel is a man's rendition of a woman's experience, and thus a man's concerns are reflected in the text. Yet the edited text is not therefore, unauthentic. Unless we are to suppose massive and highly chauvinist omissions from the taped material—an assumption justified by nothing in the text and contradicted by the editor's introductory assurance that he wrote "in essence everything that was said" (vii)—we have to accept that Miss Jane's life did not include relationships with other women whose intimacy and impact were equal to those of her relationships with men. That is not a radically unusual female experience. Furthermore, she is clearly sensitive to the feelings and oppressive experiences of other black women: Molly, Mary Agnes, Verda, Vivian, and Lena. Even to the white Amma Dean Samson and the Cajun Adeline Cluveau she gives the sympathy of one woman for another who is suffering under a domineering and immoral man. Her intuitions and philosophy of life are often distinctly feminine. For example, it is scarcely masculine to consider levees and spillways as punishable infringements on the freedom of rivers. Women readers, especially black ones, have recognized the authenticity of Miss Jane's personality and experience.[8] Gaines has never been excoriated for crossing gender lines as William Styron was for crossing those of race in *The Confessions of Nat Turner.* If Miss Jane's editor omitted anything, he seems to have done so in recognition of his own limitations and in the interest of authenticity.

In *Miss Jane Pittman* we have a man's book in the sense that the actual author is male. And he had the good sense to be forthright about his viewpoint in creating a woman protagonist by also creating a male editor. The latter is distinct from Gaines himself yet obviously incorporates many of Gaines's own experiences and concerns: listening for hours and months and years to his aunt Augusteen Jefferson and other old folk, leaving home and returning, exploring the definitions and possibilities of authentic black manhood, seeking valid and humane ways to understand and change the patterns and rules that have historically governed Southern culture. Just as Gaines listened to and learned from Augusteen Jefferson, so did his teacher-editor from Jane Pittman. Gaines has said that he told the story through Miss Jane's own voice partly because he had "fallen in love with my little character" and he has acknowledged that he acted "as her editor. Never her advisor" ("Miss Jane and I" 37). The same may be said of his character-editor.

The final result of this novel's form, of Gaines's simulation of an extensive editorial process, is, ironically, to have made Miss Jane so real and her story so absorbing that the editor recedes in the reader's mind, although perhaps never fully. Chapter divisions, the attention to chronology, and the very fact of written form all keep the thoughtful reader aware of the intermediary. Yet the spell of Miss Jane's voice tends to block one's constant awareness of the editor. As Marcia Gaudet observes, Miss Jane "takes over as narrator and seems to take on a presence and life of her own" ("Miss Jane" 23). Indeed, several readings may be required before even the most critical reader might think to ask, "How could she know that? Or how could she remember what she heard so long ago?" At that point of questioning the form, the reader encounters the editor, the challenge and pleasure of examining what he tells about his sources and his use of them, checking *his* text—his composition from the tapes—to see if he has indeed made all things possible, tied up all loose ends. And he has, or has so nearly done so that readers have typically assumed Miss Jane's factual reality. Gaines continually has problems persuading reviewers, students, and people on the street that she is fictional, that *he* didn't tape her (or his great-aunt or his grandmother), and that he can't supply her photograph ("Miss Jane and I" 23).[9]

What he has supplied is a vibrant and memorable character, an old woman of much experience, ripe in her insight and wisdom. In presenting her, he has, not incidentally, added much to our knowledge of fictional edited autobiography as a form, about when and how it must be used if the resultant work is to have formal and moral coherence and credibility. In addition, he has demonstrated its possibilities for creating both characters and special meaning. Miss Jane and her editor, by their interaction, create a vision of human collaboration. In the introduction, he tells of her initial reluctance to talk, then her defense of his insistence despite Mary Hodges's threats, even her eagerness to begin. Though she requires other folks' assistance to keep going, may at times be forgetting on purpose, and insists on taking her narrative in any direction she wants, she never quits. And after the last interview, she apparently trusts the young teacher to do with the tapes whatever he wants. When she dies eight months later, his work is unfinished. Apparently he felt no compulsion to edit in haste and obtain her approval. She trusted him to be accurate; he trusted her to trust him. At her funeral he corroborates her story by the testimony of others. In recounting his entire process, he makes clear his reverence and gratitude for Miss Jane and the other people who collaborated. Across boundaries of age, sex, and education—often as divisive as race could be—they have gathered "all of their stories," a history of their people. Cooperatively, they have shaped it for transmission to another generation, presumably of both blacks and whites, who will understand more fully their human unity. Gaines has often said that understanding is his goal. Miss Jane, other elderly residents of the quarters, and the teacher-editor have accomplished it for him and embody his vision of the future.

Notes

1. In particular, see Bates, Blasing, Clark, Eakin, Mansell, Morris, Olney, Pascal, and Weintraub.

2. The following account of Gaines's experiments with form is based on my interview with him. Similar information can be found in Tooker and Hofheins 89–90 and Gaines, "Miss Jane and I" 35–37.

3. Beckham 104–6 refers to Miss Jane's need to keep the listener's attention through the long tale. By implying that she is telling it at a single session, he overlooks the work of the editor in both taping the individual interview sessions and editing the material.

4. For a full discussion of roles and voices in the African-American storytelling tradition and in *Miss Jane Pittman*, see Callahan, *Grain* 15–21, 194–99.

5. Evidence for such commemoration in oral tradition can be had today near Oscar, Louisiana, where a Professor Plantevigne, the prototype of Ned, is commemorated in the conversations of older people ("he taught my husband") and in a marker beside Route 1, where he was shot.

6. Bryant, "Gaines" 861. Foley sees the novel as a pseudodocumentary used to arouse skepticism about a previously accepted version of American history. In a broad sense, her interpretation reflects the editor's purpose, but everything Gaines himself has said in interviews indicates that, as author, he was concerned not with history as such but with presenting people as he knew them.

7. See Gaines's comments in Tooker and Hofheins (91) on Jane as an observer and recorder rather than a person directly involved in the action. He said much the same to me in our 1983 interview. J. Hicks says the story is the history of men who risk action and die and of women who remember, tell, and move along the new paths opened up by the men ("To Make" 18). Neither author nor critic has noted explicitly Jane's return to active leadership at the end; yet she recalls Big Laura at the head of the people moving out in the road (cf. 14 and 243, 16 and 245–46).

8. Miss Jane's representation, in either the novel or the television film, has been discussed and commended by Doyle ("Heroines"), Giovanni, and Hunter. A strong dissent on the television version was registered by Harrington, who did not question Gaines's own textual creation.

9. Foley, who knows the book is a novel, nevertheless believes its goal is "to convince the reader that the historical personage Miss Jane Pittman did actually exist and triumph" (399). Gaines does not agree, but after answering questions about Miss Jane as a historical person in nearly every interview he has granted, he says he is so tired of defending his creation as a fiction that he has stopped trying.

A "Slow-to-Anger" People: *The Autobiography of Miss Jane Pittman* as Historical Fiction

Keith E. Byerman

The Autobiography of Miss Jane Pittman has been seen from its publication as a historical novel, involving as it does the re-counting of black experience from the Civil War to the civil rights movement.[1] But such a categorization can easily be a curse, as the term *historical novel* carries connotations of mass-market period romances. The potential for such association was reinforced when the novel be-came a made-for-television movie starring Cicely Tyson. It thus entered popular culture in the company of *Roots, North and South,* and *Winds of War,* all appeals to simplified versions of both the past and patrio-tism. Heroes, villains, and historical issues are clearly defined in such works, with the utilitarian purpose of making viewers and readers proud of some aspect of the American experience. Even when the heroes are black, the mass audience can easily identify with their courage, loyalty to family, and perseverance—all good American qualities.

There is, however, another tradition of the historical novel, one that includes Sir Walter Scott, Honoré de Balzac, and James Fenimore Cooper and is the subject of *The Historical Novel,* by Georg Lukács. The authors of such fictions undertake to portray the past in a way as to make both it and the present more comprehensible. They seek to rep-resent the full complexity of social relations and conflicts and to show how realities of the past have created the present. For Lukács, the seri-ousness of historical fiction lies in the concreteness of its representation of social reality and its exploration of the dialectic of freedom and ne- 107 cessity (41). His underlying assumption is that literature is a product of its social, political, and economic contexts, and therefore fiction reveals the conflicts and ideological assumptions of the author's own time. Moreover, when that author takes the past as his subject, he validates his writing by representing concretely the historical context as well as his immediate subject matter. In doing so, he necessarily reveals both the universality of human experience, which for Lukács is grounded in historical materialism, and the processes of change that constitute history. Thus, for Lukács, serious historical fiction is a means of revealing the truth of human experience.

In these terms, *Miss Jane Pittman* is clearly serious fiction rather than popular literature. Its characters and their actions are limited by historical conditions. The principal subject of the book is the everyday lives of ordinary people under such conditions. The tension between freedom and necessity is so fully developed that the book has a cyclical pattern. And, finally, out of this cycle, a present is shown to emerge from the past. The story of Jane Pittman is the story of the black masses and their coming to a consciousness of their role in history; but, as shall be seen, the very complexity of the reality and the dialectic created raises questions about the plausibility of the novel's "progressive" conclusion.

The recreation of social reality is for Lukács the sine qua non of serious historical fiction: "The novel's aim is to represent a particular social reality at a particular time, with all the colour and specific atmosphere of that time. Everything else, both collisions and the 'world historical individuals' who figure in them, are no more than means to this end. Since the novel portrays the 'totality of objects,' it must penetrate into the small details of everyday life, into the concrete time of the action, it must bring out what is specific to this time through the complex interaction of all these details" (150–51). In this sense, the function of the historical novel is not antiquarian. That is, its purpose is not to produce the illusion of some moment in a real or imaginary past that is of interest primarily for its exoticism or romance. Rather, the historical novel reproduces as accurately as possible through language the human experience of a given time and place. Such representation is accomplished through depictions of ordinary rather than extraordinary reality, through portrayals of the lives of common people of all classes in their usual ways of living, and through the recreation of the whole rather than some outstanding part.

For Lukács, the writer's task is the creation of a world in its concrete totality. *Miss Jane Pittman* performs this function in a variety of ways. It depicts the economic conditions of the post-Civil War period, the complex and slowly changing racial relationships of a particular Southern community, the folk culture created by blacks in response to their situation, the heroic figures who emerge from that culture, and, most important, what Lukács calls a "mediocre" protagonist, Jane herself.[2] By fully integrating these elements in fiction, Gaines produces a work superior to others written around the same time. Margaret Walker's *Jubilee* (1966) covers similar ground, but its historical details frequently do not become part of the lives of its characters. Alex Haley's *Roots* (1976) was much more successful with the popular audience precisely because it simplified relationships and gave its characters essentially modern sensibilities. The irony, of course, is that it was presented as the most "historical" of such books. Through the aspects mentioned above, Gaines avoids these problems. While *Miss Jane Pittman* does not consistently provide the quantity of detail of other works, the detail that is used very effectively creates a sense of an authentic past continuous with the present.

The economic structure of the South is evident from the beginning in the scenes of life under slavery. The abuse and exploitation of Jane by her mistress concretely represent the realities of the system. Moreover, the point is reinforced when Jane is forced to give up her dream of Ohio in order to provide for Ned and herself. Such material is integrated into the structure of the novel in terms of thematics, plot development, and characterization. Throughout the novel, Gaines links consciousness to economic and ideological systems. The connection to plot is evident in the use of postwar economic desperation to explain why Jane gives up her quest for the North. Survival in a South devastated by a war that destroyed its economic system requires a total commitment to the present rather than the future. So she must go to work, not to create new opportunities but to obtain minimal food and shelter. Thus necessity generates a story of the South and a larger tale about living in a primarily static world rather than questing for some alternative reality.

The most concentrated depiction of economic matters comes in the story of Joe Pittman. Although one of the heroes of the novel, Pittman is less important for challenging racism than for defining his manhood and individuality through confronting and conquering nature. In this sense, he is an archetypal economic man, wresting his identity and livelihood from struggle with unmediated materiality, the origin of all value. His effort to master the wild horses to make them productive for human purposes is emblematic of a fundamental human drive not merely to dominate the natural world but also to give it meaning.

Pittman's heroic character is first apparent in his escape from the economic slavery of the postwar plantation system. He must, in effect, buy the right to create himself by paying off the debts the owner says he owes. To do this, he and Jane sell virtually all their possessions. His decision to clear the debt rather than walk away from it suggests a cleansing ritual and, in economic terms, getting a clear title to himself. Having rid himself of all the accoutrements of that system, he is free to create a new structure by which he returns to the origins of human signification. He reconstructs both human economy and human identity simultaneously.

His reputation as a horse breaker is legendary, so it is appropriate for his greatest challenge to come from a horse that Jane describes in mystical terms: "He was the devil as far as I was concerned. . . . He was stronger and faster than any horse he had ever seen. Run for days and wouldn't get tired. Leap over a canal that a regular horse wouldn't even try. After they had been after him about a week some of the men started saying he was a ghost. Maybe even a haint" (91). Appropriately, she turns to the power of hoodoo to prevent what she clearly foresees as a fatal confrontation. But as the conjure woman explains, such confrontation is "man's way." Although this confrontational style carries connotations of Hemingway's grace under pressure, it has more universally human implications as well. Without such encounters with nature's power, humans cannot create value and meaning. Through Joe Pittman, Gaines is suggesting the truly fundamental economic reality of postwar life for blacks. The achievement of authentic freedom and identity in an environment of social, economic, and political chaos required a return to human origins. Pittman's true heroism, then, lies in his understanding of historical conditions and his willingness to sacrifice himself in the quest for true mastery.

Gaines's grasp of the mythic nature of this episode is indicated by its displacement from the Louisiana setting of the rest of the novel. Its unmediated character cannot be contained within the historically and socially determined world of the plantation. While its function is precisely to define the boundaries of that world, the novelist clearly understands that myth must stand outside history in order to clarify it. Within history, economy and identity are always "contaminated," infected as it were with institutions and ideologies of the past. By moving Joe Pittman's story to a pristine West, Gaines can not only reveal the origins of economy and identity but also elucidate the complex historicity of the Southern world he is recreating. Myth gives history its meaning by being on its margins.

Virtually all the other characters of the novel, both heroic and ordinary, black and white, remain within the historical and economic context. The blacks labor in a sharecropping system barely removed from slavery. The narrative reveals a black community that, from the announcement of emancipation to the civil rights movement, seeks first and foremost to maintain whatever economic security can be had under such a system. This concern helps to explain the essential conservatism of that community in political and cultural as well as economic matters. Its members see these spheres as integrated and realize that survival depends on not arousing white hostility in any of them.

Racial hostility is the second aspect of the social reality Gaines depicts. Blacks are cautious precisely because they know what whites are capable of doing. Here the author works primarily within the black literary tradition; violence against blacks is shown to be arbitrary, impersonal, and "natural." In a scene early in the book, a roaming band of anonymous whites savagely attacks a group of recently freed blacks. Their motivation for this brutality appears to be no more than the fact that the blacks are free. The text does not indicate that the whites suffer any consequences of their behavior. Such things just happen. Nearly a hundred years later, the killing of Jimmy Aaron, a civil rights activist, is similarly depersonalized. The murder itself takes place offstage, the killers are unknown, and neither the whites nor the blacks apparently expect any legal action to be taken.

Ned's assassination is a different kind of case, but it nonetheless confirms this pattern in many ways. The murderer, Albert Cluveau, is a distinctive character with his Cajun speech, his relationship with Jane, and his personal idiosyncrasies. Within this characterization, however, is the crucial element for the narrative: he is a hired killer who methodically and impersonally goes about his work. Cluveau warns Jane when he is ordered to kill Ned, for whom she has been a surrogate mother since his own was killed by "patrollers" when he was very small. But friendship does not make Cluveau loyal enough to Jane to consider refusing the assignment. His feelings of guilt for the crime involve a form of displacement; rather than acknowledge his responsibility, he accuses Jane of putting a curse on him. His increasing madness and grotesque death are presented in gruesome detail. But the effect of the story is to reinforce general white indifference to black victimization, since Cluveau's conscience and its effects, by their very grotesqueness, are shown to be aberrations in the white South. The norm is represented by the unconcerned sheriff and Cluveau's coconspirators, who remain unidentified and uninvestigated.

Gaines similarly shows other forms of racial interaction to be fundamentally antagonistic. The story of Tee Bob Samson and Mary Agnes LeFabre reinforces the principle. Tee Bob, a member of an important and wealthy white family, falls in love with the beautiful black Creole Mary Agnes. Ignoring the tradition that would allow them a private but never a public or legal relationship, he seeks to take her away and marry her, dismissing the advice of both friends and authority figures. He is stopped only because Mary Agnes herself rejects his plan; she knows that "the rules" cannot be broken. According to Jules Raynard, Tee Bob's *parrain*, or godfather, "She was a nigger, he was white, and they couldn't have nothing together. He couldn't understand that, he thought love was much stronger than that one drop of African blood. But she knowed better. She knowed the rules. She was just a few years older than him in years, but hundreds of years wiser" (194). But Tee Bob does not merely refuse to give up his dream. According to Raynard's hypothetical reconstruction of events, after Tee Bob strikes Mary Agnes in confused anger, she looks at him in such a way that he knows that she sees him as another white who, if he chooses, can exploit, abuse, and rape black women with impunity. Because he cannot tolerate such an identity, he commits suicide.

This episode implies that the social order structures even the most intimate of relationships and that there is no possibility of stepping outside historically determined reality except through death. Even the most powerful of individuals are bound by the unspoken rules. While blacks suffer most (Mary Agnes has her life threatened by Tee Bob's father simply for being the object of desire), whites are imprisoned as well within this order and must, like the young man's parents, suffer remorse and loss because of a caste system their ancestors created and they maintain.

If Gaines had presented only the story of racial oppression, as many black (and white) writers have done, his work would be useful for ideological purposes, but it would not capture the full complexity of the history of the Southern black experience. If blacks were only victims, then his work could not be what Lukács calls a "prehistory of the present," since the transcendence of oppression through the civil rights movement would be unexplainable. Folk culture is the aspect of the social reality enabling blacks to survive with some degree of human dignity and integrity. As represented in the novel, it comprises religious beliefs and practices, speech patterns, views of nature and society, and a system of ethics and morality that values survival strategies and endurance. Gaines does not introduce folk material merely for local color effects but makes it a part of the fabric of the society he is representing.

The fundamental source of value for this folk community is religion. They believe that what happens is the will of God and that their duty is to know how to accept events. Jane comments, "The colored has suffered in this world, and that is true, but we know still the Lord's been good to us" (211). The local church is the center of their world, and the rest of life is read in terms of its symbols. When Jimmy Aaron is born, they begin asking if he is "the One," a modern Moses or Christ who will provide moral leadership. They do everything they can to make him become what they need him to be; they watch him and discipline him, trying to keep him pure for his role. And when he returns to encourage their participation in the civil rights movement, he makes his appeal in the church. But because that appeal is essentially secular, the people reject it. As Elder Banks states, "All we want to do is live our life quietly as we can and die peacefully as the Lord will allow us. We would like to die in our homes, have our funerals in our church, be buried in that graveyard where all our people and love ones are" (226).

Such a faith both reinforces social passivity and gives moral value to the endurance of suffering. The latter becomes clear in the chapter titled "The Travels of Miss Jane Pittman." Her story of religious conversion describes an encounter with a white Jesus, who instructs her to carry a load of bricks across a river if she wants to save her soul. She does so despite the offers of Ned and Joe (presented as disguises for the devil) to carry it for her and despite the fear of walking through a space filled with briars, snakes, and alligators. The church accepts this story as evidence of her "comin' through" because it validates the folk view that life is a burden to be endured and, further, that any claims that life can be different (as in the offers of Ned and Joe) are cruel deceptions.

It is Jane's voice that most effectively grounds the representation of the folk world. She presents us with details about conjure and hoodoo beliefs and practices, about the respect that should be given nature, and about attitudes toward events in the larger world, such as Huey Long's power and the athletic triumphs of Joe Louis and their significance for black people. She records the interactions of life in the quarters: the births and deaths, the jokes and sermons, the religious politics and secular entertainments. Through her we learn of the daily lives of ordinary rural poor blacks. The mundane nature of much of her narrative is precisely what gives it the sense of reality Lukács considers necessary for historical fiction.

Beyond providing such information, the voice creates a sense of authenticity. It is the classic folk storyteller's voice, full of apparent self-deprecation and rich in allusion and folk wisdom. The story is told in the folk manner, with digressions, lapses, seeming discrepancies, multiple layers of telling, and clever twists of meaning. It is a voice that often appears unsophisticated, as when Jane claims in the prologue not to understand why anyone would be interested in her story. But it also displays a hard-won dignity, as when she explains why she liked Huey Long: "I agree he did call the colored people nigger. But when he said nigger he said, 'Here a book, nigger. Go read your name'" (151). This is a voice historically grounded in the agricultural landscape of late-nineteenth- and twentieth-century Louisiana.

Jane's voice gives a particular twist to Lukács's insistence that the historical novel must focus on ordinary life to explain effectively the social and historical forces at work: "And it is a law of literary portrayal which at first seems paradoxical, but then quite obvious, that in order to bring out these social and human motives of behaviour, the outwardly insignificant events, the smaller (from without) relationships are better suited than the great monumental dramas of world history" (42). Creating a narrative voice such as Jane's compels Gaines to report history from a local perspective. Events and movements of the larger world must be explained in terms of her small, relatively isolated community. Readers see wars, natural disasters, social and political change, and other historical phenomena from the bottom up and thus know in concrete terms the effects of history.

Consistent with such a perspective, *Miss Jane Pittman* presents local figures as heroes. Rather than show the actions of "world-historical individuals," the novel foregrounds the stories of Big Laura, Ned Douglass, and Jimmy Aaron. Their brave actions emerge from the values of the community—family, education, and freedom. Although they all must transcend the self-protectiveness of that community in order to act, they do so in the name of the community. Ned leaves but then returns to provide the education and sense of dignity he knows the people want and need. After he has been assassinated by Albert Cluveau, he becomes part of the oral history and folk belief: "For years and years, even after they had graveled the road, you could still see little black spots where the blood had dripped" (116) when he was carried home in the wagon. His story suggests that heroism is not abstract or ahistorical but is, rather, specific to its social context and historical moment. Ned and his actions are meaningful as embodiments of historically determined ideals and values. Moreover, these embodiments become part of the history, concrete validations of those ideals. Thus the hero, shaped by the community, also gives shape to its experience.

But it is Jane, not these heroic individuals, who is the central character in the book, and her status helps to explain the nature of the novel as historical fiction. In talking about Sir Walter Scott's work, which Lukács considers a model of serious writing in the genre, he observes:

> The principal figures . . . are also typical characters nationally, but in the sense of the decent and the average, rather than the eminent and all-embracing. . . . It is their task to bring the extremes whose struggle fills the novel, whose clash expresses artistically a great crisis in society, into contact with one another. Through the plot, at whose centre stands this hero, a neutral ground is sought and found upon which the extreme, opposing social forces can be brought into a human relationship with one another. (36)

Jane Pittman can be seen in precisely these terms. She is "mediocre," to use Lukács's term for such figures (33), in the sense of being an ordinary, average character and thus very much embedded in her world rather than set apart by unusual traits. She is also in the middle of virtually every conflict, not as a combatant, but rather as part of the ground on which the conflict occurs. She stands between blacks and whites, progressives and conservatives, the religious and the secular, the traditional and modern worlds. She is both the mother figure for Ned Douglass and the friend of Albert Cluveau, his assassin. She helps to raise Tee Bob Samson, the plantation owner's son, and shares her house with Mary Agnes LeFabre, for whom he commits suicide. She defends Jimmy Aaron's civil rights program in the church but then explains to him why the old people will not participate. She has made her religious "travels," but she loses her position in the church because she likes to listen to Sunday baseball games on the radio.

Her placement at the center of competing forces makes each of these a concrete, human, historicized conflict, dramatizing the fact that tensions of race, politics, religion, and economics are not abstractions but everyday realities handled by ordinary people. Moreover, her involvement provides the author the opportunity to make each side comprehensible in ways that otherwise would not be possible. The reader, for example, can know what motivates Albert Cluveau to commit acts of murder. Even though, in this novel, to understand all is not to forgive all, the complexity of forces creating such violence is clarified. Similarly, because Jane is a part of the church, we are privy to the members' fears that inhibit positive action. In contrast, because she helped to raise Jimmy and told him stories of Laura and Ned, he can explain to her why he must act even without their help. In each case, Gaines undertakes to humanize historical forces and thereby show their human effects. Jane both focuses and makes concrete these elements of reality through her position within the narrative.

One of the tasks of the historical novel is to portray the social reality of a given time and place. But such a portrayal has little more than antiquarian significance unless the author also has a philosophy of history. In fiction, such a philosophy is seldom explicitly articulated but is nevertheless evident. Lukács defines this idea in terms of the dialectic of freedom and necessity: "Thus, whereas drama concentrates the correct dialectics of freedom and necessity in a heroic catastrophe, epic [narrative] gives a broadly unfolded, entangled picture of the varied struggles—great and small, some successful, some ending in defeat—of its characters, and it is through the totality of these that the necessity of social development is expressed. Both great forms, therefore, reflect the same dialectics of life" (147). In his view, every society is engaged in a struggle between sheer survival—getting the basic requirements of life—and a transcendence of necessity into a realm of choice and control. Every serious work of historical fiction, because it portrays social reality, must therefore represent this dialectic in some form. Harry Henderson has categorized the two principal perspectives of American historical fiction as progressive and holist. A "progressive imagination" emphasizes the importance of reason and ideas in human experience and sees a steady movement toward their realization (36). In Lukács's terms, this is a resolution of the dialectic in favor of freedom, since it implies that human intelligence can be successfully applied to the problems faced by human beings. Humanity is, in other words, capable of using its abilities to transcend necessity. The holist perspective, in contrast to the progressive imagination, "sees society as a seamless web of relationships" (36). Culture in the broadest sense, rather than reason, shapes human nature and history. The holist view thus suggests a much larger role for necessity since there is no escape from one's place and time. Freedom itself is defined and bounded by culture and history.

In terms of these ideas, Gaines tries to provide a progressive way of reading a reality he depicts as holist. Because he blends the two perspectives, as Henderson has indicated is common in historical fiction, *Miss Jane Pittman* contains tensions and problems that are difficult to resolve. The freedom-necessity pattern is clear throughout the work. The heroic figures consistently espouse a notion of freedom in the realm of social reality. This affirmation begins in the opening of Jane's narrative when she herself asserts the right of self-naming at the moment of her liberation from slavery. She will no longer be addressed by the slave name Ticey. Although she is repeatedly punished, she does not budge from her stand. Likewise, in the next major episode, Big Laura undertakes to lead a band of freedmen to the North. Her heroism consists of rejecting a return to the old system, even though freedom means loss of economic and social security: " 'Before y'all start out here heading anywhere, what y'all go'n eat?' Unc Isom said. 'Where y'all go'n sleep? Who go'n protect you from the patrollers?' " (13). As freedmen, Laura and her group do not have a white master to provide either protection or necessities in return for their labor. Laura unflinchingly leads them into such uncertainty. Her experience of the realm of freedom is short-lived, because she and most of the others are killed by white night riders who will not tolerate black emergence from necessity.

The response of Joe Pittman to his dialectical condition is, as has already been suggested, archetypal. He confronts the limitations presented by nature in order to wrest both economic stability and personal freedom. The horse Jane considers to be haunted symbolizes the uncontrolled nature that must be mastered in order to move into the realm of freedom. Thus while in one sense Joe's story is a replication of Laura's, it is also an important variation since, for him, freedom is not merely movement away from the control of others but is in fact the exercise of his own power. This concern is why he rejects both the use of conjure to control the horse and also Jane's pleas that he avoid the animal altogether, both of which would defer the achievement of freedom by precluding true mastery.

The freedom-necessity dynamic takes a more mediated form in the narratives of Ned Douglass and Jimmy Aaron. Their stories emphasize physical force and economic power within the Southern social matrix. Necessity comes to be defined as accommodation to the existing social structure. For blacks, this fact means not merely avoiding violence and working for a living but also concealing any appearance of full humanity. Necessity takes on social and ideological dimensions in such circumstances. In this sense, Ned's effort to educate the black community would implicitly violate the social order even if he were not encouraging them to seek political rights. From the perspective of whites in power, any black achievement threatens the reality that has been created. Thus the necessity of maintaining the status quo requires eliminating any impulse to generate black freedom. So, like Laura and Joe, Ned, as the emblem of freedom, must be destroyed.

Like Ned in both his significance and his fate, Jimmy also illuminates Gaines's reading of history by requiring the involvement of the masses in the quest for freedom. His story makes clear the nature of the folk, the character of historical change, and the author's efforts to make the past the prehistory of the present. In each of the moments of dialectical tension, some or all of the people hold back, choosing necessity over freedom. Unc Isom, Jane herself in Joe's story, and the black community in Ned's work establish the pattern of basic black conservatism. In the latter case, the choice is presented as actual physical separation: "They didn't want go near him when he was living, but when they heard he was dead they cried like children" (116). The folk believe that they have survived by adaption to their environment—in other words, by accepting necessity. They have a fatalistic worldview in which suffering is inevitable and therefore a religious virtue (as in Jane's "travels") and in which social-political invisibility enhances the probability of survival. They regard activism as courageous but futile and, moreover, dangerous to all. They will keep alive the memories of Laura and Joe and Ned but will not imitate their efforts. As Jane explains to Jimmy, "The people here ain't ready for nothing yet. . . . Something got to get in the air first. Something got to start floating out there and they got to feel it. It got to seep all through their flesh, and all through their bones. But it's not out there yet. Nothing out there now but white hate and nigger fear. And fear they feel is the only way to keep going. One day they must realize fear is worse than any death. When that time come they will be ready to move with you" (228).

In articulating this view of the folk, Jane also expresses a possibility of social change, a motive for moving from necessity to freedom: "People and time bring forth leaders" (228). If a leader from the people can enable them to see beyond their fear, then change will occur, for the masses cannot be stopped. Nevertheless, Jane understands that the process is slow, and she urges Jimmy to expend his energy in talking to the people, in making them see his vision. Her view takes into account the accretions of social and psychological inertia that have to be overcome. Both white oppression and black accommodation must be counteracted, and, in Jane's view, the latter is nearly as formidable as the former. From this perspective, history and society are organic, and even intentional change must be made part of the process.

If the narrative followed Jane's wisdom, then a clear continuity would be established between past and present. The triumph of the civil rights movement that had occurred by the time Gaines wrote the novel would be shown to be an extension of the world of the folk. Puzzlingly, the text does not demonstrate such continuity. Jimmy claims that there is not time to do what Jane says, and his death is the price for his impatience. He thus falls into the pattern of those rebels who die for their beliefs. Like Laura and Ned, he will stand alone if necessary in the face of oppression. And if the history recorded up to this point in the novel in fact supplies an ongoing pattern, then he would become part of a heroic narrative passed down by the submissive folk.

This time, however, the pattern is broken, and history is disrupted. Instead of remaining part of the background, Jane engages in her own act of rebellion when she hears of Jimmy's death. She insists on going to town as planned, and, despite Robert Samson's threats, she begins that journey into the present in the book's last lines. In doing so, she rejects not only Samson's power but also the meaning of her own narrative. Her survival to tell the story to the history teacher, who interviews her and establishes the novel's frame, implies that she has escaped the fate of all previous rebels. At the time of the telling, she is still on the plantation, though Samson had threatened to evict anyone who disobeyed him. Although Gaines prepares us for such a conclusion by having Jimmy argue that Miss Jane could be the parish's Rosa Parks, the book does not offer adequate motivation for her playing such a role. Neither the transcendence nor the success of her act is grounded in the patterns elucidated by the narrative. While she has engaged in small acts of resistance and kept alive the stories of greater ones, she has primarily been the character in the middle and the recorder of stories of the suffering that accompanies such courageous acts.[3] Therefore she violates her function and her wisdom in order to become the unpunished radical we see at the end. Through her, the author in essence imposes a progressive resolution on a holist tale.

One reason for such disruption is evident. The social reality and dialectic revealed by the novel *cannot* explain the emergence of activism by the black masses. The forces of white oppression and black conservatism are represented as simply too strong to allow for the rapid, almost immediate, black political development shown in the last pages. Gaines consistently makes clear that "the rules" have nearly totalitarian power; both blacks and whites are destroyed when they try to challenge them. At the same time, he seeks to valorize the folk culture that enabled blacks to survive such circumstances. But the social reality and ideology at the time of the book's composition privileged black activism rather than endurance. Thus the folk ought to be shown to have helped generate and participate in the civil rights movement.[4] Because the historical reality Gaines has created does not clearly demonstrate such continuity, he must impose a connection. Thus Jane, emblem of the folk world, acts in the tradition of rebellion and does not suffer for doing so. By an act of narrative sleight of hand, the folk, locked for so long in a repressive reality, leap forward into the progressive present. Black submission magically becomes black power.

Ironically, this violation of Lukács's definition of historical fiction itself reveals the historicity of narrative. In 1971 Gaines could not come to the essentially conservative conclusions implied by the body of his text. At that moment, such meanings could not be spoken, and so the genuine admiration he expresses for the folk had to be shaped to fit the necessity of his own historical moment. If we compare *Jubilee* and *Roots* to what happens to Gaines's narrative, it is possible to see the complexity of his problem. Both of these other works focus on the exceptional character of an individual rather than on than the nature of the social reality. The authors depict Kunta Kinte and Vyry from childhood as special and not "mediocre" in Lukács's terms. Their strength seems innate rather than a product of the environment; they absorb only those qualities that are positive. Such narratives do not allow for the elucidation of historical forces.

This lack means that there can be neither psychological development nor true dialectical tension. Kunta Kinte from his birth is shown as a distinguished person. The name itself connects him with his grandfather, one of the most distinguished of African holy men. As the child develops, the rituals through which he goes serve only to confirm his excellence. The text never suggests any real possibility of his failure or inadequacy; the misfortunes he suffers are consistently the results of chance. Similarly, in *Jubilee,* Vyry's name carries clear connotations of virtue and truth, and nothing she does contradicts these meanings. She too is special; her near-white color and beauty are repeatedly noted as making her qualitatively different. The only true internal conflicts she faces are between strong virtues: her devotion to her children and her desire for freedom. Yet her choice of the children is never permitted to compromise her integrity. Her belief in freedom remains unstained. Unlike Jane Pittman, Vyry, though she must make adjustments to necessity, does not accommodate herself to historical reality. Like Kunta Kinte, she remains a pure rather than typical, "mediocre" character.

Just as these characters are static, so the worlds in which they live are largely fixed and undialectical. Kunta Kinte's Africa and much of the world of American slavery are unaffected by history. Despite the presence of slave trading, the society of the Mandinka remains much the same as it has been for centuries. Haley's Africa is mythic in the sense that all its activities are ritualized and ahistorical. Even the actions of necessity, such as drought, recur in a regular pattern and thus do not generate change. In addition, when Haley does present history, as in the case of the American Revolution, he shows it to be external to the world in which his characters are living. Likewise, Margaret Walker devotes sections of her novel to expositions of the economic, social, and political conditions of black life after the Civil War. However, even when her characters experience these conditions, they have little meaningful impact on the lives being described.

In sum, these two narratives do not demonstrate the concern for historical process that is evident in Jane Pittman's story. They are tales of resistance to outside evil, typified by slavery in *Roots* and by white racism in *Jubilee*. They are heroic narratives in which unchanging characters enact their virtue by struggling against the forces of evil. In this sense, they come closer to the classical epic than to the historical novel as described by Lukács. Their purpose is less to show the past as the prehistory of the present than it is to depict the glory of that past. Such a purpose reveals a commitment to the pastness of the past rather than a revelation of its connection to the present. It is perhaps significant in this context that both Haley and Walker claim to be telling the stories of their own ancestors. To establish a proud and honorable lineage suggests, ultimately, a commitment to individual rather than social experience. History thereby becomes the story of great individuals and not a dramatization of historical reality.

In contrast, what Gaines attempts is social revelation. The problem for him is that such a revelation cannot necessarily be made consistent with certain political values. Klaus Ensslen has attacked *Miss Jane Pittman* precisely because, he believes, Gaines has deemphasized the ideas of social criticism and resistance in African-American folk culture (152). The point of the present analysis, however, is that Gaines *does* incorporate such material in his work but, in contradistinction to Haley and Walker, understands that it is only a part of the story. Freedom for him is not an abstraction or a pure quality; it is a concrete part of the human experience and therefore has to be understood in tension with necessity. He chooses to show history as something happening in and through Jane Pittman and her community. Because he reads their story in an authentically dialectical way, he cannot make it come out exactly as he would prefer. Thus the very flaw of the conclusion gives the book its strongest claim as historical fiction.

Notes

1. See Andrews; Bryant ("Gaines"); Byerman (*Fingering* 87–94); Hicks ("To Make"); Jackson; and Pettis.

2. Lukács's clearest articulation of such a figure comes in his discussion of Sir Walter Scott: "The 'hero' of a Scott novel is always a more or less mediocre, average English gentleman. He possesses a certain, though never outstanding, degree of practical intelligence, a certain moral fortitude and decency which even rises to a capacity for self-sacrifice, but which never grows into a sweeping human passion, is never the enraptured devotion to a great cause" (33).

3. Compare Babb 94–96. Babb offers the view that such resistance suggests Jane's heroic nature. Although this behavior indicates one source for the actions of the rebel figures, it must also be judged as a strategy of survival within the context of a long life of accommodation to, if not acceptance of, the existing social reality. Unlike Babb, I see such a strategy of survival rather than one of resistance as being central to the narrative.

4. For a discussion of the influence of the black nationalism of the 1960s on Gaines's depiction of the characters in *Miss Jane Pittman,* see Hogue 64–85.

Voice and Perspective in the Film
Adaptations of Gaines's Fiction

Mark J. Charney

Three of Ernest J. Gaines's works have been adapted into film for a television audience: "The Sky Is Gray," from the short-story collection *Bloodline* in 1980; *The Autobiography of Miss Jane Pittman* in 1974; and *A Gathering of Old Men* in 1987. Strong characterization and compelling narrative lines make Gaines's fiction appealing to filmmakers. Each story contains a strong protagonist or group of protagonists, a central conflict, and a variety of regional voices. Each describes a situation that not only interests readers but almost forces them to take sides. And each presents characters who are likeable and universal in their struggles—perfect subjects, especially for television drama. Despite the subtleties of Gaines's use of voice and the complexity of his characters, the plot lines of his works seem deceptively simple to adapt to screen.

Possibly because of the potential visual appeal of Gaines's strong narratives, the three movie versions remain faithful to the primary narrative lines of the original works in spite of inevitable discrepancies between the fiction and the film. *The Sky Is Gray* is the most literal adaptation. Written for the screen by Charles Fuller and directed by Stan Lathan, the film retains from the story most of James's adventures on his journey to the fictional town of Bayonne. In the movie version of *The Autobiography of Miss Jane Pittman*, director John Korty condenses many of the novel's significant narrative incidents to accommodate a two-hour television time slot, but he borrows most of the novel's string of climaxes. Although Volker Schlondorff, director of *A Gathering of Old Men*, significantly changes the opening and conclusion of the novel, he too uses the emphasis in the adaptations on literally translating the plots from fiction into film ultimately contributes to the failure of each.

The test of a good screen version of a novel lies not in its literal transference of the words to the screen but in the director's ability to rethink the work in visual terms. In adaptations of novels such as D. H. Lawrence's *Women in Love* or John Fowles's *The French Lieutenant's Woman,* directors Ken Russell and Karel Reisz, respectively, create a cinematic form that reinvents the novels upon which they base their films. Likewise, John Huston, in film versions of Flannery O'Connor's *Wise Blood* and James Joyce's "The Dead," invents new visual metaphors to replace verbal ones and uses camera angles and juxtaposition of scenes to replace narrative voice. All three directors successfully adapt novels by using an understanding of perspective to create irony and theme on film.

To describe each of the four perspectives in *Women in Love,* for example, Russell associates the protagonists with distinct visual symbols to reveal their inner nature. Gudren and Gerald share an appreciation and understanding of the violence inherent in relationships, but while Gerald believes in a traditional form of violence—one that involves force—Gudren uses art to deflect and to avert violence. Rather than use voice-over or casual dialogue to reveal their differences, Russell defines them by showing each character in a scene with animals. Gerald uses spurs to attempt to force his horse to run headfirst into a moving train, an act that both frightens and excites Gudren. Gudren overcomes a herd of bulls by performing a primitive dance, an act that bewilders Gerald. Gerald raises blood but fails to accomplish his mission; Gudren effortlessly defeats her male antagonists by more accurately understanding the implications of violence. Such scenes serving as visual metaphors in *Women in Love* not only foreshadow Gudren's eventual triumph over Gerald but also define character motivation and inner voice.

Reisz and Huston translate narrative into cinematic perspective by rethinking the shapes of the novels upon which they base their films. To replace the contemporary narrator in Fowles's *The French Lieutenant's Woman,* whose discussion of Victorian life and values contrasts with twentieth-century philosophy, Reisz and Harold Pinter, who wrote the screenplay for the film, cut back and forth among three stories: the Victorian love story, the film being filmed within the movie, and the relationship of the contemporary actors performing roles in the movie.

The narrator is gone, but the conflict between centuries and values remains. In *Wise Blood,* Huston intimately associates the camera with the minister of the First Church Without Christ, not only to elicit sympathy but also to explain the complex relationship between the past and the present and to illustrate the overpowering influence of place upon personality. In the film version of "The Dead," Huston retains first-person narration only at the end of the film to illustrate the shifts in the protagonist's understanding of his wife, but it is the director's haunting shots of drifting snow that illustrate for viewers the influence of the past upon Gabriel's present and future.

While the television versions of Gaines's fiction retain some of the sentimental power of the stories themselves, Lathan, Korty, and Schlondorff ironically sacrifice the consciousness of the protagonists in an effort to reproduce the narrative strength and chronology of Gaines's writing. The directors of Gaines's work reproduce what they believe to be the most important details of the narratives, but, unlike Russell, Reisz, and Huston, none discovers a visual and figurative means to adapt the most inventive and significant aspect of each story: Gaines's sense of voice and perspective.

In a review of *Bloodline,* Granville Hicks of *Saturday Review* writes, "It is not surprising that Gaines likes the first person, for he uses colloquial language effectively and has a strong feeling for the rhythm of speech" (19). Ben Forkner compliments Gaines's "keen, sure ear for the vocabulary, idiom, accents, and rhythm of native black speech" in a review of *A Gathering,* but he sees voice as the central focus: Gaines "recognizes the power of language in predominately oral culture to assert, affirm, and keep hold of personal and collective values" (425). And in an interview with Gregory Fitz Gerald and Peter Marchant, Gaines admitted that his emphasis on voice, rhythm, and dialect originates from his interest in hearing people speak: "I think I am more of a listener, really. I listen. I like to listen to the way people talk, and I like to listen to their stories" (333). Each of the characters in Gaines's short stories and novels reflects his love of listening. He writes almost exclusively in the first person because the third person denies the freedom and flexibility to express the voices of his protagonists, and it is through these narrators that he reveals the struggles not only of Louisiana (where most of his fiction is set) but of an entire nation.

"The Sky Is Gray," the most widely anthologized of Gaines's works, is the second short story in the collection *Bloodline*. The tale, which chronicles an eight-year-old boy's journey from his Louisiana plantation home to a dentist in the small town of Bayonne, contributes to the collection's overall thematic movement from inexperience to experience. In an interview with John O'Brien, Gaines talked of that movement: "By the time you come to the last story there is much more experience to interpret. You have both older women and older men. You have the point of view of the white woman. There are many different experiences coming into the story. So there is constant growth from the first to the last story" (91). In "The Sky Is Gray," Gaines focuses partially upon James's mother Octavia and her need to push the boy into a position of manhood and experience as early as possible. Through the youngster's perspective, the reader sees the pride with which Octavia carries herself and the enigmatic trials she poses for her son to provide him with the skills she believes he needs for survival. The love and respect he feels for his mother are tempered with fear, confusion, and vulnerability; he feels the need to protect her while he desperately wants to be protected by her. Although the plot concentrates on James's visit to the dentist and the kindness one white woman shows him in Bayonne, the complex relationship between mother and son is the focus of the story.

For example, in the fourth section Octavia beats James when he refuses to kill two redbirds they have caught in a trap. The reader understands through James's language the disappointment James feels in himself, the fear he feels of his mother, his efforts to understand her actions, and his sympathy for the birds: "I'm still young—I ain't no more than eight; but I know now; I know why I had to do it. (They was so little, though. They was so little. I 'member how I picked the feathers off them and cleaned them and helt them over the fire. . . .) Suppose she had to go away? That's why I had to do it. Suppose she had to go away like Daddy went away. . . . They had to be somebody left to carry on" (90). Although James attempts to understand the rationale for his mother's anger, the reader knows that the answers James finds with the help of his auntie and Monsieur Bayonne do not sufficiently justify in his eyes either the birds' death or his mother's violence. The parenthetical references juxtaposing the image of the birds with that of James's weak justification heighten the conflict he is forced to experience at age eight and illustrate his hesitancy to accept the adult role of provider.

In the film version of the same scene, Lathan fails to find a visual means to reproduce the boy's internal narrative voice. The director of many American short stories, plays, and novels for PBS and Showtime including *Booker, The Trial of Moke, Go Tell It on the Mountain,* and *Uncle Tom's Cabin,* Lathan heightens the violence of the act itself in the film adaptation by cutting repeatedly from James to his mother to the caged birds, but the audience senses only James's fear and Octavia's violence, not the son's efforts to understand the actions of the mother. As the screenplay for the adaptation suggests, rather than acting from a sense of responsibility, James kills the bird to escape the wrath of his mother: "She does not hit him but her tone is final. For a moment the boy is motionless, then, quickly, haphazardly, he begins to stab into the other cage, trying not to look but increasing his pace. Jabbing. Again, and again, and again" (442). Ironically, in the movie Octavia begins to represent the very violence from which she attempts to protect James. Without the benefit of James's perspective, her actions seem cruel and pointless because Lathan makes no connection in the film between the necessity of killing the birds and the disappearance of the father. In the story, Gaines cuts from the bird incident to the trip to Bayonne, increasing the audience's sympathy for Octavia. In the film, on the other hand, the next scene shows the family eating the small birds James has killed, now creatures the size of chickens, with James trying in vain to prove that their death no longer affects him. Without the benefit of his internal voice, the viewer cannot achieve a complete understanding of Octavia's purpose.

Lathan's inability to discover a cinematic means to reveal James's perspective toward his mother's actions ultimately reduces the thematic thrust of the story adaptation. Most critical responses to the short story emphasize the significance of James's confused reactions to his mother's distance and his father's absence. Todd Duncan explains the importance of Octavia's instructions: "James is, in fact, receiving an intense education, but one outside of school. His mother is his teacher, and what he is learning is to survive his harsh environment and take on prematurely the duties of an adult" (89). Similarly, John W. Roberts writes that "Octavia has made protecting James from becoming vulnerable her primary goal in life" ("Individual" 111), and Jordan Pecile believes that "the missing father is, of course, a necessary strategy for the success of the narrative" (455).

In the ninth section of the story, James expresses this need to recover his missing father, while he and his mother look for a place to find shelter from the cold: "I used to like to be with Mama and Daddy. We used to be happy. But they took him in the Army. Now, nobody happy no more. . . . I be glad when Daddy come home" (108). In section eleven, he also displays the affection he feels for his mother and his desire to fill the void his father has left: "She's looking real sad. I say to myself, I'm go'n make all this up one day. You see, one day, I'm go'n make all this up. I want say it now; I want tell her how I feel right now; but Mama don't like for us to talk like that" (110). Like most eight-year-olds, James wants to please his mother, but readers recognize through his internal dialogue that he resists the type of pride that has caused his mother to withdraw from the world. The story's title reflects his belief that a gray exists between black and white; for James, a compromise between good and evil is still possible, but not for Octavia. The film version of the story not only neglects to explain the point of the title but also ignores the perspective that reveals James's real growth. Because Lathan never cinematically expresses the boy's internal reactions to his parents or to the trip to Bayonne through voice-over or symbol, audiences must view Octavia's final statement in the story and the movie, "You're not a bum; you're a man," as simply a sentimental device used to prompt an emotional reaction, not as a statement that ironically heightens her and her son's differing opinions of manhood.

More has been written about *Miss Jane Pittman,* both the television movie and the novel upon which it is based, than any other work by Gaines. The director, John Korty, best known for his Oscar-winning documentary *Who Are the De Bolts? . . . and Where Did They Get 19 Kids?,* began making amateur films at age sixteen and has directed and produced independent, low-budget feature films and television movies since the mid-1960s (Katz 666). *Miss Jane Pittman* won much acclaim because Korty sensitively presents in it an absorbing story and a compelling protagonist. Pauline Kael believes that it "isn't a great movie, though with more directorial freedom and a better script it might have been. But it's quite possibly the finest movie ever made for American television" (76); Joseph Kanin of *Atlantic* feels that "the film is as moving and powerful a study of black life in this country as has yet been produced. . . . Unquestionably the finest film to have been made for television" (117). Indeed, it is difficult to disapprove of a film that boasts an outstanding performance by Cicely Tyson as Jane Pittman and attempts honestly to approach sensitive and controversial subjects on television. But like Lathan, Korty sacrifices the voice and perspective that make the novel successful in favor of a series of moving and disturbing emotional crescendos. Because the final film project is a sequence of climactic vignettes, it lacks the novel's depth of character and sense of place, time, and oral tradition.

Miss Jane Pittman has the form of a folk narrative. Keith E. Byerman points out that "the key question, for Gaines and others, is how to make use of the black folk material that is so crucial to the experience they recreate in the process of inventing factual worlds" ("Afro-American" 49). To recreate the black experience, Gaines presents his fiction as folk biography; he invents a protagonist who at the age of 110 reveals aspects of her life and the lives of others in Louisiana from the Civil War to the civil rights movement. Byerman points out that the recurring pattern in the novel is a buildup from violent climax to violent climax: "An act of resistance is held by a heroic figure who is ultimately killed by opposing forces; in the aftermath, Miss Jane is left to preserve whatever has been gained, including the legend of the hero, and to prepare a new generation of rebels" ("Afro-American" 50). In this fictional autobiography, Miss Jane is always either a proponent or an observer of change; she becomes a vehicle through which history lives, especially in the eyes of the young black history teacher who finds her tales fascinating.

The novel's success depends more heavily on oral tradition than "The Sky Is Gray." To capture honestly the sounds and expressions of a former slave, Gaines read WPA interviews of ex-slaves recorded in the 1930s: "After reading them . . . I got a rhythm, a speech, a dialogue, and a vocabulary that an ex-slave would have" (Rowell, "This Louisiana Thing" 46–47). Most reviewers of the novel attribute its success to a strong sense of oral folk tradition. Danny Beckham writes that Gaines "goes beyond the mere cherishing of that specialness of Southern dialectical pronunciation, syntax, and diction to incorporate qualities of voice and storytelling which have placed *The Autobiography of Miss Jane Pittman* in that rare category of American novels which talk to the reader" (102). Hoyt W. Fuller emphasizes that the voice of Miss Jane connects the past to the present, making her struggle timeless: "Her language is the plain, rich, soulful speech of unlettered and relaxed country people, laced with the basic wisdom, insight and humor which have been vital weapons in the battle of Black survival. The accent and rhythm of her speech are in the streets, on the radio, in the movies, on TV, echoing the convoluted, sad, and inadmissible past, haunting the natural psyche, narrowing the distance between the time of slavery and today" (89). Through this convincing use of the oral tradition, Gaines chronicles not only the tales of one woman, but more importantly, the shifting black perspective from the late 1800s to the mid-1960s. He does so in a style that seems more fact than fiction.

In the television version, Korty retains the novel's basic narrative movement from climax to climax, and he uses Miss Jane's voice-over to provide transitions between the present and the past. In the script, however, Tracy Keenan Wynn reduces the interview time frame from "eight or nine months" (vii) to a few days and transforms the young black history professor into a middle-aged white journalist who finds his consciousness altered by the power of Miss Jane's story. To fit the material within a two-hour television slot, Wynn emphasizes the violent sections of the novel: the death of Big Laura; the Ku Klux Klan's destruction of the plantation school; and the murders of Joe, Ned, and Jimmy. After each act of violence, Korty builds to create the next until the controversial end of the film, when Miss Jane triumphantly drinks from the "whites only" fountain outside the courthouse. Many critics, such as Alvin Ramsey and Vilma Raskin Potter, disapprove strongly of the false sense of closure this sentimental ending brings to the film. They also object to the shift from a black to a white interviewer. Gaines himself has pointed out the technical weakness of the film as narrative: "So what you have in the film now is peaks—a lot of peaks. But you don't have the valleys and slopes as you would have had, had the film been longer" (Rowell, "This Louisiana Thing" 49). The "valleys and slopes" represent the meat of the novel—Miss Jane's descriptions of the shifting values, lifestyles, and perspectives of her people. Without these sections Korty limits the film's visions to a string of violent occurrences. He may recount more than one-hundred years of history, but he indicates none of the subtle changes in vision and personality that occur during that century.

For example, after the death of Ned, Miss Jane describes in detail the personal dreams and visions that led to her salvation: "I had a load of bricks on my shoulders and I wanted to drop it but I couldn't. It was weighing me down and weighing me down, but I couldn't let go of the sack. Then a White Man with long, yellow hair—hair shining like the sun—came up to me. (He had a long white robe, too.) He came up to me and said, 'Jane, do you want to get rid of that load?' I said, 'Indeed, indeed. But how come you know me? Can you be the Lord?'" (13). The move by Miss Jane and her friends toward religion as a source of answers not only interrupts the story of purposeless violence that drives the novel's momentum but also represents the movement in the early 1900s by blacks, especially in the South, to attempt to use religion both to face and understand the violent struggles of the past. Religion provides Miss Jane with a means to avoid violence and hatred, and as she begins to believe in a divine structure and purpose in the universe, she replaces youthful anger and resentment with a calm sense of resolve and pride. Book 3 of the novel, "The Plantation," focuses upon subtle shifts in religion, culture, and society—changes that are ignored as the film moves quickly from Ned's death (the end of book 2) to set up Jimmy's eventual murder in book 4. In Wynn's efforts to include each of the climaxes, he overlooks the equally important quiet moments that reveal the sources of Miss Jane's inner strength and philosophy of survival.

Even more destructive to the film is Korty's objective and distanced use of the camera to indicate Miss Jane's subjective and intensely personal account of the black struggle for pride and independence in Louisiana. Like Gaines, Korty incorporates the taped interview format as a frame. He begins with the journalist's visit, and through flashbacks resembling those in the novel, he recounts Miss Jane's biography in chronological order. In spite of Miss Jane's voice-over to narrate the incidents and provide transitions, Korty abandons her position as controller of the vision. Instead, he manipulates viewers' emotions by using the camera to emphasize the randomness and general destructiveness of the violent scenes.

For example, in the second section of the novel, "Reconstruction," Miss Jane describes how the Civil War ironically encouraged only external changes in the slavery system: "It was slavery again, all right. . . . You didn't need a pass to leave the place like you did in slavery time, but you had to give Colonel Dye's name if the secret group stopped you on the road. Just because the Yankee troops and the Freedom Beero had gone didn't mean they had stopped riding. They rode and killed more than ever now" (70). Part of the power and honesty of the novel originates from the fact that Miss Jane always offers as universal truth her Louisiana-based perspective of history. Gaines's careful research is obvious, but by filtering it through Miss Jane's perspective, he avoids force-feeding history to his readers. About the film, however, John Callahan writes, "Despite Gaines's complex, concrete account [of Reconstruction], the screenwriter slaps into Jane Pittman's mouth a vision of Reconstruction right out of D. W. Griffith's *Birth of a Nation*" ("Image-Making" 57). To describe Reconstruction, Korty uses a montage of visual clichés: burned schools, random violence, and lynched mulattos. Such a sequence is visually distanced from Miss Jane's perspective despite her voice-over: "But Reconstruction never really worked. It wasn't too long 'fore carpetbaggers, black and white, moved in to take from the South what the war didn't." The shots avoid a personal perspective and thus elicit from audiences a textbook sense of guilt. Ironically, by concentrating heavily on the violence in the book without creating a method to tie it more closely to Miss Jane's voice and perspective, Korty loses all but the sentimental power of the novel.

Very little has been written about the most recent adaptation of Gaines's work, although in many ways Schlondorff's version of *A Gathering* captures atmosphere and perspective better than the other film adaptations. Once an assistant to directors Louis Malle, Alain Renais, and Jean-Pierre Melville, Schlondorff began his career with television reports from Algeria and Vietnam. In the mid-1960s he returned from France to Germany, where his first feature film, *Der Junge Torless* (Young Torless) (1966), "a keen psychological study of the cruelties of boarding school life in turn-of-the-century Germany," established him as a leading director (Katz 1023). *A Gathering*, his first film for American television, offers fifteen black-and-white first-person narrators who describe the consequences and aftermath of the murder of a young Cajun, Beau Boutan, from a powerful and violent local family. Believing the murderer to be the proud and quiet Mathu, Gaines's community of old black men gather at the Marshall plantation, the scene of the crime, hoping to prevent Mathu's arrest by each claiming responsibility for the deed. For most of the men, the incident represents a chance to make up for the injustices of the past by allowing them to retain a measure of dignity in the face of certain danger. The novel inevitably ends in violence between the blacks, who attempt to protect their community, and the Cajuns and rednecks, who feel they have been wronged. *A Gathering* is effective in spite of Gaines's overbearing reliance on almost mythic forms of good and evil because he sensitively describes the perspective of each of the individuals—from the stubborn white landowner Candy to the proud and friendly Chimley.

As in Gaines's other fiction, much of the success of A *Gathering* lies in the author's ability to combine a compelling tale with a strong sense of perspective, but he represents a multitude of perspectives in this single work for the first time since the story "Just Like a Tree." Reynolds Price attributes the power of the novel to the fifteen individually drawn voices: "They are nicely distinguished from one another in rhythm and idiom, in the nature of what they see and report, especially in their specific laments for past passivity in the face of suffering" (15). Lloyd W. Griffin similarly emphasizes Gaines's ability to capture the speech patterns of a community: "He has a marvelous ear for speech rhythms, context, and dialect; a deep knowledge of the people, black and white, of the region; and a rich fund of humor, compassion, and understanding" (2690).

Through effectively casting real Louisianans and a rustic use of the camera often resembling that in a home movie, Schlondorff captures the strong sense of Louisiana's backwoods atmosphere so significant to the theme of the novel, and he also succeeds by visually emphasizing the struggle and power of the group of men. But he loses the delicate balance between the community and the individual that creates much of the thematic strength and humor in the novel. Like Korty, Schlondorff fails to find a cinematic method that effectively distinguishes one old man's voice from the next, except through actions and/or dialogue. The novel emphasizes the individual by focusing on the specific consciousness of each participant in the gathering. The sense of community that grows is surprising and somewhat ironic in the novel, especially considering the individual motives each man has for joining the group. However, the television script, written by Charles Fuller, glosses over the individual reasons the men have for backing Mathu. Unlike the novel, it implies that the community is formed as quickly as the men gather. Although the men verbally express individual reasons for their participation, the viewing audience has trouble distinguishing one man's consciousness from that of the next.

In the novel, for example, Gaines concentrates upon voice and internal perspective to individualize each character. Chimley decides to go to Marshall and join Mathu because he senses the needs of his friend Mat: "I looked him in the eyes. Lightish-brown eyes. They were saying much more than he had said. They was speaking for the both of us, though, me and him" (32). Mat reveals his reasons for joining the gathering by expressing the physical changes he experiences when facing the possibilities of revenge: "My chest started heaving, heaving, just heaving. Like I had been running up a hill, a steep hill, and now I had reached the top" (37). Cherry comes partially because he admires the strength and pride that he recognizes within the community: "After that [climbing on the back of the truck to travel to Marshall] we didn't do much talking. We was just feeling proud. I could see it on Yank's face; I could feel it sitting next to Chimley and Mat. Proud as we could be" (42). Except for the dialogue Schlondorff and Fuller borrow from the novel, the personal histories that help to distinguish each individual from the group are lost to film audiences. As a result, the film's momentum is driven by the questions what will happen next and who will pay. The novel, on the other hand, is driven more by the transformation of the individual consciousness into a communal perspective.

Gaines has pointed to part of the problem he has with the film: "You can put action on the screen, but I don't know that you can put thoughts and dreams and, really, the depth of the personality on the screen" (Gaudet and Wooton 88). Most of his unhappiness with the adaptation centers around the director's inability to transfer the novel's emphasis on language more directly to film: "When they started taking a few lines from here and a few lines from there and putting them together in one speech, and adding their own terms to it—that's when they took liberties I did not approve of" (90). He also believes that because Schlondorff is not from the South, he missed the novel's potential for humor that depends heavily on how the speakers use language, particularly their "sense of pausing" (91–92).

Gaines's criticism seems especially insightful when he is examining Schlondorff's adaptation of the core of A *Gathering,* the epiphanic flood of accusations each of the men pours out against Sheriff Mapes, revealing years of repressed hatred for the misdeeds of whites and Cajuns. Johnny Paul laments the passing of the land and its variety of flowers because of abuse by white greed and technology; Tucker reminds Mapes of the unsolved murder of his brother; Yank resents the local community because technology and progress have ended his profession, horse breaking; and Coot describes the forgotten blacks who died for their country in Vietnam but are not allowed to be buried next to the whites. In the television script, Fuller retains and combines a few of these stories.

Yank's and Johnny Paul's tales of progress become one, for example, and Tucker's description of the death of his brother is delivered by Clatoo. Yet Mapes stops the stories before they either build to an emotional climax or help to distinguish one character from the next. Rather than relying on close-ups or originating flashbacks to define individual perspective, Schlondorff more often uses the slow pan to heighten the common emotions of the group. To accommodate a two-hour time slot, he also concentrates the novel's fifteen voices into three or four, thus narrowing the scope of the work. Although, like Lathan and Korty, he retains most of the major narrative incidents from the novel in chronological order, from Lou Dimes's presence to Gil's pleas with his father for mercy, Schlondorff visually undermines the individual to emphasize the density and power of the group.

As in the adaptation of *Miss Jane Pittman*, sentimentality in *A Gathering* overshadows subtleties of characterization and complexities of emotion. The problems created by sentimentality are strongly exemplified in the changes made for the ending of the television adaptation. In the book, the struggle between blacks and whites ends inevitably in violence, as Snookum describes in one of the final sections: "They was shooting everywhere. Soon as the sheriff went down, they started shooting. Shooting out the front door, shooting out the window, shooting up the ceiling—shooting everywhere" (200). Charlie, Beau's murderer, is killed, as is Luke, and most of the men are injured, but violence helps to stir a sense of accomplishment within the old men. It not only reminds them of the glories of victory, but more importantly it symbolizes a final stand, a risk that is worth the potential danger. In the film, however, Schlondorff omits the violence entirely and thereby fails to express the story's reality and establish the men's victory. Threatened by the number of old men who have gathered with shotguns, the drunken rednecks and Cajuns who have come to wreak vengeance upon the blacks uncharacteristically flee. Mathu yells, "Lord have mercy. We done did it," and the film ends with the sound of gunshots used as fireworks, celebrating the all-too-easy victory encouraged by the sense of community created. The novel ends triumphantly for the men, but that success is as internal as it is overt in the shoot-out. In spite of the violence they have encountered and the number of men who have been wounded and killed, most regain dignity either from actions that have been taken or words that have been spoken in the course of the day. In contrast to the book, the movie falsely implies that, for blacks, a strong sense of community can prevent the inevitable struggles with violence.

The film versions of "The Sky Is Gray," *Miss Jane Pittman,* and *A Gathering* share problems similar to those in other adaptations of works by African-American authors. To appeal to a large audience, filmmakers translate novels by black authors into cinematic terms acceptable to white viewers. Like Korty in *Miss Jane Pittman,* Stephen Spielberg in *The Color Purple* sentimentalizes the novel he adapts; he transforms the bleak landscape of Alice Walker's epistolary novel into pastoral greens, browns, and pinks, evoking an unrealistically nostalgic picture of rural tranquility. While he retains the bigotry and violence of the men in the novel, he stresses only those conflicts most easily acceptable to white audiences. For example, he deemphasizes the incest scene with which Walker begins the novel but intensifies the poignant separation of Celie and her sister; he largely ignores the homosexual relationship that initiates Celie's move toward independence but concentrates dramatically on her husband's mistreatment of her. Korty and Spielberg both build their films to climactic acts of personal revenge—Miss Jane drinks from the whites-only fountain, and Celie escapes from her husband—thus undermining the more subtle resolution of the novels. In most films adapted from novels written by black American authors, sentimentality and a false sense of closure override the more honest and less stirring resolution in the novels upon which they are based. Audiences are made to feel good, to believe that the struggles and successes of Miss Jane and Celie suggest the promise of racial equality.

Also virtually untranslated in film adaptations of works by black American writers is the sense of internal struggles pervasive in their fiction. In Jerold Freedman's adaptation of Richard Wright's *Native Son,* Bigger Thomas's self-realization comes too quickly. In the novel, Wright suggests that Bigger's months in jail ironically offer him his first peaceful opportunity to reflect on his background, motives, and influences. Lengthy discussions between Bigger and his mother, his lawyer, and his minister contribute to his epiphany. The film version, on the other hand, emphasizes the murder trial and the final resolution, not Bigger's painful struggle to accept and understand himself and his actions. The murder in the novel is only the means to inspire an end; in the film, the murder *is* the end in itself. The epiphanies reached by James in "The Sky Is Gray" and Celie in *The Color Purple* are equally false on film. Both Lathan and

Spielberg focus primarily on the external events that influence character, omitting the internal voice that defines character and traces change in the fiction. Finally, directors who have adapted the writing of African-American authors largely ignore the significant cultural and ritualistic elements that influence and direct their characters' actions. Korty omits those sections of *Miss Jane Pittman* that examine the influence of religion and the supernatural in the community's growth, while Spielberg downplays descriptions of Africa that ultimately help to build Celie's pride in *The Color Purple*. The deterministic elements of place that influence Bigger's act of murder in *Native Son* and explain the community's sense of degradation in *A Gathering* are overlooked in efforts to advance the plot and strengthen the narrative line. Lathan, Korty, Schlondorff, Spielberg, and Freedman seem to be so obsessed with illustrating that blacks and whites share similar problems and struggles that they ignore the cultural differences contributing to racial inequality and prejudice. Ironically, each filmmaker undermines the value in the original work of fiction by stressing the sentimental over the realistic, omitting the internal voice and sense of perspective, and slighting the cultural and historical elements.

In each of the adaptations of Gaines's fiction, many of the narrative incidents are translated literally and chronologically to the screen. But perhaps because of time and budget constraints, or possibly because of the perceived demands of a television audience, Lathan, Korty, and Schlondorff fail to bring to their adaptations the imagination necessary to transform the power of the verbal into equivalent visual terms. Each director retains and intensifies only those narrative aspects of the stories that translate easily to film and appeal surely to a broad audience. None reinvents the internal voice and sense of perspective that drive the characters to understand both their actions and the cultures that influence their growth.

Black Women: Race, Gender, and Culture in Gaines's Fiction

Marcia Gaudet

Ernest J. Gaines portrays some of the central experiences and concerns of women in his fiction. In particular, he shows how black women shape their identities and deal with social relationships in a rural folk community. Elizabeth Fox-Genovese says that "race and gender lie at the core of any sense of self" (28). While race and gender are dominant, culture often defines or determines how they affect identity. This dynamic is particularly true for rural black women rooted in a place, knowing only one set of cultural rules.

Feminist scholars have recently focused on the depictions of communities of women in the fiction of black female writers and in black culture in general. Such scholarship draws on both black feminist critical theory and the cultural politics of black women. Hazel V. Carby's *Reconstructing Womanhood: The Emergence of the Afro-American Woman Novelist* "embodies a feminist critical practice that pays particular attention to the articulation of gender, race, and class" (17). Judith A. Spector and others insist, however, that male authors must be included in a study of gender in literature. Spector says, "The study of male authors is wholly legitimate for the feminist scholar" (378). She calls for awareness of all writers' attitudes toward gender and for studies "of characters of opposite gender in works of female and male authors" (377). Trudier Harris's book on black women in James Baldwin's fiction is an excellent example of such a study. She concludes that few of the black women in Baldwin's fiction are "spiritually healthy" (5) and that they "almost invariably allow the men to determine their paths in life" (8). In terms of

technique, she notes that Baldwin uses a woman narrator only once—
Tish in *If Beale Street Could Talk*.

Gaines's portrayals of black women seem to be, in general, much
more complex and much more positive than Baldwin's. Gaines says of
his early reading of fiction about the South, "I did not care for the way
black characters were drawn. . . . Whenever a black person was mentioned in these novels, either she was a mammy, or he was a Tom; and
if he was young, he was a potential Tom, a good nigger; or he was
not a potential Tom, a bad nigger. When a black woman character was
young, she was either a potential mammy or a nigger wench. For most
of these writers, choosing something between was unheard of" ("Miss
Jane and I" 26). Gaines's women characters show not only "something
between" but also something more complex, both as individuals and
as character types. Frank Shelton notes that "women are a preserving,
conserving element in Gaines's world" ("*In My Father's House*" 343),
certainly characteristic of the aunt and grandmother figures, yet there is
also a diverse range of women characters. Portraits of black women in
Gaines's fiction reveal individuality and a compelling sense of strength
in dealing with the world. They possess devotion to their family and
a commitment to the culture in which they live, despite the need to
question or negotiate cultural rules. Three issues Gaines deals with concerning women—the influence women have over men, violence toward
women, and women's communities—reveal that he creates female characters with an awareness of the complexity of attitudes toward gender
and culture.

Certainly the most popular, positive, and pervasive women in Gaines's
fiction are the elderly aunts or aunt figures. They have positions of
power and respect within the community, and they seem to combine
strength, humanity, and an assured wisdom about life. The "auntie" who
raises her nieces and nephews, or more often her great-nieces and great-
nephews, is a common figure in black fiction and in black culture, and
Gaines himself was reared by a great-aunt. The title "aunt" is usually
used for an older woman even by those who are not really related to
her, especially if they have known her all their lives. Though generally
identifying themselves in terms of relationships to men, these women in
Gaines's works are not passive servants but are influential in the development of these men. The aunt figures are often sources of strength and
wisdom, but they can also be a stifling influence, especially when trying

to protect the boys or men from danger, real or imagined. The older women generally seem to have a confidence and sense of place within their community that the men lack. They create a sense of continuity and cohesiveness among their people. Nevertheless, there are important limitations, in Gaines's view, in what they can offer.

Miss Jane Pittman is, of course, the most fully developed "aunt" figure, but this type appears as a significant character already in Gaines's first novel, *Catherine Carmier*. There, Jackson's Aunt Charlotte cares deeply for those close to her, and she has achieved respect and wisdom, though her perspective is limited by the circumscribed life she has lived. Her understanding of the human condition does not go beyond the world she knows. Only her love for Jackson enables her to accept his decision not to fulfill her dream that he remain in the community as a teacher. In "Bloodline," Copper's Aunt Amalia ('Malia) is another strong aunt figure. Her influence, however, cannot compensate for Copper's madness, and she is unable to direct or change his actions. In *In My Father's House,* Angelina Bowie is the godmother or *nanane* of Reverend Phillip Martin, the central character. When he goes to her for advice and sustenance, she tries to talk to him but does not understand him at all. She says, "Phillip, you done gone plumb crazy?" (114).

Aunt Caroline and Aunt Margaret in *Of Love and Dust* both display a strong sense of right and wrong, yet they have gained prudence from having lived in the white-dominated culture, and they realize that sometimes it is safest to ignore or forget what is going on around them. Aunt Caroline overhears the white overseer, Bonbon, carrying on his affair with her neighbor Pauline but maintains a pretense that nothing is happening. Aunt Margaret works for Bonbon and overhears the lovemaking of Marcus and Louise, Bonbon's wife. While she fears the consequences of this affair for the other black people and she confides in Jim, the narrator, hoping that he will intervene, she later chooses to forget that it ever happened. Caroline and Margaret—like Charlotte, 'Malia, and Angelina—are similarly unable to influence men, and they choose to act as if they were ignorant about affairs in order to avoid creating racial conflict in the community.

The short story "Just Like a Tree," collected in *Bloodline,* is Gaines's first work to use an older woman as the central character. Aunt Fe's niece has come from "up north" to take her away from Louisiana because of the bombing of a black person's house nearby, part of the violence in the area resulting from the civil rights movement. She is clearly loved and respected by the people in the community, who consider her part of an extended family, and she has no desire to leave. Aunt Fe has reached the age and position at which her wisdom and strength in her own community serve her well, but she seems to realize that she knows only this small world. Leaving would not only make her vulnerable to change but also deny her the sustaining strength of community. Aunt Lou, her closest friend, is much more assertive than Aunt Fe in trying to maintain her position of authority. Aunt Lou shows a need to control her son and his family, both in her attempt to discipline the children and in her warnings to her son when he loses patience with the mule, Mr. Bascom, who refuses to pull the wagon on which the family rides. Though she insists on her way with her family, she is a very tender and caring friend, like a sister to Fe. Aunt Clo is an older woman who puts events in a philosophical context, saying that taking Fe away is like "jecking" up a large tree and trying to plant it somewhere else. Though their styles are different, all three are strong women, resolute in not giving up control of their lives. Fe tells Lou, "I ain't leaving here tomorrow, Lou," and then, "No, I ain't going nowhere" (248). They also have the respect of the young people in the community, even those who do not agree with them about the civil rights movement.

In Gaines's latest novel, *A Lesson Before Dying*, there are two important aunt figures, Tante Lou (Aunt Lou) and Miss Emma. Tante Lou continues to have considerable influence on her nephew, Grant Wiggins, even though he is in his mid-twenties. Though he has a college degree, he returns to the quarters to teach and lives with his aunt. At times, she attempts to control him with her "looks." Grant says, "She looked at me the way an inquisitor must have glared at its poor victims" (99) and "My aunt knew how to make you feel that she was of a lower caste and you were being too kind to her. That was the picture she presented, but not nearly how she felt" (115). Grant feels respect and duty toward his aunt but also becomes frustrated and impatient when she manages to persuade him to do what he has no desire to do—to visit a young convict regularly during the months prior to his execution. In contrast to the typical aunt figure in Gaines's fiction, Tante Lou is successful in forcing an adult male, whom she has raised, to comply with her demands. Earlier aunt figures seldom retained that kind of power to control the actions of their "boys" after they had become men. The other aunt figure, Miss Emma, is nanane to Jefferson, the young black man convicted of a murder he did not commit. Though she is not as forceful as Tante Lou, her strong sense of dignity and her determination to have her nephew achieve a sense of manhood before he dies, to "stand" with dignity himself, are characteristics of the aunt figures throughout Gaines's work.

Jane Pittman is certainly Gaines's best-known character. Although more complex than the other aunts, she shares many of the characteristics of their type. Keith E. Byerman describes her as "perhaps the ultimate 'aunt' figure in Gaines's fiction," noting that she is "old and respected" and has "undergone a full range of experiences in the world of the folk" (*Fingering* 87). It should be noted, however, that Jane is never *called* "aunt," possibly because she did not remain in the same community her whole adult life. In general, the people who call her "Miss Jane" were already adults when she met them, though much younger than she. As she narrates the story of her life of over a hundred years, which includes a childhood in slavery and old age during the civil rights movement, we learn that even as a child Jane feared nothing and no one. Her stubbornness and determination as a child are shown when she keeps her new name, given her by a Union soldier, and refuses to answer to the old one, Ticey. These incidents and her foolhardy search for Ohio are recognized by the adult Jane for what they are. She is an individual with intelligence, wit, courage, determination, and integrity. She has also fulfilled the role as an Auntie in rearing a child not her own and in continuing to be a source of guidance to the young in the community. Jane is mature in her concern and caring for Ned and also realistic about her relationship with his young schoolteacher. But when Ned becomes involved with the struggle for black people's rights, Jane (following Colonel Dye's orders) tells him to stop. Ned does not listen, "said he wouldn't stop" (74). When Ned tries to get her to leave with him, she refuses, saying, "We doing what we both think is best" (76).

Jane is independent and hardworking, with a sense of humor. She also has a position of respect and prestige. When she wants to move from the cook's house to a house back in the quarters and Robert Samson protests, she says, "I told him at my age I did what I wanted to do" (201). At the end, she openly defies Samson when he warns everyone on his plantation that they will have to leave the place if they participate in civil rights demonstrations. When she decides to go to Bayonne to meet Jimmy, even though he is dead, she says, "Me and Robert looked at each other there a long time, then I went by him" (246).

In an interview, Gaines said, "I like Miss Jane because she's small, she has fantastic courage, and she is an individual" (Laney 8). Elsewhere, Gaines described her as "an uneducated person, an illiterate person, but someone with a tremendous sense of being, of knowing. Miss Jane is very intelligent from a folk, non-educated point of view" (Blake 3). Miss Jane's place in the community as an older woman and aunt figure is enhanced by such qualities as intelligence, verbal acuity, and independence, all of which contrast to her small size. Barry Beckham points out her verbal wit and clever rejoinders and her readiness to do verbal battle. He notes that "the only way the black Southerner can assert her womanhood short of rebellion may be through the *word*. And often this practice of signifying or verbally abusing another is also necessary to preserve one's humanity against the hostility of other blacks" (106). Like other aunt figures, Miss Jane has gained strength and wisdom from life experiences that have earned her a position of near-veneration in the black community.

A second category of female characters Gaines portrays is the mother. His mothers are strong, mature women concerned with young children and their needs. They sacrifice for their children, who almost always are boys. Amy, the mother in "A Long Day in November," is unusual in Gaines's fiction because she is not on her own but is raising her family along with her husband. She is presented through the consciousness and narrative voice of her young son, Sonny. She cares for and protects him, though at the same time she is trying to cope with her own marital problems. Amy shows tenderness for Sonny by smiling at him and calling him her "baby." He says, "She hugs me real hard and rubs her face against my face" (4).

Octavia in "The Sky Is Gray" is perhaps the fullest development of the strong mother figure, intent on teaching her children how to survive with dignity. She is unsentimental and harsh because survival and manhood for her son are her goals. In addition, she is raising her children alone, since the father is in the army. Octavia has strength and dignity, but she lacks warmth and the ability to show love openly to her children. She is so determined to teach them how to survive that she will not allow them to cry or to be afraid, nor does she condone tenderness or open displays of affection. In spite of her harshness, James (the eight-year-old narrator) understands that she loves them and they love her. James says he loves her and wants to buy her a red coat. Gaines has said that in the rural black culture of the late 1940s, the first duty of a mother who loved her children was "To show us how to live, to show us how to survive" (Gaudet and Wooton 65). Octavia does this by forcing her son to kill animals for food and by defending herself from a pimp by pulling a knife on him.

In addition to strength and courage, pride and dignity are goals mothers have for their children. Octavia refuses "charity" from the old lady Helena while she and James wait for the dentist—they must repay her for what they get. Byerman notes that "an act of kindness must be carefully negotiated" (*Fingering* 78) as social conventions and pride must be balanced. Later she tells Helena, "Your kindness will never be forgotten." This is in sharp contrast to their treatment by the nurse in the dentist's office who completely ignores their humanity. Todd Duncan says, "In the tradition of many a black mother under the South's system of caste and class, her own system may be stern, but it is consistent and understood by her son, hence a reliable guide for his development" (91). When Octavia says, "You not a bum . . . You a man," she expresses confidence that her methods, though harsh, will lead her son to survival with dignity—a common theme in Gaines's fiction.

Big Laura, Ned's mother in *The Autobiography of Miss Jane Pittman,* gives a very different view of motherhood, though she certainly seems as devoted to her children as Amy. Leading the freed slaves north from the plantation, she is more masculine than traditionally feminine in her approach to protecting others, especially her children and Jane. She protects Jane from being raped by the "nitwit" while the men in the party do nothing. Jane says of her, "She was big just like her name say, and she was tough as any man I ever seen" (16). After patrollers kill Big Laura and her baby, Jane says, "I didn't cry, I couldn't cry. I had seen so much beating and suffering; I had heard about so much cruelty in those 'leven or twelve years of my life I hardly knowed how to cry" (23). Despite Big Laura's death at the hands of the armed poor whites, women as mothers in Gaines's fiction seem to have the ability to make decisions, to protect and provide for themselves and their children, and to deal with the realities of life. Their strength, wisdom, and dignity come through confronting the hardships of their lives in a racist culture that shows little, if any, compassion for them and their children.

Gaines's fiction has many portraits of women at work. They earn a living, not only for themselves but often for their family, as hoodoo ladies, boardinghouse keepers, fieldworkers, domestics, waitresses, and schoolteachers.

It is interesting that Gaines's earliest portrayal of women workers was as prostitutes in "The Turtles," which appeared in 1956 in *Transfer,* a literary magazine at San Francisco State College. A widow, Mrs. Diana Brown, and her niece Amy live away from town. Max, the young narrator, says, "None of the other womenfolks associated too much with her or Amy" (93). Max and his friend Benny are taken to Mrs. Brown's house by their fathers for their sexual initiation when Max is fourteen. His "Pa" tells him: "I want you to go into the house, and go into the first room on your right. Just push the door open and go in there" (94). Max obeys his father, but Benny is overcome with fear, threatened by his father when he refuses to enter the room, and finally reduced to tears. This story presents women as frightening, yet having sexual intercourse with them is an essential part of attaining manhood.

The hoodoo ladies are liable to seem caricatured unless they are viewed in relation to their culture, in which even those who do not accept the power of their cures recognize their special status. These women demand respect from the skeptical, and, in fact, create fear in them. Madame Toussaint in "A Long Day in November" is the hoodoo woman to whom Eddie goes, after the minister proves ineffective, as a source of wisdom about how to get his wife to return home. Eddie has no faith in her powers, but all else has failed him. After Reverend Simmons tells him he must solve his problems the best way he can, Eddie says, "When you want one of them preachers to do something for you, they can't do a doggone thing. . . . I hate to go to that old hoo-doo woman, but I reckon there ain't nothing else I can do" (44). Specializing in marital problems, Madame Toussaint gives the men advice on how to treat their women and how to communicate with them. She says, "You men better learn" and "Y'all never know how a woman feels, because you never ask how she feels" (61). She acts as a facilitator in the community between women and men, but her sympathy is clearly with the women. Another hoodoo lady, Madame Gautier in *Miss Jane Pittman,* is similarly consulted when all else fails. Miss Jane says, "I didn't believe in hoo-doo, I never have, but nobody else wanted to listen to me" (92). Though Madame Gautier gives Jane some white powder to sprinkle for protection, her main role seems to be to advise Jane to accept reality. She says, "Nothing can stop death, mon sha . . ." (94). Like Madame Toussaint, she is consulted as a last resort, but she has no solutions. Though she offers some temporary comfort, she recognizes that she is powerless to change the inevitable.

Women fieldworkers are included in several short stories and novels. Octavia in "The Sky Is Gray" cuts cane, and Amy in "A Long Day in November" says she is not afraid of working in the fields, if necessary. Miss Jane works there as a young girl and also later in life, even when she could chose to be a domestic. Her story about the episode involving Black Harriet and Katie Nelson is Gaines's most emotionally intense portrayal of women fieldworkers. It shows women in competition and conflict—against nature, white men, and other black women. Black Harriet does not have "all her faculties, but still she was queen of the field. . . . Could pick more cotton, chop more cotton than anybody out there. Cut more cane than anybody out there, man or women, except for Toby Lewis" (131). When Katie challenges Black Harriet to a race in hoeing the rows of cotton, the other workers encourage the competition. Jane acknowledges the responsibility they all share for the tragic results of such sport: "I got to say it now, we was all for it. That's how it was in the field. You wanted that race. That made the day go. Work, work, you had to do something to make the day go. We all wanted it. We all knowed Katie couldn't beat Harriet, but we thought the race would be fun" (131). When Black Harriet begins leaving wire grass behind in order to stay ahead of Katie, the overseer, Tom Joe, warns her and then begins to beat her with a whip. The support from other women comes only after this physical attack from an outsider. When Grace Turner tries to defend and protect Black Harriet, Tom Joe beats her also. Bessie Turner then threatens Tom Joe with her hoe, and finally all the workers get involved. In the end, Black Harriet is taken to the state mental hospital while Grace and Bessie are fired by the plantation owners, who "didn't do a thing to Tom Joe" (133). Here, Gaines shows that black women must endure a torturous kind of labor that can destroy them, and he suggests the psychological damage all suffer from a life in the fields. This dark scene is an indictment of the economic exploitation of black women in this culture.

Black women working as domestics in the homes of white families were traditionally thought of in the black communities as having more prestige and an easier lot than the fieldhands. Their jobs gave them access to the white employers on a more personal basis, and therefore, these women often had to act as go-betweens or contacts across racial lines. Among those who work as domestics are Aunt Margaret in *Of Love and Dust,* 'Malia in "Bloodline," Miss Jane Pittman, and Janey in *A Gathering of Old Men.* Aunt Fe is a retired domestic in "Just Like A Tree," and her story seems to conform more than that of the others to the view of the harmonious relationship between domestics and their employers. While there are no open conflicts in the homes, the other women have no illusions about their employers and certainly no false admiration. The caring of the black woman for the white child—for example, Aunt Margaret's concerns for Tite—is a humanistic response to a child who lacks adequate parenting. The older domestics, such as 'Malia, have a certain freedom in speaking to their white employers and the liberty of expressing their disapproval directly. 'Malia realizes that her position and her employer's reliance on her enable her to say things to him that others could not say and that she herself would not have said when she was younger. This advantage gives the older women a freedom and strength in dealing with others.

Women schoolteachers in Gaines's fiction are almost all Creoles, a category of women that perhaps should be dealt with separately. Gaines's first novel, *Catherine Carmier,* considers the problems of cultural mores that keep the French-speaking Creoles of color apart from the black community in south Louisiana. The Creoles are separated not only by language but also by intense pride in their ancestors, many of whom were free persons of color in the Old South. They enjoyed the legal right to own land and slaves, and, up until Louisiana's statehood in 1812, also the right to vote. Catherine, Lillian, and Della (their mother) are all beautiful women, fitting the Creole stereotype, but they are not developed as strong female characters. Thadious M. Davis has pointed out that Catherine "locks herself into a life of conformity to her father's ways" and is "trapped by her own feelings, values, and beliefs" ("Headlands" 10). The retired Creole schoolteacher in the book is much more positively portrayed. Madame Bayonne, confidante and adviser of the central character Jackson Guerin, understands more about the world than the other women, but she stands apart from the black culture in which she lives. For Jackson, she provides a broader perspective since she, like he, knows a world away from their community. Valerie Babb suggests that Madame Bayonne also provides coherence: "Her knowledge of past and present and her analytical abilities allow her to create a perspective for Jackson, one that links many disparate elements of race, ethnicity, class, and communal history" (144, n.9).

Another schoolteacher, Miss Hebert in "A Long Day in November," is almost certainly Creole, both because she has a French name and because the story is set in the 1940s, a time when almost all the women teachers in black schools in south Louisiana were Creole. Though the young narrator is afraid he will be whipped by the teacher because he does not know his lesson, Miss Hebert's response is guided by sympathy because of the marital discord in his home. She seems genuinely concerned about the students in a community where educational standards are low.

In *Miss Jane Pittman,* the first woman schoolteacher in the quarters, Miss Lilly, is described by Miss Jane as "a little bowlegged mulatto woman from Opelousas" (153). Gaines recognizes the culture's distinction between Creoles of color (those of mixed racial and ethnic identity, including some French or Spanish heritage) and mulattos in his fiction. As Miss Jane says of Creole Place, "No matter how white you was if you didn't have Creole background they didn't want you there" (159). Miss Jane later tells about Mary Agnes LeFabre, a young Creole schoolteacher whose family disowned her because she insulted their caste consciousness by teaching black children on the plantation. She leaves the plantation to return to New Orleans after the plantation owner's son falls in love with her and later kills himself because he realizes that, in his culture, love across racial lines is doomed. Mary Agnes is a beautiful and intelligent young woman, caught between two worlds, with little control of the circumstances of her life. Although respected, she and the other Creole schoolteachers are regarded as outsiders by the black community because of their ethnicity, not their higher level of education.

Gaines's most positive portrayals of young professional women are Beverly Ricord in *In My Father's House* and Vivian Baptiste in *A Lesson,* both Creole schoolteachers. Beverly is typical of Gaines's strong women, even though strength and wisdom such as hers characterize only mothers or older women in Gaines's earlier works, rather than young, single women. Beverly is a mature, intelligent woman to whom the men listen and whom they also perceive, at times, as their equal. Her character shows a deepening complexity in women characters in

Gaines's work over the years. She is educated and knows a world away from the quarters. She admires the courage of the civil rights leaders and believes she and the other teachers should be protesting, too. Yet she is still isolated from the community that employs her. Virginia Colar tells Shepherd, Beverly's fiance, "She's a nice girl, even if she is Catholic and Creole" (24). Gaines continues to develop this character type in *A Lesson*. There the schoolteacher, Vivian Baptiste, a young mother, is separated from her husband and involved in a serious love affair with Grant Wiggins while her divorce is pending. Gaines shows her negotiating the conflicting demands of her status in the community as an educator and her personal desire for an intimate relationship.

Because Gaines portrays black women firmly rooted in a definite historical and geographic place, we must look at the culture's mores regarding gender roles in order to understand more fully the foregoing character types. To date, the subject of fathers and sons has received almost all the attention of scholars focusing on gender roles in Gaines's works. Indeed, he has spoken about this theme repeatedly in published interviews. Nevertheless, the influence of women on men, violence toward women, and women's communities are important gender issues in Gaines's fiction.

The most important aspect of relationships between the genders in Gaines's fiction is the attempts of black women to influence the black male in his quest for manhood. Rather than having their paths in life determined by men, women in Gaines's fiction are more likely to try to help determine the paths for their boys and men. The image of the boy or young man achieving direction is almost always connected to his mother's or aunt's strength and teaching. For example, when the mother in "The Sky Is Gray" tells James, "You not a bum. . . . You a man," she is attempting to teach him a lesson about attaining manhood. Although mothers and aunts try to train their youngsters, in general, older men cut themselves off from female influence. Thus Gaines's women, despite their strong sense of self, have only limited ability to influence men in making decisions and in establishing their sense of self-identity and manhood. A clear exception to this pattern of the inability of women to shape the behavior of adult males is depicted in "A Long Day in November," to be discussed below along with other stories involving violence.

Sometimes fear impels women to try to control their men's behavior. For example, the danger Joe Pittman and Ned face in their work scares Miss Jane. Ironically, when she tries to ensure Joe's safety, she inadvertently becomes responsible for the escape of the wild horse that, in turn, causes his death. Later on, when Ned returns to Louisiana to teach, she unsuccessfully tries to get him to go back to Kansas with his family because she knows he will be killed. In trying to influence Jimmy in book 4, Miss Jane's motivation is not personal fear but rather a sense of threat to the community's survival. She cannot control Jimmy and ultimately comes to understand not only his need for her support but also the necessity for his actions. Like other women, she helps the young males achieve manhood, but she is essentially powerless to shape their actions as men.

In *In My Father's House,* Phillip Martin's nanane is unable to give him the direction he needs or to help him find solutions to the problems in his adult life. His commitment to civil rights is a course chosen beyond her, and his earlier rejection of family is also something she could not prevent. Alma, his wife, is no more successful in helping or influencing him. A possible exception to this inability to influence men is the schoolteacher who appeals to him with reason and intelligence in the final pages. After Phillip Martin has given up on his life and civil rights work, Beverly Ricord reasons with him to stay away from Adeline Toussaint, a "scarlet woman" from his past. The men fight Phillip to keep him from leaving the house, but Beverly appeals to reason to accomplish the same goal. She is decisive, wise, and strong. Frank Shelton points out that it is significant that a woman reasons with Phillip in the end. Shelton says that Phillip's betrayal of women is significant in the context of Gaines's fiction: "In his past life he sexually used and abused women in order to convince himself he was a man, but even in his more enlightened present it is suggested that he has little use for women except as they admire him and support his ego" ("*In My Father's House*" 343). Shelton concludes that "if Martin begins approaching women on a different, more humble footing, perhaps he will then be open to the sustenance which they often provide in Gaines's fiction" (344). Beverly tells Phillip Martin he has to continue his work: "You wanted the past changed, Reverend Martin. . . . Even He can't do that. So that leaves nothing but the future. We work toward the future" (213). In admonishing a man to face reality, Beverly's voice has something in common with that of the hoodoo woman in "A Long Day in November."

A Gathering, a novel in which the men finally achieve manhood, clearly demonstrates the absence of women's influence on black men's behavior. For example, when Mat Brown's wife tries to stop him from going to the Marshall plantation, he threatens her with violence. He acknowledges her fear, but he will not be stopped: "Pray if you want to. Pray for all us old fools. But don't try to stop me. So help me, God, woman, don't try to stop me" (38). Though boys and young men may need women to help them understand the nature of being men, ultimately women cannot make them men. They must do it on their own. In *A Gathering,* the men acquire the courage, albeit in old age, to stand. They achieve an independence and maturity more typical of mothers, and women in general, in Gaines's fiction.

In contrast to *A Gathering,* in which women have no influence, *A Lesson Before Dying* depicts women who do control. Here Gaines shows for the first time the direct influence of women on a mature man. The alienation of Grant Wiggins from his culture is bridged by both the influence of his aunt and the support of his fiancée. In this novel Gaines also attempts to bridge the gender gap he has typically presented in this culture. Here a man is influenced by women without compromising the dignity or integrity of either gender. Events influenced directly by the aunt lead Grant not only to a perception of his own manhood but to his ultimate understanding and acceptance of his role in providing some possibility for another black male to achieve manhood. The situation of the aunt figure who raised a now educated young black man who returns to the quarters is reminiscent of that in *Catherine Carmier,* but there is a direct change in the influence women are able to assert. The characters and the dynamics of *A Lesson* show a much more mature writer's awareness of the ambiguities and complexities of real life.

Violence in Gaines's fiction reflects complex, often ambiguous cultural norms. Gaines believes that violence, in some form, is inevitable when there is no other outlet for frustrations and little chance that any hopes can be realized (Gaudet and Wooton 43–45). Women are generally the catalysts for violence among males. Both Marcus in *Of Love and Dust* and Procter in "Three Men" kill another man in a bar because of an argument over a woman. Similarly, Jackson and Raoul fight because of their conflict over Catherine Carmier. Generally, except in the case of rape, violence does not touch the women. Though beatings are sometimes threatened, they are not carried out. Jane Pittman says, for example, that when she wanted to quit working in the big house because of conflict with the old cook, "Joe told me if I didn't get back up to that house he was go'n take a stick and run me back up there" (88).

The only instance of violence by a husband against a woman is the ironic beating, done at the wife's insistence, in "A Long Day in November." This story often gives readers difficulty because it seems to imply that women want or need to be beaten or otherwise abused by men. Such an interpretation, however, disregards the culture and the time in which this story is set. Amy knows that she has humiliated Eddie in the eyes of their neighbors by insisting that he burn his car to prove his devotion to her. So that night she insists on being beaten in order that he can put her back in her place and become, once again, the man in the family. The appearance of masculinity is all she really gets, since she is clearly in control, but such appearances are essential, in Amy's view, for maintaining her own position in the community. As Byerman says of Eddie, "Like his son, he must be taught the meaning of manhood by a woman" (*Fingering* 76). Eddie had earlier been threatened by his mother-in-law with a knife, the dog, and a shotgun. She clearly questions his manhood until he finally burns his car. Then she says, "I must be dreaming. He's a man after all" (71). The cultural rules demand that a husband and father act "like a man." One of Eddie's problems is that he is a basically good person who understands neither his wife's needs nor the rules of the culture regarding manhood. Amy understands that to live and function with respect in a community one must at least follow the form of the code. When Eddie asks Amy why he had to beat her, she says, "Because I don't want you to be the laughingstock of the plantation." Though Eddie says he does not mind if they laugh, she replies, "I do mind" (75–76). As she correctly interprets their culture, she knows that her status as wife and mother is dependent on Eddie's being perceived as a man. To interpret her actions as self-demeaning or disgraceful is to apply middle-class feminist perspectives to a culture in which a woman had little opportunity for education or access to other roles, and her only option was often simply to do the best she could. Ironically, Amy is following an outmoded code in a community that is clearly more matriarchal than patriarchal. Although strong father figures are absent from Gaines's fiction, patriarchy as an ideal continues.

The culture Gaines is portraying seems not only to condone but to demand a husband's use of force or threatened force to maintain his authority over his wife. The characters in "A Long Day in November" apparently admire a husband's use of physical punishment for a wife's disobedience. Although the rights of a husband in this culture are clear and maintaining order in the family takes priority over a wife's independence, violence toward women is not generally accepted. With equal clarity, the culture censures violence in the form of rape. Rape of black women by white men is one of the many tragedies of the plantation tradition from which black men could not protect their women, as shown when the son of the plantation owner in *Miss Jane Pittman* rapes the Creole schoolteacher.

Johanna Rey's daughter in *In My Father's House* is the only woman in Gaines's fiction to be raped by a man of her own race. Interestingly, the sexual attack occurs after the family has moved away from south Louisiana. The mother of Reverend Phillip Martin's first children—Etienne, Antoine, and Justine—Johanna has lived in San Francisco for twenty-one years, since Martin deserted her. Life there is brutal, and she has suffered from violence. Johanna's lover rapes her daughter, and the son Antoine, in turn, kills him. The rape of a daughter by the mother's lover is a common theme in black literature that seems to mirror a real threat in black life. Maya Angelou, in *I Know Why the Caged Bird Sings,* and Alice Walker, in *The Color Purple,* deal with similar situations. It is interesting to see how Gaines handles such a situation as opposed to black women writers. With Gaines the focus is clearly on the brothers and how they react to the violence against their sister. In the foreground are the issues of family honor, duty, and justice as perceived by the brothers and the devastating effect of the rape on them. Rape is never culturally acceptable, and in the black culture it further emasculates those men who believe they should have been able to prevent it.

Gaines's fiction seems to suggest cultural mores that require men to protect women from sexual threats, yet men are seldom successful in doing so. Women must, in fact, protect themselves, as Octavia does in "The Sky Is Gray" when she defends herself against the pimp with a knife. When as a young girl Jane Pittman is threatened by the "nitwit," she is rescued and protected not by a man but by Big Laura.

A final issue to consider is Gaines's depiction of women's relationships with each other on the basis of shared gender identity. Gaines has no single-sex communities of women like those Nina Auerbach discusses in *Communities of Women.* However, the women in Gaines's fiction seem to provide the sense of community in the society generally. Gaines's ability to understand and record the sense of unity women create and sustain among themselves also reveals the limits of community. In *Catherine Carmier* there is a failed sense of relationship between Catherine and her mother and a working relationship between Aunt Charlotte and Mary Louise. Not only does Mary Louise help Aunt Charlotte when she is sick, but more importantly, they spend time together and share thoughts and feelings. Aunt Charlotte tells her, "Just sit here with me a minute," and Mary Louise knows "that Miss Charlotte had something to say, and she would not leave until Miss Charlotte had spoken" (34). Perhaps the best depiction of a network of women in Gaines's fiction is in "Just Like a Tree." The close relationship among Aunt Fe, Aunt Lou, and the other women suggests a genuine community spirit of sharing and caring. Though men are also involved, the women have the kind of intimate, confiding friendships and cross-generational relationships that provide the sustaining strength of community. It is significant that such a sense of community among women is much more evident among the older women in Gaines's fiction. Young women in general seem to be isolated. There are no strong mother-daughter relationships, just as there are no mature father-son relationships.

As Gaines's characters age, they seem to move toward more comfortable interactions among women and across generations. This fact is particularly evident in the progression of stories in *Bloodline*. The main characters progress not only in age but also from isolation to shared relationships with other women. In "A Long Day in November," Amy's mother seems to be an adversary, and Amy does not have any women available to her as confidantes. Octavia in "The Sky Is Gray" is a young mother who must work out solutions to her problems on her own because her husband is away doing military service. In "Just Like a Tree," however, the women share a strong emotional bond with one another and a sense of intergenerational responsibility. It is worth noting that the feelings of community and obligation are not directly associated with close kinship ties. Such feelings seem to work best with age, and the bonding occurs in the homes rather than in the workplace. In *A Lesson* the close relationship among the older women is particularly evident as they have coffee and cake in Tante Lou's kitchen. Vivian knows that in order for her relationship with Grant to develop, she must be accepted by these women. Gaines shows her helping to serve coffee and speaking quiet words of comfort, simple acts that cause the women slowly to open their circle to her.

In *Miss Jane Pittman* the community of women is apparent, both on the porch as the frame is set for Miss Jane to tell her story and in the quarters at the end with Mary, Lena, and others. Scenes of Miss Jane talking with other women, however, are strangely absent from her life story. She goes to the hoodoo doctor as a client, not to create community. Nor does she join the other women at church later in her life. Work has provided neither her nor any of the other women in Gaines's fiction a place to sustain a separate women's community. The impression of Miss Jane's isolation from other women given in her narrative contrasts with the information in the frame and in the facts of her relationships at the end. This situation reflects the inherent conflict in literature between community and the individual voice narrating her own life story.

Underlying the various roles women play in the culture and the themes discussed above is the technical matter of voice, central to Gaines's craft of fiction. In portraying women and issues that matter in their lives, Gaines presents several female characters who are able to tell about their lives and their roles in their own voices. Gaines uses women as narrators in "Just Like a Tree" (four of the ten are women), *A Gathering of Old Men* (two of the fifteen are women), and *Miss Jane Pittman*. Clearly, his most complex woman narrator is Miss Jane. She is someone who has become somewhat of a legend in her own folk community. The history teacher comes to her to record her story. Not only is her life a long one, but the community feels it is worthy of being recorded because Miss Jane has the capability to "form" and narrate her life. Babb notes that it is appropriate for Gaines to allow a black woman's voice ("a largely overlooked viewpoint") to recall and interpret cultural history because, as she says, "Gaines's women provide the nurture that enables individual, familial, and communal survival" (77).

Given the success of Miss Jane's first-person narration, it is somewhat surprising to realize how few of Gaines's narrators are women and that none of the female narrators is a child, a narrative stance he handles well with several young boys. In addition, Gaines virtually limits the woman's narrational voice to the elderly. Anne Robinson Taylor's study of the female narrators created by male novelists, *Male Novelists and Their Female Voices*, is concerned with the "revelations these so-called women actually make about their authors, the extent to which they are versions of their creators in skirts" (3). It would seem that female narrators are a reflection of the male author's experiences and relationships with women in his life rather than true reflections of women's experiences. Gaines has been extremely successful in creating older female narrators, and his comments in interviews suggest that these are versions of the older women in his life who were of great importance to him in his formative years. Gaines has said that he got his own values from the old ones who raised him, particularly his aunt, and that his mother and his maternal grandmother were incredibly strong women: "I was raised by older women as a child. . . . I was around older women much more than I was around the men who came around the place where I lived" (Gaudet and Wooton 39; see also 64–71). Of Miss Jane, Gaines says, "She is not my aunt. . . . Maybe I had my aunt in mind when I was writing about her, but I had other old people in mind as well—those who sat on our gallery in the 1940's, and those whom I've met on the road since then" ("Miss Jane and I" 37). In the case of women narrators, Gaines hears the voice clearly only with older women. Thus they are the only women he allows to "take over" and narrate his fiction. Perhaps the elderly women's roles as conservators of culture and facilitators of community distinguish them in Gaines's fiction as particularly appropriate female voices through which to present and interpret African-American life.

Gaines's fiction presents black women in relation to a rural folk community unique in the South because of the Louisiana French Creole culture. Race, gender, class, and culture are inexorably bound to questions of identity, just as a sense of place is tied to pursuit of individual needs. While there are varieties of adaptations, it is clear in Gaines's fiction that despite being black, female, and poor, the women gain strength and wisdom from life experiences. Moreover, survival with dignity leads in old age to a secure position of prominence within the community.

"Haunted by the Idea": Fathers and Sons in *In My Father's House* and *A Gathering of Old Men*

Daniel White

In his early works, Ernest J. Gaines focuses primarily on the young black male, tracing the growth of this character from early childhood to young adulthood. In the short story collection *Bloodline,* Gaines begins with six-year-old Sonny Howard, moves through adolescence with nineteen-year-old Procter Lewis, and in Copper Laurent portrays the young man. In the first two novels, *Catherine Carmier* and *Of Love and Dust,* Gaines probes deeper into the characters of his young males. Jackson Bradley from the first novel is a naive version of Copper Laurent; the second novel continues the story of Procter Lewis, whom Gaines has renamed Marcus Payne. Though the names may differ, one similarity among these characters remains: they all rebel in the face of oppression. Through their rebellious actions, which often result in violence or death, Procter, Copper, Jackson, and Marcus all become instruments of change in Gaines's stagnant plantation world where the whites rule and the blacks fearfully submit.

The older characters, usually in the persons of the elderly aunts—Aunt Charlotte from *Catherine Carmier* and Aunt Margaret from *Of Love and Dust,* for example—seek to restrain the young rebels. They act to protect themselves and "the people" from violence, but however noble their intent, they are working also to stifle change and preserve a decadent system beyond its time.[1] This conflict between the generations continues in the third novel, *The Autobiography of Miss Jane Pittman,* in which Ned Douglass, Miss Jane's surrogate son, and Jimmy

Aaron, whom the old people designate "the One," their unofficial spiritual leader, both must fight not only white oppression but the fear in older blacks. However, the end of the novel marks a significant change in Gaines's fiction. The decision of 110-year-old Jane to go into town and join a civil rights demonstration shows that the elderly in Gaines's world may finally be realizing the necessity of rebellion. Though this ending reflects the achievements of Gaines's blacks, an apparent union of young and old against the white oppressor, we find in the next two novels that, despite this success, other conflicts remain unresolved.

Perhaps the main reason that Gaines's early protagonists are young males and elderly women is that these characters were inspired by his experiences before leaving Louisiana at age fifteen. Though young Gaines sometimes worked in the fields with the men, his closest ties to adults were with the older women who raised him, his Aunt Augusteen in particular.[2] And even after moving to California to live with his mother and stepfather, Gaines still did not develop a close father-son relationship because his stepfather was in the merchant marine and seldom at home. (Gaines does, however, credit his stepfather for getting him off the streets and into the library.) It was not until Gaines began visiting his Louisiana home that he developed close ties with older men, especially during his research for *Miss Jane Pittman*. Trying to get an idea of how Miss Jane would remember her life, Gaines talked with the old men still living on the plantations, spending hours on their galleries sharing their pasts. In an interview with Marcia Gaudet and Carl Wooton, Gaines has said, "I think I became closer to older men when I started coming back to the South and wanted to write about things. And it seemed the older men were the ones who were there, the ones who had survived" (*Porch Talk* 39). Gaines's observations stuck with him after the completion of *Miss Jane Pittman* and undoubtedly led to his new protagonists— the Reverend Phillip J. Martin of *In My Father's House* and Mathu, Chimley, Coot, Uncle Billy, and all the other old-timers in *A Gathering of Old Men*.

The shift in focus from the young male rebel to the mature and aging man does not indicate a change in philosophy. Rather, Gaines is using new knowledge to approach an old theme—the separation of fathers and sons. Throughout Gaines's earlier works, we see this separation from the point of view of sons without fathers. In "Three Men" Procter Lewis, abandoned by his father, finds a substitute in Munford Bazille, the old convict. Copper Laurent from "Bloodline" will never find a father because he was the product of a white man's lust. Marcus Payne from *Of Love and Dust* is Procter Lewis without a Munford Bazille. The list goes on, but perhaps the best example is young James in "The Sky Is Gray." In his journey of initiation, he encounters many of the symbols and practices of small-town Southern racism, but the void left by his missing father is the root of his greatest hardships. As Valerie Babb has noted in her book *Ernest Gaines,* "the psychic state of Gaines's male characters is a direct result of paternal presence or absence" (98). Most often, this state is the result of absence.

In an interview with Mary Ellen Doyle, Gaines has explained that the rift between black fathers and sons originated with slavery:

> The father and son were separated when they were brought to this country over three centuries ago. The white man did not let them come together during slavery, and they have not been able to reach each other since. Despite the revolution, the black father is in a position of non-respectability, and the white is still in control. The black man is seldom the owner, still is not the public defender in court, not the judge. The young black man almost always sees a white in these positions, not an older black man, not his father. . . . So the son cannot and does not look up to the father. The father has to look up to the son. That is not natural. And the cycle continues, and continues, and continues. A few of our black fathers make it, but the majority do not—and I doubt they will in our time. ("*MELUS* Interview" 73)

According to Gaines, the problems between black fathers and sons originated with white slave owners who literally separated father from son by breaking up families to put individual slaves on the auction block. And despite the civil rights movement, black fathers have not totally rejected submission, and they have not attained positions of power in white as well as black society. Black fathers must acquire this power before they can regain the respect of their sons, a prerequisite for reunification. Gaines presents an in-depth exploration of these ideas with *In My Father's House,* which focuses on a father. "It is a book I had to write," he has said, "because I was haunted by the idea [of the separation of black fathers and sons]. It cost me more time (seven years) and pain than any other book I've written" (Doyle, "*MELUS* Interview" 72).

One reason that Gaines may have devoted so much energy to finishing

In My Father's House is that he had experienced life without a father. The head of Gaines's household when he was a child was a woman, as is true of many black families in America today. After the separation of Gaines's parents, his father moved to New Orleans. According to Gaines, "He was never there when I was a kid growing up. He was there when I was a very small child, but not after I was on my own. From the moment I was on my own, which was when I was about eight years old, he was not there" (Gaudet and Wooton, *Porch Talk* 62). The struggle to complete *In My Father's House* probably reflects Gaines's struggle to come to an understanding of his own father's absence. Other black male writers have faced similar experiences. Ralph Ellison was three years old when his father died; Richard Wright was the same age when his father deserted the family; and James Baldwin was born to an unmarried woman and never had a father, only a stepfather, with whom he had an ambivalent relationship. In *Black Boy,* Wright expresses rage at his father for leaving the family to face the hardships of poverty and hunger. Baldwin's novel *Go Tell It on the Mountain,* which at one point was entitled "In My Father's House," shares more than a working title with Gaines's novel. It contains Baldwin's own attempt to work through the problems of a failed relationship with his father. In Gaines's *In My Father's House,* the author consciously set out to explore his ideas about the split between black fathers and sons. In focusing on a mature black father in this novel and on elderly fathers in *A Gathering,* Gaines is able to draw from a large pool of black male experience. He uses this range of experience to illustrate how black fathers and sons have become separated and why they have had limited success in reuniting.

In My Father's House opens at Virginia Colar's boardinghouse, where a mysterious young man calling himself Robert X has just arrived. Once settled in, he fishes for information about the Reverend Phillip J. Martin, pastor of Solid Rock Baptist Church and the civil rights leader of St. Adrienne, Louisiana (which Gaines calls Bayonne in other books). But once Robert X gets his information, he spends all of his time walking in the cold winter rain and lingering in the road in front of Martin's house and in the doorway of his church. Out of curiosity, Elijah, a young teacher who lives with Martin and his family, invites Robert X to a party at the minister's house. There Martin rallies his followers for their planned demonstrations against Albert Chenal, the largest employer in town and the least moved by the idea of civil rights. When Martin sees

Robert X and realizes the young man's identity, he falls to the floor, then allows his white advisors to tell his people that he has collapsed from exhaustion. For the next few days, Martin, confiding in no one, agonizes over his weakness at the party but primarily over his weakness twenty-one years earlier when he abandoned Johanna Rey, the woman he loved, and their three children. And he agonizes because he cannot remember the given name of his oldest son—who has taken the name Robert X.

In revealing Martin's secret past, Gaines shifts his focus from the enigmatic stranger to the celebrated father. If it were not for the eerie presence of Robert X, we might, in the beginning, be lulled into thinking that Gaines is presenting a celebration of the civil rights movement and of a dynamic leader. Robert X hears only praise of Phillip Martin. Virginia proudly recites Martin's accomplishments and expresses the community's desire to see him elected to Congress: "People thinking 'bout sending him on to Washington. Would be the first one from round here, you know" (10). Elijah calls the reverend "our Martin Luther King" because of "his leadership, political and moral. His character" (16). "The man's beautiful, so much courage" (20), says Beverly Ricord, a young teacher. Her boyfriend Shepherd, also a teacher, dubs the reverend "King Martin" (30). And when Gaines finally introduces us to the imposing presence of Phillip J. Martin, we could easily believe that the man deserves his renown. Though sixty years old, Martin is a model of power and virility, often being compared to a prizefighter. He stands over six feet tall, weighs around two hundred pounds, and has "thick black hair" and a "thick well-trimmed mustache" (34). Because of his age and his leadership abilities, Martin may at first appear to be an ideal father figure, something missing in any form from Gaines's previous works. The presence of such a mature role model, a respectable elder statesman in the black community, could perhaps suggest the achievement of some sense of normality, and perhaps many observers wanted to believe that civil rights did indeed establish a greater degree of normality.

However, Gaines suggests that one decade's worth of political and social reforms did not and could not repair the damage of more than one-hundred years of slavery and oppression. As evidence, he presents Robert X and the young teachers. Robert X, with his terse, abrasive, cryptic comments, supplies the first indications that Phillip Martin may not be the savior his followers believe him to be. When Virginia boasts of her minister's accomplishments, Robert X cuts her off: "It sounded from the tone of his voice that he didn't believe what she was saying" (10). The young man's skepticism is less subtle in response to Elijah's tribute to Martin's superior character: "His character? . . . Do you ever know a man's character?" (16). The teachers, the only other young people we see, wallow in fear and self-pity, spending every evening in the Congo Room drinking themselves into a collective stupor. Even Beverly, who applauds Martin's courage, admits she has none of her own: "I think it's a shame. . . . We being the teachers, we ought to be the ones out there in front" (21). Chuck answers with all of the bitterness and cynicism of the post-Martin Luther King young: "That shit's over with kiddo. Them honkies gave up some, because of conscience, because of God. But they ain't giving up no more. Nigger's already got just about everything he's getting out of this little town. Anything else he want he better go look somewhere else for it" (21). Gaines ends the discussion tersely: "The bartender brought the bottle" (21). Thus, the cycle of despair and drunkenness continues. But nothing could be more damning than Robert X himself, a twenty-seven-year-old exoskeleton. He represents the future—all the hopes and aspirations of the movement. Yet he has received no inspiration from the leaders and only pain from the great father figure—the Reverend Phillip J. Martin—his flesh-and-blood father. "My soul is sick," he says, comparing it to the piles of garbage in the alley below his boarding-house window: "Used to be something good in them bottles, in them cans. . . . Somebody went through lot of pain making them bottles round—red and green. Look at them now. Busted. Cans bent and rusted. Nothing but trash. Nothing but trash now" (27). Despite Martin's civil rights demonstrations, he will never be able to restore the "something good" he destroyed when, twenty-one years earlier, he discarded his eldest son like one of the bottles in that alley.

Although Phillip Martin seems an ideal father figure, someone that a son should respect, some of the details of his position reflect a disturbing weakness. First, he is still only a preacher in a local church. The talk of his becoming a U.S. Congressman would probably be a fantasy even without the appearance of Robert X; St. Adrienne is, after all, a tiny constituency. Furthermore, Martin must depend on two white allies, one of whom is a lawyer. Deacon Howard Mills, speaking to

Jonathan Robillard, Martin's suspicious assistant pastor, defends these associations by saying, "We ain't got no black attorney round here who can do what Anthony can do. And Octave's the only friend we have on the board of education" (33). Of course, whites and blacks working together is an accomplishment in itself, but here the whites are still the only ones with positions of any real power. Frank Shelton observes that Martin's character fits into Gaines's "pattern of classical tragedy" and points out the tragic flaws of pride and selfishness—"ego gratification"—that afflict the reverend and his lieutenants ("*In My Father's House*" 343). Martin is no Oedipus, for his flaws are numerous. Though as a minister he is supposed to be a humble servant of God, Martin, like the intolerant preacher in "The Sky Is Gray," loves material things. His house is "the most expensive and elegant owned by a black family in St. Adrienne" (28). In the driveway of his beautifully landscaped yard sit his "big Chrysler" and his wife's station wagon (28). He wears expensive clothes, and Shepherd notices his showy jewelry—"the two big rings on his fingers and the gold watch band round his wrist" that "sparkled in the light" (35).

Even if Martin's character flaws could somehow escape the attention of Robert X, the older man's actions, past and present, still would probably preclude any feelings of respect in his son. Twenty-one years earlier, Phillip Martin had the chance to be a husband, a father, a man. But by not standing up and going to his family, by staying in the bed of a woman for whom he cared nothing, Phillip chose to live the way whites expected black men to live—as something subhuman, not guided by reason or normal emotions. When Phillip accepted this definition of his status, he had license to act as a brute—to indulge his lusts and shun the responsibilities of fatherhood. As he admits, "I was an animal before I was Reverend Phillip J. Martin" (211).

Years later Martin discovered God. He was converted, eventually using his pulpit to fight for reform. And he took a young wife and started a new family. He accomplished many things for his people and earned respectability for himself, but these feats do not, as Martin has believed, compensate for deserting his son. The fragility of his self-deception becomes apparent when, preparing for the biggest demonstration of his life, he receives a second chance to claim his son and fails pathetically.

When Martin faints at the party after recognizing that the uninvited guest Robert X is his son, he makes a few feeble efforts to rise from the floor. But instead of standing, Martin allows Octave Bacheron's "small white hand" to keep him on the floor. Instead of explaining his fall, Martin babbles gibberish: "Don't let me deny him again" (41). Dooming himself further, Martin allows Bacheron and Anthony to tell the people that he fell because of exhaustion, and the two white men "made him lean on them" as they put him to bed (42). Martin then broods constantly over his mistakes, especially this latest one: "Why didn't he knock that white man's hand away from his chest? He could have done it easily as flicking away a fly. Wouldn't that have been the right thing for him to do—brushing away that white man's hand and getting to his feet? Being leader, wasn't that the thing to do? If not the leader, who then? Who? But no, like some cowardly frightened little nigger, he lay there and let them do all the talking for him. He even let them push pills down in his mouth" (54–55). Martin realizes that he should have stood and asserted his independence by acknowledging the presence of his son, so he laments his weakness and his dependence upon his two white allies. All of this self-torture inevitably leads Martin to question his own manhood, but it will take a journey into his past for him to discover just how erroneous his entire concept of manhood has been.

However, we can already see where he has erred. Giving to the community is not the same as giving to a son. Other characters in Gaines's works give of themselves and achieve real nobility—Munford Bazille, Jim Kelley in *Of Love and Dust,* and Jane Pittman—but these people do not have their own children. Miss Jane, with her relationship to Ned, comes closest, but she is a mother figure, not a father. Even without natural children, these characters act on the need to establish what Erik Erikson terms *generativity,* which is "the concern for establishing and guiding the next generation" (*Identity* 138). To achieve generativity, the individual must move beyond personal needs and take steps to ensure that successive generations have a hopeful future.

As Todd Duncan has shown in discussing *Bloodline,* Erikson's theories on human development—the "eight ages of man" in particular—provide an enlightening context in which to explore Gaines's fiction. With the progression from six-year-old Sonny to the death of elderly Aunt Fe, *Bloodline* is largely a depiction of the human life cycle. Gaines has said that he wrote and arranged the stories with this end in mind (Ingram and Steinberg 341–42). Gaines's two novels under discussion here similarly lend themselves to interpretation based on Erikson's ideas because the characters' problems parallel the eight crises, each of which must be resolved for the individual to mature and then face death with courage and dignity.[3]

Phillip Martin, like Jane, Munford, and Jim (who have no children of their own), tries to achieve generativity through "other forms of altruistic concern and creativity which may absorb . . . parental drive" (Erikson, *Identity* 138). For Jane and the others, this substitution is not overly drastic, as they become substitute parents to Gaines's young, fatherless rebels. Martin's civil rights work, on the other hand, reflects a complete departure from parenthood, which is especially significant because he does have children of his own. Even his ties to his St. Adrienne family are tenuous; the narrative never portrays Martin with these children. And the complaints of his lawful wife Alma suggest that Martin has stumbled in a previous developmental stage, the one Erikson calls "intimacy—which is . . . a counterpointing as well as a fusing of identities" (*Identity* 135). Alma senses the distance between herself and her husband, finally telling him, "You come to me for this bed, for nothing else" (134). With his failures as a father and a husband plaguing his every thought, Martin questions even his role as a civil rights leader: "Lately I've been having my doubts. . . . If you not reaching the young, what good you doing?" (58). Thus, Martin's failures as a father merge with his failures as a leader.

Finally deciding that he must reach out to his son, the minister sacrifices the march against Chenal to get Robert X out of jail, a move that produces unfortunate consequences. Robert X is unimpressed, especially since his father still refuses to accept personal responsibility for the results of his desertion. Instead, Phillip Martin blames "that world out there" for Robert X's pain (100). He cannot even remember Robert X's real name. It bears mentioning here that Robert X's chosen name parallels that of Malcolm X, while Phillip Martin's surname and his activism have echoes of Martin Luther King, Jr. By renaming himself, Robert X apparently repudiates his father and his father's King-inspired ideals. He comes to St. Adrienne seemingly as a son of Malcolm X and his more militant vision. Certainly Robert X's rejection of his father includes a promise of violence. With mixed pain and hatred, the son walks away from the father—but not before telling Phillip that he is going to kill him. Returning home, Martin finds that word of his deal with the sheriff has reached the members of the civil rights committee, who promptly oust him as president in favor of pretentious, overly ambitious Jonathan Robillard.

With the future of his committee looking bleak and his own survival in doubt, Martin journeys into his past, searching for some kind of redemption. One of his goals on this quest is to talk with his old friend Chippo Simon, who has recently seen Johanna in California. But first the search leads Martin into the roadhouses and juke joints of his youth, where he confronts his past sins and the universality of his problem. Sexy seductress Adeline Toussaint represents Phillip's lusty past; it was his irresponsible appetite for sex that led him away from his first family. And when Martin meets Billy, a young radical, he learns the extent of the failure of black fathers. Billy asserts that blacks must join together for one day and burn the country to the ground: "Burn it down, you destroy Western Civilization. You put the world back right—let it start all over again" (162). Sensing a source of the young rebel's anger, Martin asks Billy about his father. The young man replies that their relationship is " 'bout average. . . . I don't bother him, he don't bother me" (165). Through Billy's bitterness, Phillip realizes as truth what he had been suspecting: "Then the civil rights movement didn't bring us together at all?" (166). Martin sees that civil rights may have improved relations between blacks and whites but that black father-and-son relationships remain unaffected because of lack of communication. Gaines has addressed this point directly in an interview: "Sitting at a counter with whites does not bring father and son together. Just because they are sitting there does not mean they are communicating" (Doyle, "*MELUS* Interview" 73).

From Chippo, Phillip finally learns the extent of the damage caused by his abandonment. Johanna, always hoping that Phillip would return to her, would not establish a permanent relationship with another man. Instead she had a series of brief affairs: "Never one too long," says Chippo. "Two, three months, then he had to go. . . . She let them know that from the start. Number one was still in Louisiana" (195). So not just the son has suffered; the mother also has been scarred. Phillip's desertion left her incapable of establishing intimacy with another man. Therefore no one ever assumed the role of father to the children. Johanna's last lover, a scoundrel named Quick George, turned his attentions to the daughter, savagely beating and raping her. The youngest boy, Antoine, demanded that Etienne (Robert X) shoot the rapist, but Etienne refused to take such action. So Antoine killed Quick George himself. "But now he was the man," says Chippo, "and he let Etienne know it" (198). Robert X's shame emasculated him. Yet the responsibility for the boy's pain and for the destruction of the family belongs to Phillip Martin. Martin realizes that if he had lived up to his family obligations, neither of his sons would have had to carry the burden of manhood that was prematurely unloaded on Robert X the day Phillip deserted them. The conversation with Chippo also verifies that his son does indeed plan to kill him. During Chippo's visit, Robert X discovered his father's whereabouts and decided to seek revenge—with Johanna's money and her blessings.

Robert X's vengeance, however, comes about differently from the way he had planned it. While Phillip's visit with Chippo continues, Alma, Beverly, and Shepherd arrive with the news that Robert X has jumped from the "trestle over Big Man Bayou" (203). Realizing that killing his father would not restore his manhood, the young man destroyed himself, ironically in the waters of "Big Man" Bayou. A bullet from Robert X's gun could not have hurt Martin as much as this news because he was hoping that what he learned from Chippo would help him move closer to his son. Now Robert X is lost forever.

But is Phillip Martin also lost? Gaines offers two different answers to this question as the novel concludes. Already drunk and now angry and wounded because of Robert X's suicide, Martin wants to rush back into the sins of the past, to Adeline's waiting bed, but settles for a brawl with Chippo and a reluctant Shepherd, who stop him from leaving. The result is a standoff, leaving Phillip with no easy outlet for his frustration. He feels beaten, and Gaines uses the image of a defeated boxer to describe him. Phillip surrenders, casting off his faith in God and everything else. Beverly, however, offers a different perspective. Once ashamed of her own timidity in comparison to Martin's strength, she now tries to give him courage. She reminds Martin that he has a son at home, Patrick, who needs a father's attention: "You wanted the past changed, Reverend Martin. . . . Even He can't do that. So that leaves nothing but the future. We work toward the future. To keep Patrick from going to that trestle. One day I'll have a son, and what we do tomorrow might keep him from going to that trestle. That's all we can ever hope for, isn't it, Reverend Martin?" (213). Beverly believes that the minister's painful experience with Etienne will give him the courage and the wisdom to forge a strong relationship with Patrick. But Beverly's hopeful words do not immediately reassure Phillip. "I'm lost," he tells his wife, Alma. "Shhh," she responds. "Shhh. We just go'n have to start again." The novel ends with these words, and we are left wondering whom to believe, the despairing Phillip Martin or the two optimistic women.

In a review of *In My Father's House*, Alvin Aubert sees the ending positively—"a reconciliation of past and present, of private and public man" ("Self-Reintegration" 133). Such a statement may seem overly optimistic, given Phillip Martin's state of mind. But the possibility does remain open for him to go back home and become a real father to Patrick, the kind of father of whom the boy can be proud. Gaines allows Alma to have the last say in the novel, and her strong words suggest that Phillip has, indeed, been given a second chance at fatherhood and that he will take advantage of this opportunity to "start over" in his relationship with Patrick. Patrick, in turn, may then be a good father to his own sons. And perhaps the future sons of Beverly and Shepherd will be able to know and respect their father; after all, Gaines chooses the young couple over everyone else to accompany Alma and share in Martin's experience. As is typical in Gaines's work, a tragedy eases the way for the slow but steady advance of progress.

This progress is not apparent at the beginning of *A Gathering,* which Gaines sets a few years beyond the end of *In My Father's House.* As the novel develops, however, we find more reason to be hopeful about Gaines's fathers and sons than ever before. For the setting of this novel, Gaines returns to the Louisiana plantation world that he captures so effectively in his earlier works. Most of the action in *A Gathering* takes place in the quarters of the Marshall plantation, where Beau Boutan, a Cajun farmer, has been shot and killed on a hot day in the late 1970s. Before calling the sheriff, young Candy Marshall, owner of the plantation, summons all willing black men to come to Mathu's house—where Boutan lies dead—with a twelve-gauge shotgun and an empty number five shell. When Sheriff Mapes arrives, he finds something that he never would have believed—a crowd of blacks in Mathu's yard and on his gallery, including close to twenty old men with shotguns, each claiming that he pulled the trigger on Boutan. Even Candy Marshall claims responsibility. But Mapes believes that Mathu is the only one with courage enough to have shot Boutan, and he tries to force a couple of the old blacks to confirm his supposition by slapping them around. They will not budge. Meanwhile, everyone waits for Fix Boutan, the dead man's father and a notorious vigilante, to ride in with his family and friends to avenge his son's death. But lacking the support of two of his sons, the old Cajun stays home. Then, in a surprise ending, all of the characters—black and white—learn something new about each other and about themselves.

The lives of the blacks still on the plantation tell us much about the lives of all blacks, including the state of father-and-son relationships. As the plantation system has deteriorated, the young adults have moved to the cities seeking opportunity. The elderly people have stayed behind to live out their lives and to raise the grandchildren left behind. The fact that children have been left to be raised by grandparents suggests that much remains to be done in bringing fathers and sons together. The old men on the plantation are clearly separated from their sons, geographically as well as emotionally. Some of them have also lost sons to racial violence. The only father-son relationship that we ever see on the plantation is that between Mathu and Charlie, but Mathu is actually Charlie's *parrain,* or godfather, not his biological father.

These old fathers have done nothing in the past to acquire the respectability that Gaines believes is necessary for a man to become a strong father figure. On the contrary, they have done everything possible to avoid conflict and remain invisible, primarily because of fear. They have allowed the white people's violence to intimidate them into complete submission. They have no respect for themselves. Therefore, their sons could not possibly respect them either. The old men are aware of their cowardice, and they burn with bitterness and shame.

A lifetime's worth of these pent-up emotions suddenly erupts in the stories the old men tell while gathered at Mathu's house. The story most relevant to this discussion is Gable's. Fighting back tears, he recounts his sixteen-year-old son's execution. Like Tom Robinson in *To Kill a Mockingbird,* Gable's son was accused and convicted of raping a white woman although he was obviously innocent. Everyone knew that if the boy did have sex with her, she must have seduced him. Gable still agonizes over failing his son all those years ago:

> And what did I do about them killing my boy like that? What could a poor old nigger do but go up to the white folks and fall down on his knees? But, no, no pity coming there. Some went so far to say my boy shoulda been glad he died in the 'lectric chair 'stead at the end of a rope. They said

at least he was treated like a white man. And it was best we just forgot all about it and him.

But I never forgot, I never forgot. It's been over forty years now, but every day of my life, every night of my life, I go through that rainy day again. And that's why I kilt Beau, Mr. Sheriff. . . . He was just like that trashy white gal. He was just like them who throwed my boy in that 'lectric chair and pulled that switch. (102)

Gable's narrative reveals that Beau, along with the rest of the Boutan family, has become a symbol of all the cruelty and injustice that Gable and the other blacks have endured throughout their lives. So Gable, like all the other old men, confesses to killing Beau Boutan as a means of regaining his lost manhood. His confession is an attempt to reach out to his dead son and in some way exact justice.

We can never know if Phillip Martin takes advantage of his second chance, but the old men of *A Gathering*, though clearly frightened, welcome theirs and decide to stand with Mathu against Sheriff Mapes and the Boutans. Mat sees this opportunity as a gift from God: "He works in mysterious ways. . . . Give a old nigger like me one more chance to do something with his life. He gave me that chance, and I'm taking it, I'm going to Marshall. Even if I have to die at Marshall" (38). In an interview, Gaines has echoed his characters by stating that the crisis at Marshall is "God giving them a second chance to stand up one day" (Doyle, "*MELUS* Interview" 76). Whether or not this opportunity reveals divine intervention, Erikson's theory about the final stage of life helps to show that the old men's willingness to sacrifice their lives is not merely senile foolishness but a natural response to their developmental crisis.

The successful resolution of this final crisis—ego integrity versus despair—is essential to the individual and to his children. Erikson defines ego integrity in part as the "acceptance of one's one and only life cycle and of the people who have become significant to it as something that had to be and that, by necessity, permitted of no substitutions" (*Identity* 139). When the individual approaches his death, he must be at peace with himself and satisfied with his life. The flip side of ego integrity is despair, the sense "that time is short, too short for the attempt to start another life and to try out alternative roads to integrity" (*Identity* 140). The old people gathered at Marshall, continually haunted by their past cowardice, have certainly been leaning more toward despair than toward integrity. An early speech by Mat to his wife epitomizes this feeling: "The years I done stood out in that back yard and cussed at God, . . . the times I done come home drunk and beat you for no reason at all—and, woman, you still don't know what's the matter with me?" (38). What is wrong with Mat is despair, but the gathering provides him and his friends with that little extra time they need to travel one of what Erikson calls the "alternative roads to integrity." To achieve that goal, the men must regain what has been taken from them—their manhood. Without it, they cannot be at peace with themselves, nor can they be good fathers. Before they can be fathers, they must first be men. Despair involves the fear of death, but with ego integrity, the individual faces death with dignity and courage. In doing so, he sets an example for his children to follow. Erikson says that "healthy children will not fear life if their elders have integrity enough not to fear death" (*Childhood* 269). Gaines's old men set such an example for young Toddy and Snookum.

The day's events have a significant effect upon these children, as we can see by looking at how Snookum changes. In narrating the first section of the novel, he comes across as a somewhat timid little boy with a limited awareness of the world around him. He gets angry with Toddy for laughing at him but does not do or say anything because he fears that Toddy will tattle on him for "playing mama and papa" with Minnie (3). When he runs off to call the people to Mathu's house, as Candy asks him to do, he goes by Mathu's himself and sees Beau's body on the ground. He notes that something strange is happening, but he has no idea how important this day will be. Nevertheless, Snookum sets the events in motion by rounding up the people of the quarters. Later in the day he witnesses the old men's newfound courage and emulates them. He even speaks up to Mapes and tells the sheriff to arrest him, too: "I don't know about Toddy, but I'm ready to go. . . . Wish I was just a little older so I coulda shot [Beau]" (109). When Mapes tries to trick him into admitting that he called everyone to Mathu's house, Snookum does not fall for the ploy: "I ain't got no more to say. . . . You can beat me with a hose pipe if you want" (109). He may not know precisely why he is standing up to the sheriff, but he is acting courageously nonetheless— because he has seen the old men acting courageously. This Snookum is not the little boy who was afraid of his brother's tiny revenge just a few hours earlier.

At the same time, though, we have one father-and-son relationship that seems to defy the idea that a father figure's courage transfers to the son. Mathu's manhood has never been doubted by anyone, black or white. And unlike Phillip Martin, Mathu has not shied away from his responsibilities. Yet Charlie apparently has learned nothing through his parrain's example. Charlie is unusually big and strong, and Lou Dimes, Candy's boyfriend, describes him as "the quintessence of . . . the super, big buck nigger" (186). Ironically, Charlie has never performed one manly act in his life. Unlike Mathu, Charlie runs from trouble and allows himself to be abused by blacks and whites alike. After Charlie has returned and revealed himself to be the true killer of Beau Boutan, he says that he knows Mathu was trying to make a man of him by beating him: "I'm fifty now, and I'm sure I musta run when I was no more than five, 'cause I know Parrain was beating me for running when I was six. 'Cause I can remember the first time he beat me for running. You remember the first time you beat me for running, Parrain? That time Ed-de took my 'tato on my way to school?" (188). Charlie may not have realized Mathu's intentions at the time, however. Beating is not communicating; in fact, beating would seem to destroy communication. In "The Sky Is Gray," James's mother beats him because he does not want to kill his redbirds, and James understands her motives only after his aunt explains them to him. In this story, Gaines implies that communication cannot be established through force. Therefore, communication between sons and fathers has to be based on something more than manhood and power. Compassion and mutual respect are also important.

In the past, Mathu has had little compassion and no respect for anyone. When he addresses the old men assembled in his house, he tells them: "I ain't nothing but a mean, bitter old man. . . . No hero. Lord— no hero. A mean, bitter old man. Hating them out there on that river, hating y'all here in the quarters. Put myself above all—proud to be African. You know why proud to be African? 'Cause they won't let me be a citizen here in this country. Hate them 'cause they won't let me be a citizen, hated y'all 'cause you never tried. Just a mean-hearted old man. All I ever been, till this hour" (182). Though Mathu retained his manhood by standing up for himself against Fix Boutan and other whites, he lost something else along the way. Bitterness and hate took away most of his capacity to feel and express affection for other people, including Charlie. Mathu's perpetual anger kept him from tempering authority with understanding, though he always acted in Charlie's best interests.

But this watershed day on the Marshall plantation offers Mathu a second chance, too. "I been changed," he tells the other old men. "I been changed by y'all. Rooster, Clabber, Dirty Red, Coot—you changed this hardhearted old man" (182). Thus the old men's stand produces yet another transformation. Mathu is so touched by his newfound allies' standing up for him that he rediscovers the part of his heart that had been taken over by hate.

This change in Mathu coincides with a change in Charlie, who returns just as Mathu is preparing to give himself up to Mapes. Charlie reveals that while working in the field earlier that day, he decided he had taken enough abuse from Beau Boutan: "I was doing my work good. Cussed me anyhow. . . . I told him no, I wasn't go'n 'low that no more, 'cause I was fifty years old—half a hundred" (190). After fifty years of being a boy, Charlie finally decided that the time had come for him to stand up and be a man. But his conversion remained tentative. After hitting Beau with a stalk of cane, he ran, and he wanted to run again when Beau came after him with a shotgun, but Mathu stopped him with threats of his own. After steadying himself and shooting Boutan, Charlie ran again, leaving his parrain to assume responsibility for the killing. However, Charlie finds that he cannot escape this time: "Something like a wall, a wall I couldn't see . . . stopped me every time" (192). Keith E. Byerman writes that Charlie's "nascent manhood . . . prevents him from escaping" ("Ernest Gaines" 95). As we have seen in *In My Father's House* and other works by Gaines, accepting responsibility for one's actions is an essential part of becoming a man. Charlie's emerging manhood thus leads him back to the quarters.

When Charlie asserts his manhood for the first time, he and Mathu move closer together emotionally. Charlie wishes to be called "Mister. Mr. Biggs," as a symbolic affirmation of his manhood (187). Sheriff Mapes willingly agrees: "At this point, anything you say . . . Mr. Biggs. That goes for the rest of y'all around here" (187). For all his faults, Mapes respects a man, and suddenly he realizes that he is surrounded by men. According to John F. Callahan, Mapes has freed himself from the "social and psychological conventions" of his white society in accepting Charlie and the others as men ("One Day" 39). As sheriff, Mapes serves as a strong representative of this white society, and his recognition of Charlie's manhood places the black man in a position of respectability for all of those in the room to witness. Throughout the scene

Mathu is obviously pleased with the new Charlie: "Mathu was looking at him as though he was not absolutely sure he was seeing him there. He nodded his head" (188). And Charlie acknowledges that he understands Mathu's treatment of him: "You tried to make me a man, didn't you, Parrain? Didn't you?" (189). The two men now understand and respect each other as they communicate across the crowded room. Thus we have the beginnings of a better kind of father-and-son relationship. But at eighty-two Mathu is nearing the end of his life, and Charlie will die before the novel ends. So for their relationship to have any lasting meaning, they must make an impression upon the children, specifically upon Snookum and Toddy. Snookum is present in the room, and he wants to hear every word Charlie says. When he goes to get ice water for Mapes, Snookum says, "Don't start till I get back, hear, Charlie?" (187). Charlie drinks some of Snookum's water before he tells his story. As he relates the story and day passes into night, Charlie becomes a father figure himself.

Though Charlie has already demonstrated his manhood to Mathu, Mapes, and the old men, he has to pass one more test before his legacy to the next generation is complete. Luke Will and his gang of rednecks, who represent an ugly past that is too ignorant to die out, are determined to avenge Beau's death. In discussing the novel's ending, Gaines has said, "I still believe in the old Chekovian idea that if the gun is over the mantle at the beginning of the play, the gun must go off by the time the curtain comes down. And I thought that the only way the gun could go off in my book was Charlie and Luke Will out on the street shooting at each other" (Gaudet and Wooton 97). Indeed, many guns go off as Luke Will and the rednecks shoot it out with Charlie and the old black men, who have been anticipating such an opportunity to unleash their anger against their white oppressors. While the old men become warriors, Charlie becomes a general. Even Luke Will soon realizes that Charlie controls the situation: "Mapes ain't in charge no more. . . . Charlie is. We got to deal with Charlie now" (206). Charlie has become an intimidating presence to the white men, just as they have always been to the blacks. Through this reversal in power, Charlie gains even more respect for himself. And even though he and Luke Will destroy each other in the gunfight, Charlie retains—perhaps enhances—his status. His death makes him a hero and a martyr. All the men touch Charlie's body, "hoping that some of that stuff he had found back there in the swamps might rub off" (210). Most importantly, the children come to Charlie: "Glo told her grandchildren they must touch him, too" (210). This inverse laying on of hands symbolizes how the children will carry on what Charlie has started.

Gaines presents a similar ritual in *The Autobiography of Miss Jane Pittman*. When Ned Douglass is murdered for teaching the black people to stand up for their rights, his body becomes something sacred as well: "They wanted to touch his body, they wanted to help take it inside. The road was full, people coming from everywhere. They wanted to touch his body. When they couldn't touch his body they took lumber from the wagon. They wanted a piece of lumber with his blood on it" (116). James R. Giles and Albert Wertheim both point out that Ned's death parallels Christ's crucifixion. The people even build a little shrine out of Ned's gravesite to commemorate the tragedy. According to Jane, "It is for the children of this parish and this State. Black and white, we don't care. We want them to know a black man died many years ago for them. He died at the end of the other century and the beginning of this century. He shed his precious blood for them" (113). Jane's assertion of the inspirational nature of this monument suggests the impact of Ned's death on future generations. In comparison, Charlie's death may not be loaded with the Biblical significance of Ned's murder, but the people's reactions to both imply that they will have a similar impact on the future. The memory of Charlie Biggs will serve as a source of strength for Snookum and Toddy. Perhaps this strength will help them to become good fathers someday. The hope in this possibility recalls the hope expressed by Beverly at the end of *In My Father's House* when she tells Phillip Martin to go back home and work to be a better father to Patrick so that no more sons will be "going to that trestle" (213).

While Gaines's black fathers and sons seem to be making progress, their white counterparts are growing apart. The white fathers cling to the past and the established codes of behavior and remain inflexible when their sons wish to move forward. We first see this conflict between Robert and Tee Bob Samson in *Miss Jane Pittman*. Tee Bob's love for a Creole girl violates the age-old code that prohibits such feelings between the races, a code upheld by Robert Samson. Unable to escape the confinement of tradition, Tee Bob commits suicide, and Robert Samson loses his son forever. In *A Gathering*, a similar conflict develops between Fix Boutan and his son Gil. Gil, however, is stronger than Tee Bob and manages to stand up to the past and to his father.

Gil Boutan represents the future of the white man of Louisiana. As a star running back for the LSU Tigers, he shares the backfield with Cal Harrison, a black, and the two are good friends. Gil and Cal represent a hopeful vision in which the races work together to achieve shared goals. "On the gridiron they depended on each other the way one hand must depend on the other swinging a baseball bat," says Sully, their friend and teammate (115). Gil has found that cooperation leads to success, but he is also aware that his partnership with Cal has meaning beyond the playing field, as is evident in his desire to see both of them named All-Americans. He wants to set an example of racial cooperation for the South and the entire country to see. But unless Gil can reason with his father and keep the old Cajun away from Marshall, his dream may be finished.

Reason, however, will not prevail, because Gil and Fix have so diverged that they can no longer communicate with each other. Gil struggles in vain to explain his feelings to his father: "Papa, I'm not putting things right. . . . But do you understand what I'm trying to say? Do you understand, Papa?" (138). Fix does not understand. While Mathu responds to Charlie's new assertiveness with pride, Fix's reaction to Gil is hostile. Fix sees Gil as betraying the family: "Your brother's honor for the sake to play football side by side with the niggers—is that so?" (142). Fix's ideas are mired in the past, and he communicates better with Beau's friend Luke Will than with his own son. Nevertheless, Gil continues to try to reach his father. He tries to tell him that the world no longer tolerates vigilantes: "Those days when you just take the law in your own hands—those days are gone. These are the '70s, soon to be the '80s. Not the '20s, the '30s, or the '40s. People died—people we knew—died to change those things. Those days are gone forever, I hope" (143). Fix hears but does not listen. His failure to communicate with his son suggests a failure in his attempts to achieve the developmental stage of generativity. Instead of guiding Gil toward his destiny as an athletic hero, Fix blindly, selfishly pushes for Gil's involvement in violent actions that would destroy the boy's future. Fix can speak only of "family responsibility" (143), and indeed he does care deeply about family, as we see in the loving way he holds Beau's young son. However, his love for family has been distorted by racial hatred, and his idea of "family responsibility" is really irresponsibility. By going after Charlie with a shotgun, Beau brought on his own death, and as we have seen already, in Gaines's fiction a character must accept the consequences of his actions. So the responsible thing for the family to do is to mourn Beau's death and, rather than seeking to punish scapegoats, learn something that will help them avoid such grief in the future. Fix, however, has learned nothing. He disowns Gil, tells him he never wants to see him again, and orders him to leave the house at once. Thus the breakdown of communication leads to this ultimate separation of father and son.

The disintegration of Gil's relationship with his father greatly upsets the young man, but with the guidance of Deputy Russell, Gil realizes the need to look to the future of the Boutan family. Gil Boutan's developmental crisis is that of "identity vs. role confusion," the resolution of which results in an individual's establishing his place in the adult world (Erikson, *Childhood* 261–63). Gil's future identity depends upon his continuing to work with Cal to achieve success on the gridiron. Russell, apparently speaking for Gaines, advises Gil that the best way to help his family is to play in the big game the next day: "You want to do something for your dead brother? Do something for his son's future—play in that game tomorrow. Whether you win against Ole Miss or not, you'll beat Luke Will. Because if you don't, he'll win tomorrow, and if he does, he may just keep on winning. That's not much of a future for Tee Beau, is it?" (151). Because of Gil's athletic achievements, he has become a hero to the people on the bayou. Parents want their children to grow up to be like Gil Boutan, and the children adore him. If he lets his problems with Fix keep him out of the game, he will lose much—if not all—of the admiration and respect he has gained, and the children will lose a role model. However, by playing in the game and working with Cal, Gil will prove his strength in the face of adversity and establish himself as a father figure to his dead brother's son. He is certain to have a more positive influence on the boy than Beau would have had.

In comparing what Gaines has to say about black and white fathers and sons, we see two opposing ideas. The blacks, separated because of slavery, are striving to come together. Gaines measures their progress by the steps they have taken to reunite. The white son, on the other hand, initiates progress by separating himself from his father. With this severance, he rejects the stagnant racial codes of the past and forges a new tradition of racial cooperation and harmony. This white son can then become a new kind of father, and a separation between white father and son may no longer be necessary.

Although Gaines's fathers and sons have a long way to go, they have begun to make substantial progress toward reconciliation. At the end of *In My Father's House,* Phillip Martin has an opportunity to reach out to his son, Patrick, but we do not know if Martin will take advantage of this second chance at fatherhood. In *A Gathering,* the black fathers act when given an opportunity, and in the case of Mathu and Charlie, a son and father come together. Though Mathu is not Charlie's biological father, he did raise Charlie, and their union, coupled with the old black men's new manhood, suggests that black fathers and sons are moving slowly toward reunification. The whites also are able to reunite in *A Gathering.* In the courtroom scene that concludes the novel, Gil sits with his family; Fix has accepted him back as his son again. Thus Gaines presents us with a resolution more optimistic than in previous novels. He even allows us to find hope in the outcome of the football game: "LSU beat Ole Miss, twenty-one to thirteen. Both Gil and Cal had over a hundred yards each" (212). For the sake of the future, Gil took Russell's advice and played in that game. His and Cal's success is one more omen of a brighter future for blacks and whites. The emergence of Gil and Cal as powerful role models represents Gaines's vision that blacks and whites can share respectability in the world, creating a society that draws together fathers and sons of both races.

Notes

1. Bryant deals extensively with this conflict in "From Death" and "Gaines." Bryant sees the old aunts as being largely successful in preventing change, more successful than I believe the evidence indicates.

2. In interviews, Gaines frequently mentions his aunt's courage and its impact on his life. *Miss Jane Pittman* is, in part, dedicated to her: "To the memory of my beloved aunt, Miss Augusteen Jefferson, who did not walk a day in her life but who taught me the importance of standing."

3. Erikson presents his ideas on development and the life cycle in two books: *Childhood and Society* outlines the stages in "Eight Ages of Man" (247–74); *Identity: Youth and Crisis* includes most of the same ideas in "The Life Cycle: Epigenesis of Identity" (91–141), generally with clearer explanations. The latter also includes "Race and the Wider Identity" (295–320), which deals with the problems of blacks in establishing "identity," a predominant concern in Gaines's works.

Image, Act, and Identity in *In My Father's House*

Karla F.C. Holloway

When Ernest J. Gaines's *In My Father's House* appeared in 1978, Kenyan writer Ngugi wa Thiong'o had already abandoned English as the language of his creative work. A year later, Ngugi's detention in a maximum security prison was understood to be a direct consequence of his efforts to bring an indigenous language to African theater and to confront the biases inherent in the language of colonialism. His objective seemed to be an uncomplicated one—to place the voices of Africa back into its literatures. But Ngugi's was a radical act that eventually led to his imprisonment.

In this chapter, I focus on what I see as a symbolic parallel between Ngugi's decision to abandon the language of colonialism and to write in his own language of Gikuyu and the thematic activity in *In My Father's House*. I believe that the opposition between orature (voice) and literature (text) in this novel contributes to the negotiation of its thematic issues. Ngugi's act of linguistic decolonization mirrors the tension Gaines's novel explores.

Gaines's novel focuses on the behavior of a minister and the trauma that his unacknowledged son has experienced. It concerns itself with the nature of sin and redemption and the frustrations that arise when motive and desire collide. But it is as important to see Gaines's work as representative of a subtle, deceptive, and sometimes even subversive tendency in literature by African-American writers to underscore a vision of black America as a decentered community. However, because this novel foregrounds its themes of individual quest and identity, the reader may be diverted from this equally critical, although somewhat obscured, issue of the novel—that activity Ngugi calls "decolonizing the mind."

Phillip Martin, the minister and father in this story, carries these roles by title but offers them little substance. He has physically abandoned his first family and is emotionally absent from his second. Scattered children, by "three or four other women" than his wife, evidence his trifling familial responsibility (150). The reader is encouraged to juxtapose the figure of his tragically lonely son Etienne (his self-chosen name "Robert X" signifies the loneliness and isolation he has experienced) against the figure of the community whose welfare Martin has also sacrificed for his own gain. The community shares a figurative space with Etienne because their victimization is intimately related to his presence. Etienne's presence subjectively represents the loss that Martin's fractured family has endured, and Martin's flawed ministry is expressively represented by the objectified and vulnerable African-American community.

Martin's selfish focus on his own stature and security eventually excludes him from the community that had been responsible for his identity. For example, the men whose shared laughter and talk behind his godmother's house underscore their camaraderie, and who once would have shared this bond with Martin as well, are no longer "comfortable around Phillip Martin": "He would have liked to go out there and take his turn with the axe. It had been like that once—years ago. He and other young men had gone from house to house to help out each other. It was always easier and more fun than working alone" (110). However, at this point in his life, when Martin has had some success at manipulating a careful projection of a selected identity (spiritual leader, father, and community activist), those commodities that display his distance from his past—among them his expensive clothes and ostentatious jewelry—betray his comfortably self-satisfying lifestyle. Ironically, they also separate him from the very community he needs in order to maintain his identity. His abandonment of the urban community's objectives (the boycott of Chenal's store) is not far removed from his self-imposed material distinctions from the rural community's identity. Because of the figurative relationship between Etienne and the community, the loss Martin experiences after failing to conceal his identity as Robert X's (Etienne's) father is one that indicts his privileged status in the community as well.

The novel's events capitalize on the symbolic imagery that extends from a blurring between subjectivity (the returned son) and objectivity (the dependent community). Robert X's intimate but severed connection to his father's house ironically identifies him as a subjective Other. The community's forced exteriority—because of Martin's separation from them—objectifies their presence in his life. The novel's structure encourages a certain murkiness to emerge from this collapsed opposition. The result is that the meanings held within the power of the opposed pairs are essentially deconstructed. As a consequence, the novel assumes its structure not from the hegemonic tension that a sustained oppositional structure would maintain but instead from the space between this pair—a depth region where indeterminant meanings reside. What seem to be images of propriety, what appear to be honest and real, and even the presentation of a sufficiently empowered gathering of men are all revealed to be little more than masques—a pitiful parody of potential.

In My Father's House thematically represents how a fragmented community's loss of creativity is due in great measure to its individual members' pursuit of personal identity and individuation. There is a symbolic parallel and a disconcerting echo between this creative loss and the loss predicted for the African creative writer by David Diop. It is important to Ngugi's thesis in *Decolonizing the Mind* that he remind his reader of Diop's prediction: "The African creator, deprived of the use of his language and cut off from his people, might turn out to be only the representative of a literary trend of the conquering nation . . . [but] in an Africa freed from oppression, it will not occur to any writer to express, otherwise than in his rediscovered language, his feelings and the feelings of his people" (25). Even though Gaines foregrounds what is essentially a neocolonial theme of personal identity and individuation, the interior thesis of a community's substantive creative loss worries the interior text. Its fracture, as Diop anticipates, is the consequence of an individuation that feeds off of the energies of the community's spiritual and physical unity. Phillip Martin may, as a minister, "represent" the gathered Christians, but their vulnerability and his own are intertwined in this novel. Critical attention to this dilemma opens a new dimension of *In My Father's House*.

It is useful to consider Martin and his nameless, unacknowledged son Robert X as illustrations of the polarity that exists between orature and literature. This schismatic opposition is textually reinforced by the ministerial identity of Martin, whose text-based Christianity is his seemingly reliable and faithful guide. The sacred and literate are juxtaposed against the secular and orate, represented by Robert X. One might expect that Phillip Martin, as an African-American preacher, could successfully negotiate the territories of the Western tradition that the Christian text represents and the evocative and logocentric traditions of West African spirituality that are remembered in African-American worship. However, Martin has abandoned his African community by behavior that consistently underscores what is a characteristically Western allegiance to his individual self. Therefore, his potential as a mediative presence between and within his community falls victim to the linguistic colonization that the Biblical text symbolically represents.

Here Gaines's novel speaks to the issues that Ngugi raises in *Decolonizing the Mind* and further indicts with his abandonment of the colonialist's language. Martin's self-indulgence (rather than his community loyalty) parallels his participation in a ministry that insists upon the hegemonic primacy of its literate traditions (text-based, Bible-centered Christianity). One way of underscoring this parallel is to consider the way in which Martin's abandonment of his African community is symbolically attached to the difficulty he experiences in prayer. As the unscripted, spontaneously spoken spiritual word, prayer represents the Otherness of African-American worship, the lifeline that connects to the community's cultural traditions. Having lost this nurturing link, Martin is spiritually and physically abandoned: "Phillip stood at the window looking out on the street, looking and waiting. . . . No one went by. The street, gray, empty, cold. The tree in the pasture across the street, gray leafless, cold. . . . He wanted to pray, he needed to pray, but how could he pray? If he prayed out loud, Elijah would surely hear him; and he could not get satisfaction praying in silence" (54). In the words of the African-American spiritual, Martin is literally "standing in the need of prayer." His loss figuratively represents the one Ngugi attempted to recover in turning away from the colonialist text and returning in his creative work to the language of Gikuyu. Martin is both deprived of "the use of his [spiritual] language" and separated "from his people" (Diop, quoted in Ngugi, 25). Because his participation in a ministry privileging literacy over oracy subliminally encourages his self-indulgent act of betrayal, Gaines's novel underscores the creative (generative) loss that the colonizer's text represents. It underscores as well the way in which the community's loss is irrevocably linked to Martin's betrayal and deprivation.

Even though the most prominent action of the novel narrows the reader's focus onto the way in which his troubles extend from his deceit, there is also evidence that his actions in this story are but one dimension of this troubled man. Phillip Martin's difficulties extend as well from his shaky linguistic center. The Biblical text that he grasps so firmly is finally unreliable because, beyond the issue of his selfish betrayal of his community and his family, this text is emblematic of the stifling controls exerted by colonialism. Consider, as an example of this subtextual indictment of colonialism, the sketchy character of Billy, the Vietnam veteran who is planning a radical and violent response to the racism against which Martin has organized marches. Billy instructs him, angrily explaining that "this country here is the last crutch for Western Civilization—what *they* call civilization. . . . Burn it down, you destroy Western Civilization. You put the world back right—let it start all over again" (162).

The failure of the Bible to rescue Martin from his spiritual oblivion illustrates the negative dialectic that emerges once the orate word is liberated from the literate text. Western cultures privilege literacy over oracy, and the religion that Martin's sacred text supports is itself supported by the weight of that written word. Christianity is grounded in a textual reformulation of a spoken word that had primacy ("In the beginning was the Word") until the text of Christianity insisted upon its scriptic center. In a similar way, the fundamental polarity between orature and literature is critical to the creative failures within this novel. Rather than liberating himself with language by *telling* the truth, Martin holds onto a Christianity that has abused his spirit and that has no resources to assuage his guilt. He pleads with God to explain (tell) him his predicament—"he asked the same question over and over: 'Why? Why? Why? Is this punishment for my past? . . . But I asked for forgiveness'" (69). However, because he fails to recognize the cultural and communal character of his emptiness, nothing in the literate (Biblical) word satisfies or explicates his sense of overwhelming loss. He is unable even to take solace akin to the Old Testament Job's in being a good and faithful and unquestioning servant. His "why?" and "why me?" echo soundlessly and pitifully throughout the novel.

Martin is held captive by script in the way that his son is identified by a tortuous relationship to voice. Robert X's character is affectively connected to speech. His demeanor threatens language; those around him are often afraid to talk, or their speech is constricted. We come to understand that voicing the "unspeakable" events of his past would be liberating. However, his initial activity in the story disrupts that potential, and his behavior consistently destabilizes the community's voices. When Virginia opens the door for Robert X at the novel's beginning, she starts to speak, but his discomfiting demeanor makes her "cut off" her voice (3). He, in turn, refuses to answer her eventual questions. He is a silent, brooding, and threatening presence that frightens away language and words even though the reader understands that within them lies his liberation. Recall Diop's assertion that loss of language is linked to a loss of creativity, which in this novel can be understood as a generative creativity that family and community expressively represent. Both losses are metaphorically embodied in Robert X's silence. "Virginia felt she would have been talking only to the walls if she had stood there any longer" (10). His presence promises to destroy the tenuous balance in his father's house—an event that ironically leads to the inevitable deconstruction of speech and text.

Ironically, the generative creativity that is Robert X's raison d'être is inversely consumed by the anger and rage that motivate his desire for revenge. He is, after all, an ambivalent sign of generative promise because he is the unacknowledged fruit of Martin's seed. Martin's destruction of his family (rather than his creation of it) motivates his son's revenge. However, Robert X's ambivalent relationship to language threatens and frustrates his own goal. He has an oracular (oraclelike) potential. If his father had come to him, acknowledged him, or—most importantly— *spoken* his name, the liberating, creative power of the word could have triumphed and would have prevented Martin from sacrificing his community. However, instead of learning Robert X's given name or his story from either the father or the son, the reader is left to learn the truth from Chippo, a friend from Martin's younger days, who reluctantly tells the story of Etienne's mother Johanna and frees all that tragic history by voicing the unhappy but necessary narrative.

Chippo's storytelling session is a climactic event as much because the reader is able to appreciate and respect the power vested in the spoken word as because it resolves the mystery of what happened to Johanna and her children. His narrative certainly indicates the power that comes from the revelation of the truth, but such empowerment does not obviate for the other two men the cultural enrichment that comes from embracing speech. Diop's promise of a "rediscovered language" that would lead to a recovery of "his feelings and the feelings of his people" is literally achieved when, after telling Martin about Johanna, Chippo feels finally able to return to the plantation and "see the old people." In this way the text clearly indicates the powerful potential of voice because Chippo reaps spiritual benefit from the oracular (told) text. His ability to return to the fold of the old community connects his use of the folk's language (storytelling) to an empowering, creative behavior. Because the subverted text is liberated in storytelling, Chippo retrieves the spiritually enabling legacy of the community of "old people" who assure him access to their generative creativity: "Well, I'm glad now I told you. I can go to Reno now and see the old people, and I don't have to feel guilty 'bout holding nothing from them. I feel good about it. Yes. Like somebody done gone to confession" (199).

Unlike Chippo, Martin remains separated from this healing voice. When, in earlier scenes, his *nanane* Angelina and the prostitute Adeline offer to listen to his story, he cannot tell it. Despite the almost contradictory figures recalled in these women's symbolic identity, there are parallels between them beyond the allusions in their names to the maternal Mary and Mary Magdalene. Martin's relationship with them had been severed since he became a religious leader in his community. Angelina accuses him of having forgotten she's alive since he visits her so rarely. And although his feelings for her obviously run deep—"he looked at the small, very old woman sitting back in the chair. . . . He loved her very much"—he cannot speak to her. "He wished he could tell her everything. But just as he had been unable to say it to anyone else, he couldn't say it to her either" (109). His vocal paralysis recalls his inability to pray. Martin has separated himself from the balm of language—the evocation of which could fold him back into the fabric of the community. Unlike the promise of Diop's assertion that the "feelings of his people" would assure him a celebratory creativity, note instead that Adeline's touch "made him feel" uncomfortable. The physical response she awakens in him is too close to the emotional commitments he has eschewed, and it is symbolically linked to what would be the "touch" of language. The "good warm feeling" she arouses does not release the anguish of his spirit. When she asks him, as Angelina had done, "You want to talk?" Martin shakes his head in a notably voiceless answer. His access to orature, like his use of it, has been sacrificed to his posture and his image. Although he has been "questioning himself," as he tells Adeline, his questions illustrate a selfish interiority that leads to Adeline's discomfiture—"She didn't like the way he was talking" (178).

Gaines underscores the parallel between Angelina and Adeline not only by their similar names. Neither will reclaim her earlier intimacy with this posturing, self-centered Martin. He has disrespected both of them in his narrow circumscription of their appearances in his life. Although his drunken ramblings at the story's end do make him think again of Adeline, it is a crude rather than a loving or generous reflection. She is remembered as "an old gal. . . . Pretty yellow woman. Good snatch" (204–5). Disrespect is a familiar behavior for Martin. It mirrors the way he has treated Johanna and Alma (as well as those other mothers of his illegitimate children) and testifies to his loss. Even though we sense that his losses are irretrievable, we are encouraged to believe that Martin does at least recognize the tragic dimensions of his behavior. His response to Chippo's comment that telling Johanna's story has made him feel as if he had been to a confessional is a mournful, if not a longing, question—"That's how you feel?" (199). Phillip is asking if this "telling" is the way that one learns to feel.

When the consuming opposition between voice and text is subverted so that evocation wins its cultural place, the thesis within the subtext emerges and embraces the empowering and creative activity of speech illustrated in Chippo's storytelling. This thematic subtext lies dormant but available within the figurative spaces of the story resulting from the deconstructive activity that has severed Etienne's voice, decentered the community's place, and rendered Martin's holy text impotent. The presence of this Other thesis also belies the seeming privilege of the neocolonial theme of individuation. A Eurocentric interpretive frame obscures the loss endured by the African-American community and forces attention away from them and toward the individual tragedies of Martin and his son. Nonetheless, Chippo's telling the essential story of this text is an indication that the focus on Martin and Etienne reveals only a fragment of this novel's identity.

Even more threatening than this thematic loss of the community's story is that the Eurocentric quest for individuation requires the sacrifice of the community's wholeness and power. That interpretive frame does not obscure either the destructive dimensions of the community's dependency on Martin or the vulnerability to selfishness and greed when individuals separate themselves from their source of power within the community.

Although the textual focus of *In My Father's House* is on the emotional sacrifice of one family, the physical sacrifice of another, and the loss of Martin's effective membership in either of these families and his community, the metathesis of loss embraces the sacrifice of the community as well. At the novel's end, Martin plaintively moans to his wife, "I'm lost, Alma. I'm lost." Alma radically inverts the silence he has forced upon her most of their married life by now commanding his silence: " 'Shh,' she said, 'Shh. Shh' " (214). She placates him with a reassurance that they can "start again." Her promise echoes in their figurative empty bedchamber. A man who has lost creativity, who has learned how to place himself above his family and beyond his community, has minimal resources for regeneration.

In contrast to the Western vision's focus on the story's themes of personal deprivation and loss, this novel's non-Western vision focuses on the community's discovery of the empowering and sustaining qualities of language. The frame for the resolution of this novel is not Martin's tentative efforts to begin his process of selfish individuation again. Instead, the appeal to this community of men to be creative and honest and responsible to their generations asserts itself as a necessary interpretive focus. Ironically, it is Martin who poses this question: "When will we stand up and tell our people the truth? When will we . . . protect our sons?" (201–2). Even though the narrative assigns this question to Martin, we understand that his selfish desire for individuation belies his ability to use his voice in the ancient, communal, regenerative ways. In this moment, the text assumes a "speakerly" quality as it moves toward the kind of narrative license that we see operating in Zora Neale Hurston's works.[1]

Martin's query is posed as much for the community of readers as it is for the community within the text. The gathered men remind him that he has abrogated his responsibility; they rebuke him for making the "decision [to call off the demonstration] all by yourself" (130) and betraying their collective voice with his independent one. However, because they are so easily prepared to trust Jonathan, who is the presumed next leader of this group, in the same way, we sense the injury done to this group is irreparable. Martin's behavior, as well as their reliance on that passive

Western and Christian ethic, has led to their impotence. As an example of Gaines's interest in this thesis of the vulnerability of Christianity, consider how Martin's behavior echoes that of Reverend Jameson's in *A Gathering of Old Men* and how both he and Jameson parallel the quiescent preacher in the dentist's office in "The Sky Is Gray."[2] In *A Gathering*, Jameson cannot bring himself to follow the lead of the men to protect Mathu. Jameson's selfish protectionism, like Martin's, isolates him from the community he seems to represent. Gaines's parallel between these two ministers is underscored not only in their cowardly self-indulgence but also in the scenes in which Martin collapses when faced with his illegitimate son and when Jameson falls under the abuse that the community of old men stoically endures. Recognizing that such individualism endangers everyone, the community's act of divestiture in *In My Father's House* is as critical an event in the story as the aforementioned resolution (the promise of beginning again) seems to be. Their collective behavior functions as an alternative denouement to this work—one that privileges the spiritual thesis of voice even though the physical text distracts attention away from its script.

The alternative focus represents the potential of this novel to claim an identity that moves beyond the restrictive and negative dialectic of Martin's and Etienne's entangled pasts. As the text claims a linguistic presence that respects the empowered, collective voice, it shifts towards the features of a speakerly text. In novels within the speakerly tradition, inner vision dominates, and linguistic interaction rather than individuation determines the textual frame. A speakerly text insists on the active participation of its own voice in the construction of the story. In one sense this is a voice that acknowledges the "call" of the text and the "response" of its collective readers. In another sense, one closer to the meaning I believe is represented here, this voice represents the interior audience of the collected text—its characters, events, symbolic systems, and story structures—and their acknowledgment of the community that they collectively embody. Consequently, in a text of the speakerly tradition, even though there are individual characters' voices and a distinct narrative voice, the presence of the story itself assumes a persona, an identity that must be considered when one is assessing either the events or the characterizations within the story.

Hurston's work, particularly *Their Eyes Were Watching God*, clearly privileges the interior collective voice of the text and foregrounds the creative role that it plays in the construction (and sometimes revision) of story. There is an interesting contrast between the foregrounded voice of her work and the submerged voice in Gaines's novel. For example, the storytelling tradition is so critical to Janie's cultural and gendered identity (she spends a good deal of time on the porch, listening to the community's stories and longing for her own participation) that the narrative itself assumes the storytelling mantle in order to render her experience with greater fidelity to the culture it represents.[3] Reading Gaines's work within the context of its interior voices allows characters to draw from the strength of the spoken text. Chippo, like Janie, bene-fits from this creative engagement of spirit. One difference between the two works is that Hurston consistently privileges the oracular dimension whereas, perhaps because of the foregrounded intensity of the colonial thesis of individuation, Gaines's novel struggles against this identity.

As an example of the potential subversion in the speakerly text, con-sider how the community in *In My Father's House* suffers from the loss of its speakerly ground. There are metaphorical parallels between this loss and the absence of women and women's voices from any of the novel's substantive imagery or activities. Gaines's women characters suf-fer an ephemeral quality that underscores their peripheral status. Critics have not generally interrogated this narrative positionality of women.[4] It is important, however, to understand the ways in which women's speech is frustrated throughout the story—as evidenced in the early silencing of Virginia, the silent and long-suffering posture of Martin's wife Alma, the inability of Johanna to tell her own story, and the absence of women's advice and counsel from the determinations relevant to the boycott. The position of women here is similar to the one that Janie must subvert in Hurston's novel. Janie divests the male hierarchy (represented by Jody Starks) by insinuating her voice into the guarded male domains. Her withering retort to her husband's arrogance so enfeebles him that he does not rise again from what becomes his deathbed.

Like the middle sections of *Their Eyes*, Gaines's novel persistently discourages women's physical presence. The first gathering at Reverend Martin's house collects the women into an obscure and silent audience for the business that the men have gathered to conduct. Chippo later tells Martin that he heard Johanna's story only after the shop owner's wife left the room. In a critical but telling physical absence, Johanna, the central figure in the context of Phillip's and Etienne's struggle, enters the story only through the mediation of Chippo's telling. Alma's experience with Martin is similar to the prostitute Adeline's. His wife accuses him of coming to her "for this bed, for nothing else. . . . For this bed. Cook your food. Follow you to that church. That's all you married me for. You never come to me for any kind of problem" (134–35). The isolated prepositional phrases and the deleted subjects make these sentences syntactically truncated accusations that parallel her physical and emotional absence from his life.

The narrative result of this imbalance of gender is similar to the imbalance between voice and text. Gaines's implication is that women's presence, their voices, and men's acknowledgment of or engagement with them would disrupt the tenuous imbalance of power within his frustrated male community. Women's wisdom could invert the old order of things, as illustrated in the final chapter when Beverly speaks to Reverend Martin about the importance of his young son Patrick. Her firm hold on and accessibility to truth about the positive results of protesting discrimination stymies his voice: "He didn't know how to answer her. He didn't like the way she was turning things around" (213). Even though she sees the benefits Martin's leadership has accorded the community, she also understands the weakness it will be forced to endure because of its dependency on leadership. Because she understands that the community cannot suffer the loss of any of its members—its children, its women, or its men—she attempts to restore this tired and fallen man some measure of respect—"You won't let *us* down, will you?" (emphasis added; 213).

The novel's sacrifice of the textual presence of its women and children mirrors the way in which its main character, Martin, has relinquished affection and concern for his wife and Johanna and his children. Instead of an intact community, a colonized one has tenuously survived, convoluted by the oppressive text of individuation. Within this perspective, Martin's whine at the end of the book—"I'm lost, Alma. I'm lost"—is as pathetic as it is pitiable. He has been surrounded by the potential for a community that would center him and that could identify and name his space, and his impotent lack of focus and sight engenders little sorrow and no respect. The folkloric dimensions of Gaines's novel and those speakerly elements that would connect it to novels like those by Hurston work inversely to call attention to how masking imagery, independent activity, and selfish identities betray the folk and their language. Even

though image, act, and identity are the sources of the community's generation, these foci also frame the novel's fractured scenes of creative loss.
Instead of the inner vision that Hurston's folkloric storytelling achieves,
the thematic repression of voice colonizes speech within a community
of men who barely realize the depth of their loss. Only Chippo is offered
an opportunity to escape this tyranny, but he must return to the "old
folks" in order to salvage his soul.

Because of the disparity between the dispossessed spoken text and the
fractured events within this story, the novel seems willing to acquiesce
to a Western ethic. However, what rescues it from the hegemony of the
West is that the story Gaines tells cannot escape the effects of its own
dichotomous presence. It descends, in spite of itself, into the altered
spaces of the deconstructed binary pairing of voice and script. The creativity rescued from this depth region, where plural and indeterminant
meanings lie, insists upon the flexibility of those meanings as a facet
of this novel. Thus the themes in *In My Father's House* reflect Henry
Louis Gates's argument that indeterminacy and poetic flux characterize
the African-American tradition.

In *Being and Race,* Charles Johnson describes "black protagonists
in the fictional world of recent Afro-American writing" as "people
deformed by their lack of power . . . [who] fail to sustain healthy relationships" and whose stories produce "little evidence of success" (93).
Phillip Martin's failures clearly fit this mode. Indeed, the "recent" land-
scapes that interest Johnson in *Being and Race* do not sound much
different from the earlier sites—spiritual and physical—of African-
American literatures. Johnson recalls Clayton Riley's 1978 assessment
of black writing as an exploration of "the fractured world of American racism and psychic disorder." The novels of Richard Wright and
Ralph Ellison, like the earlier literature of James Weldon Johnson
and Charles Chesnutt, explored, in different styles, these similarly disconcerting themes. The consistent focus of the novels in twentieth-
century African-American literature leads Johnson to label the "tradition of Afro-American letters as a literature of tragedy unchanged" (93).
Gaines's stories clearly follow the well-worn paths of this literature as he
explores these fractured psychic realms and the consequences of racism
and psychological disjuncture.

In *My Father's House* examines the nature of regeneration and the
dimensions that would frame the interior, psychic spaces where regen-

eration can occur. But it is also a novel that indicates what can result when individuals are forced to choose between self and community and when individuals lose access to what Diop calls "felt" language. There are consequences for replacing such language with empty narrative in which image-making means turning away from the mirror, act and activity are life-threatening, and identity is spiritually diminishing. The result is a kind of fiction that privileges behavior over voice and body over spirit. The external quest (that is, the character-in-search-of-self) thesis that seems to frame the interpretive events of this story functions as a diversionary strategy that leads away from the dissipated community who, in any other context, would center our critical attention.

Ngugi's *Decolonizing the Mind* is a political reflection directly relevant to the identity of African-American literary texts. Calling attention to the cultural communities within these works focuses an interpretive schema that is often otherwise dominated by the individualistic thrust of the West. An Afrocentric frame refocuses critical inquiry onto the community, thus unveiling an important subtext of *In My Father's House*. When we consider that the dangerous fragmentation and vulnerability the community faces come, at least in part, as a result of the linguistic colonialism that has trapped Phillip Martin and rendered him generationless, then the circumscribed story of a father and son achieves an essential interaction with its identifying community. The community's presence is an essential frame, and it has a necessary place in the struggle between Etienne and his father because their own survival is dependent on the behavior and loyalty of its membership. In this way, the male community, already a significant theme in Gaines's work, assumes a critical interpretive importance. In *In My Father's House*, the potential to "rediscover language" that expresses the feelings of the writer *and* the feelings of his people finds its own ground within the desperation of an African-American community that has suffered the loss of both of these feelings.

Notes

1. Concerning this tradition, see the chapter "Zora Neale Hurston and the Speakerly Text" by Gates in *The Signifying Monkey* and also his *Figures in Black*, especially 249.

2. For discussions of the depiction of ministers in "The Sky Is Gray" and other short stories, see Gaudet, "Failure."

3. See my discussion of this narrative inversion in *The Character of the Word*, especially chapter four.

4. Babb does engage in some discussion that calls women's positionality in this story into question. (See, for example, 108–10.) However, like Gaines, she uses women characters to give the reader further insight into Martin's psyche. For example, Babb writes that what she considers as Adeline's "innocuous duplicity" serves to magnify "the more tragic consequences of his own" (108) and that his wife's promise to him is a directive of what he "must do" to reinflate his "diminished presence" (110), not an ironic pronouncement of what he has been incapable of accomplishing. This tendency toward reviewing the presence of women in terms of their serviceability and posture in reference to the male characters is one worthy of more critical attention as it seems to appear not only in Gaines's craft but in the critic's response as well.

Strong Men Getting Stronger: Gaines's Defense of the Elderly Black Male in *A Gathering of Old Men*

Sandra G. Shannon

During the months immediately following the publication of Ernest J. Gaines's highly acclaimed *The Autobiography of Miss Jane Pittman*, he found himself having to convince the media that his protagonist—a 110-year-old ex-slave—did not exist. He also confessed to an audience at Southern University that he had "not interviewed my grandmother or my aunt who raised me when I lived in the South" ("Miss Jane and I" 23). While the accusations that prompted such declarations may have tried Gaines's patience to some degree, more importantly, his responses reflect his determination to avoid reliance upon stereotype. In its place he substitutes three-dimensional elderly blacks endowed with compassion, conscience, and intelligence.

Old black men and women are interspersed throughout Gaines's fiction in varying roles, ranging from the strong and silent to the weak and quick-tongued. Just as some may be sycophants for "old massah," others are militants prepared to die. They are not all admirable, nor are they limited to degrading stereotypes. The wide range of his characters shows Gaines's tendency to incorporate into his work black personality types previously avoided by other authors. Because of his tendency to convert into central figures characters that might otherwise seem minor, Gaines has developed a reputation for giving voice and significance to the least likely individuals—those who are too quickly viewed as irrelevant, apa- **195** thetic, or simply undeserving of recognition. In the Louisiana locales serving as settings for his fiction, old black people become Gaines's new breed of heroes.

The inclusion of elderly blacks in Gaines's fiction coincides with a much improved public image of older people in America. Moreover, his sensitive treatment of the elderly seems to mirror the positive results of recent research among leading gerontologists. Both the novelist and the social scientist realize that the second-class status of America's elderly is perpetuated by myths and misconceptions that have for too long remained unchallenged. For example, Robert N. Butler's *Why Survive? Being Old in America* analyzes disturbingly naive stereotypes that embody characteristics many believe to be actual symptoms of old age. Butler contends that the average person views aging as "little more than decline, with no redeeming personal or social value. Old age has become an absurdity, a time of life with virtually nothing to recommend it" (403). O. Z. White identifies an often mistaken perception among the younger population that the elderly are powerless. This, he notes, is the chief reason for discrimination against them. He explains that the elderly "are considered to be recipients rather than participants. The statuses they presently hold and the ill-defined roles they play are not significant to the production or decision-making process" (4). In large part because of pressure in recent years to reassess the elderly's role in society, these and similar myths have been brought into question and dispelled. Now, commanding renewed respect, the elderly enjoy vibrant new roles in reality as well as in fiction. They have evolved from the fatalistic stereotypes depicted in works such as Arna Bontemps's "A Summer's Tragedy" and Harriet Beecher Stowe's *Uncle Tom's Cabin* to latter-day militants in Gaines's *A Gathering of Old Men* and *Miss Jane Pittman*.

As indicated by the current elderly population in the United States, unprecedented in size, and its growing political clout, the elderly demand a new and better image than the images Butler and White document. No longer are older Americans limited to traditional images associating lethargy with growing old. Instead, the present mission of gerontologists such as Butler and White and writers such as Gaines is to promote a healthier and more realistic view of the elderly.

Elderly blacks appear in limited numbers and often in fairly minor roles in Gaines's body of fiction. One work, however, demonstrates a major shift in his depiction of the elderly black male. *A Gathering* is a decided departure from his previous works in which defiance is either a coincidence or a selfish choice for black men, old or young. Furthermore, it portrays a degree of camaraderie among men of similar age not found in his other works. The concentrated energy resulting from the combined protests of old black men and its effect in heightening the novel's conflict further distinguish the work from Gaines's previous fiction. Moreover, the collaboration among the old black men of *A Gathering* seems to point to a culmination of Gaines's quest to fuse black consciousness with black solidarity. He appears to suggest that success at effecting change is inseparably bound with discovering the special advantages of group strength. In this regard, the novel posits a challenging reappraisal of old black men.

In *Miss Jane Pittman* Gaines depicts, rather than the stereotypical shuffling, humming, heaven-bound elderly black, an alert and active force with whom the opposition must reckon. But the similarities between *Miss Jane Pittman* and *A Gathering* do not extend beyond the obvious parallels in the ages and charisma of their elderly characters. Even though Jane Pittman, Charlie, Mathu, and the group of old black men are alike in their refusal to conform to roles regularly assigned to elderly blacks, a variety of inhibiting gender ethics enforced by land-owning Southern whites to assure their continued control of the blacks significantly limits any further comparisons. The heroics of Jane Pittman and the collaboration among the old black men in *A Gathering* must be judged according to two separate standards of behavior tolerated by land-hungry Cajun farmers—one for elderly black women and another for elderly black men. The women are more likely to be respected, tolerated, and ultimately provided for in their old age. Older black men, at the same time, exist as weary shadows, agreeing with or ignoring their oppressors often as a concession to save their very lives. For Gaines's older black men, psychological emasculation is the option between exile or an early death. Seldom seriously challenged, defiant older black women in Gaines's fiction noticeably differ from older black men, who, because of their doubly oppressive circumstances, often appear to be mere cowards.

By virtue of age and gender, Jane Pittman transcends the dehumanizing behavior that her male counterparts endure. Although her life has been punctuated by episodes of personal horror, her narrative recalls relatively few potentially fatal occasions when she has challenged whites. Even while traveling alone with the orphaned toddler Ned in tow—begging for water, for directions to Ohio, for a ride on a ferry, or for a place to sleep—she manages to reap compassion from otherwise vicious whites. A young black girl and a small child making their way all alone from Louisiana to Ohio and an old woman, once a slave, walking to an all-white fountain for a symbolic drink pose far less danger than a group of frustrated old black men carrying weapons.

As Jane Pittman ages, she elicits concern rather than scorn from her master. Eventually she is no longer required to work in the fields and is "brought up to the big house" as cook. Here she works on her own terms, showing feisty disregard for any authority Miss Ama and Robert try to impose upon her: "I told him at my age I did what I wanted to do" (201). Not only is she shielded from backbreaking toil in the fields, but she is also able to choose her own living quarters. She even persuades Miss Ama to provide help in fixing up the place.

For the major part of her life, therefore, Jane Pittman manages to preserve at least a facsimile of her pride. When she participates in the rally to drink at the all-white water fountain in Bayonne, she does so with the protective immunity afforded by her status as a respected 110-year-old. She is not exposed to the rash verbal and physical abuse that her younger comrades and the old men of *A Gathering* have learned to expect from white antagonists. The young are the preferred targets of die-hard white racists; they pose the greater long-term threat to the status quo. Old black men likewise pose a threat to Louisiana whites, but these are threats to reverse a legacy of symbolic emasculation. Jane Pittman, on the other hand, poses no apparent danger in the eyes of whites. Although her courage in accompanying the entourage of black youths to Bayonne is admirable, her sacrifice is meager by comparison, when one considers the aggravation endured by other blacks who both literally and physically fight oppression.

Despite the fact that Gaines's older female characters seem distanced from verbal and physical abuse, they are nonetheless frequently tormented by divided consciences. While not entirely oblivious to the sufferings of other blacks, they must exist in tense environments where they are obliged to feign ignorance of various crimes. In some instances, their decisions to remain loyal to whites compromise and demean them. Thus they cannot in good faith completely enjoy their protected status without at least some degree of guilt.

Miss Amalia of the short story "Bloodline" is cursed by such a tormenting ambivalence. On one hand, as the black housekeeper, she is concerned for the poor health of her white boss, Frank Laurent, the last white heir to the Laurent property; on the other, as the aunt of the belligerent mulatto Copper (also known as General Christian Laurent), who returns to claim his birthright as a Laurent, she is painfully aware of his reasons for discontent. Son of the white plantation owner who raped Miss Amalia's sister, Copper challenges the Laurent family law that says, "Your mon was black and you can't claim a damn thing" (206). But understanding Copper is all that Miss Amalia can do. She can offer no more than her tears when she tries to stop the inevitable confrontation between him and the last remaining white heir.

> "Don't go down there [to the quarters], Mr. Frank," 'Malia said. "Please, dont' do down there."
> "I must go, Amalia," Frank said. "I can't let Copper in here [his own house]."
> "And your heart?" she said. She was crying; the water had run down her face to her chin.
> Frank stood there looking down at her.
> "Poor Amalia," he said. "We all hurt you, don't we, Amalia?" (199–200)

Similarly, Aunt Margaret in the novel *Of Love and Dust* has to endure an extremely awkward ordeal. She must pretend to ignore the frequent lovemaking sessions of the conniving Marcus Payne and his Cajun overseer's wife Louise. Caught between her loyalty to Sidney Bonbon's family and her strong disapproval of Marcus and his method of seeking· revenge on the overseer, Aunt Margaret must suppress her frustration: "It won't end good," she thought. . . . He go'n pay, she go'n pay, both of them go'n pay for this day." (162)

Jane Pittman also experiences an awkward dilemma. She is proud of her self-proclaimed son Ned, who becomes an agent of black resistance. Yet she befriends the Cajun who ultimately shoots him. She faints from the shock of learning the white vigilantes have charged Albert Cluveau to kill all black opposition, including her Ned:

> I looked at Albert Cluveau a moment, then I felt my head spinning. I made one step toward the house, then I was down on the ground. I heard somebody way off saying, "Jane, Jane, what's the matter, Jane?" I opened my eyes and I saw Albert Cluveau with his ugly face kneeling over me. And I

thought I was in hell, and he was the devil. I started screaming: "Get away
from me, devil. Get away from me, devil. Get away from me, devil." But
all my screaming was inside, and not a sound was coming out. (105–6)

She is helpless. She knows that Ned will not end his crusade for freedom.
She knows his death is imminent, and she knows at whose hands he will
die. As evidenced by the predicaments of Jane Pittman, Aunt Margaret,
and Miss Amalia, although peace and security are often within reach,
these rewards are often either elusive or conditional—subject to many
compromises and much suffering.

In *A Gathering,* female support is also conditional as well as slow in
coming. At first, several elderly black women oppose their husbands'
uncharacteristic bravery. Like Mapes and other witnesses, they have to
be convinced gradually by the spectacle the elderly group creates with its
show of force. The women are clearly distanced from their men in terms
of the degree to which they consider the confrontation to be worth the
risk of physical harm. The extreme shift from years of inactivity to total
involvement causes a debate within one of the black families: Mat cannot sneak past his wife Ella with his twelve-gauge shotgun without an
emotion-charged speech explaining why he must go to Mathu's house:
"All these years we been living together, woman, you still don't know
what's the matter with me? The years we done struggled in George
Medlow's field, making him richer and richer and us getting poorer and
poorer—and you still don't know what's the matter with me?" (37–
38). Ella is clearly moved by Mat's words, but the fact that she does not,
at first, intuit his motives after having been married to him for so long
suggests naïveté bordering upon blindness. Chimley meets similar resistance from his wife, who not only protests "cleaning fishes this time of
day" (32) but also questions his sanity after he shoots his twelve-gauge
out the window. With guarded humor and not nearly so much emotion
as Mat, Chimley clears the way for his departure: "If I come back from
Marshall and them fishes ain't done and ready for me to eat, I'm go'n
do me some more shooting around this house" (33). The women's shock
at their husbands' willingness to participate in an open rebellion reveals
how even they do not understand the extent to which these old black
men have born their hurt. The men's actions at the graves of loved ones,
in front of Mathu's house, and in their own homes dispel any notions
that Mat, Chimley, or any of their group have been cowards all of their

lives or that they simply did not care about the way they were treated. Gaines's characters show their revolutionary nature by reacting to the death of the central character on the very day it occurs. Moreover, other participants in the symbolic coup do not dally before deciding on their course of action. Events occur in such rapid succession that Gaines manages to move quickly from the initial shooting scene to the congregation of the old men at Mathu's house. Though there are several brief scenes of deliberation between the old men and their wives and each other, these conversations are but brief interludes before they resume their mission.

Age, tenure, and quality of service mean little to the Boutan family and other whites who keep both young and old black men in a state of subservience by threatening them with violence or exile at the slightest hint of revolt. Beau Boutan enforces his family's martial law in order to maintain control over Charlie and other elderly black men by frequently intimidating, cursing, and beating them. Unlike Jane Pittman, the old black men are not immune to beatings because of their age or any special grace shown them by white landowners. According to Charlie's account, "I told him [Beau] he didn't need to cuss me like that. I told him I was doing my work good. He told me he wouldn't just cuss me, but he would beat me, too. I told him no, I wasn't go'n 'low that no more, 'cause I was fifty years old—half a hundred. He told me if I said one more word, he was go'n show me how he treated a half-a-hundred-year-old nigger" (190).

In *Of Love and Dust*, Bonbon, whose task is to harass the antagonist Marcus Payne, follows a similar set of rules for handling blacks. The novel's black narrator Jim Kelly describes the overseer as "brutal because he had been brought up in a brute-taught world and in brute-taught times. The big house had given him a horse and a whip . . . and they had told him to ride behind the blacks in the field and get as much work out of them as he could (67).

In "Bloodline," Frank Laurent, the last white heir to the Laurent property, is just as faithful in executing traditional family laws as are Boutan and Bonbon. The legacy of sanctioned violence against blacks is so much a part of his life that he claims to have no alternative but to adhere to "rules" that have long preceded him. In an unusual display of emotion, he explains to his black help, Felix and Aunt Amalia, why he insists that his mulatto nephew Copper must come through the back door before they can talk: " 'What am I supposed to do?' he said, when he couldn't hold back any more. 'Change the rules? Do you know how old these rules are? They're older than me, than you, than this entire place. I didn't make them, I came and found them here. And I—an invalid— am I supposed to change them all?'" (188). In such rare moments as this, when his emotions and good judgment creep to the surface and expose his compassion, Frank Laurent quickly regains his constitution by citing tradition.

Although whipping is one of the most belittling forms of punishment executed against black men, perhaps an even more pathetic, though less obvious, form of torture is debilitating mental abuse. Having to exist with constant reminders of helplessness, old black men—from Bishop in *Of Love and Dust* to Mathu in *A Gathering*—exhibit extreme types of behavior. They become either cowards or the sole defenders against white oppression. As two noted gerontologists assert, "The impact of stress upon the aged is often greater than upon the young since the elderly as a group usually possess fewer personal resources for coping effectively with stressful circumstances. Old age is the first stage of life that brings systematic status-loss for an entire generation" (Varghese and Medinger 97). In Gaines's fiction, elderly black men who choose to survive, in spite of ever-present reminders of their shifting status as well as the threat of exile or death, must inevitably adopt a variety of defense mechanisms. They either convince themselves that they are among the select few to receive favors from the Cajuns and therefore become oblivious to rampant violations of their people, or they challenge their Cajun oppressors head-on in frequently futile attempts to preserve their land and their pride.

While holding onto flimsy promises of security in their old age (which, in many cases, amount to merely the assurance of a place to die and be buried), some old black men in Gaines's fiction appear to shuffle along as if hypnotized, not questioning or challenging their plight. The epitome of this character type appears in *Of Love and Dust*. The pathetic old black servant Bishop has throughout life been obsessively loyal to the white landowner Marshall Hebert. Although he is not subjected to beatings, Bishop is no more than an expendable commodity. Like the old men in early episodes of *A Gathering,* he abides by an unwritten agreement devised and enforced by rich white landowners: if you work hard, don't cause trouble, and remain loyal, you will be allowed to remain on the land until death. It comes as no surprise, therefore, that Bishop frantically pleads with the belligerent Marcus Payne not to jeopardize what he thinks will be a long and peaceful retirement at Hebert's home place. He has grown old there and has served Marshall Hebert with unquestionable loyalty for the major part of his life, yet in one evening he becomes an outcast:

> "Get out," Marshall finally told him.
> "No sir," he said.
> "Get out of here," Marshall told him again.
> "No sir," he said. Then he started babbling off at the mouth. "Your people say I can stay here. Your people liked me. They say long as I was a good boy I could stay here. They say if I looked after y'all and I was a good boy, this house was my home till I died. They say that room there 'side that dining room—"
> "Didn't I tell you to get out," Marshall said, coming on him. (236)

Felix, the seventy-year-old narrator of "Bloodline," similarly believes that the years of service to his white employer ought to merit special favors for him. Like Bishop, at first he seems confident that he is better than other blacks who do not have a certain understanding with their white employers. He brags about the special relationship he and Miss Amalia enjoy not only as friends but also as confidantes to the wealthy Frank Laurent: "Me and 'Malia had been there almost long as Frank had been there, and he told us more than he ever told anybody else. And that's why he never scared me. I obeyed his orders because I respected him; not because I was scared of him" (166). Nevertheless, Felix's supposedly warm relationship with Frank Laurent does not prevent him from being regarded as mere chattel. When the two elderly men discuss strategies for negotiating with the young "whipper-snapper" Copper, they are comrades; yet when matters of authority and control are in question, their relationship quickly polarizes. Frank Laurent becomes the unquestionable voice of authority, and Felix becomes just another old, insignificant black man. At such times, Frank Laurent is quick to remind Felix of their true relationship in vicious verbal attacks: "You start toward that door, Felix, so help me God I'll get that gun out of that desk drawer and shoot your goddamn head off" (188). As Felix struggles to find reasons to excuse the demeaning way Frank Laurent treats him, he becomes more and more insignificant to the work's central conflict. His passive role relegates him to the background as merely "the innocent eye"—the narrator who comments upon the conflict around him but does not alter its course.

Like Felix, the elderly black men in *A Gathering* must contend with taunts and insults from antagonists who see them not as proud humans but as clowns. Hence, their actions are, at first, perceived by their wives and the citizens of Bayonne and the Marshall plantation as a farce. Robert Butler notes the typicality of such reactions toward the elderly: "Negative attitudes toward the old range from pity and infantilization to avoidance or direct hostility. The old are forced into—and for the most part accept—a narrow definition of appropriate behavior, usually quiet and passive" (402). Indeed, both black and white residents have become so accustomed to the contagious passivity displayed by many of the old black men that any deviation from such behavior is seen as more of a confirmation of senility than of courage. Thus they are met with disbelief from those who claim to know them well. Their wives, of whom Clatoo's is representative: "You old fool. Y'all gone crazy?" (36). Their minister: "Some of y'all live far as Silo, the old Mulatto Place, Bayonne—ten, twelve miles from here. Don't y'all know Mapes go'n know half of y'all couldn't be nowhere near this place when this happened? Y'all all gone plumb crazy" (56). The sheriff: "Isn't it a little bit late for you to be getting militant around here?" (86). And Sully: "It was like looking into the *Twilight Zone*. Remember that old TV play *Twilight Zone?* You would be driving through this little out-of-the-way town, and suddenly you would come upon a scene that you knew shouldn't be there—it was something like that" (117–18). To these doubters, the old black men are fools; to the sympathetic reader, their action is an eruption of an ailment that has festered for years.

In a recent study of Gaines, Valerie Babb notes that the character Lou Dimes depicts the old black men as "warriors of an absurd war, and their appearance leaves one wondering why these men had to fight in the first place" (130). To defenders of the status quo, the term *absurd* denotes militancy, radicalism, foolishness, and having lost one's sense of place in society. It is a tempting label for those who are observers rather than participants. To such doubters (those who are not black, those who are not old, and those who do not actually participate in the standoff), the term is a quick dismissal of anything that challenges popular opinion. While *absurd* does not adequately describe the actions of the old black men, it does suggest refreshing nonconformity. When used to describe the energy used to challenge an historically racist society, the term becomes a positive and approving one rather than just another of the many indicators of dementia.

A *Gathering* not only invites the reader to examine heroism among old black men as compared to heroism in their female counterparts but also challenges an era in literary history in which depictions of black men suffer the numbing effects of negative stereotypes. By setting an older version of revolutionary black men in an explosive environment where racial tension rivals that of the revolutionary 1960s, Gaines seems to mock the virtual exclusion of the more aged generation of blacks from protest writings of the 1960s. His narrative suggests a revival of black consciousness prompted not by youthful advocates of the urban-based black arts movement but by the last-ditch efforts of men in the twilight of their lives.

As a protest novel, *A Gathering* challenges the legacy of violence endured by small-town black residents of southern Louisiana. It protests the increasing loss of their land to the Cajuns, threats to their cemeteries, and both the blatant and the disguised forms of racial oppression demonstrated against them by white bigots and their more liberal yet misguided white allies. Just as importantly, it protests the much-maligned image of old black men as nonparticipants in the quest for racial justice.

Black artists from the 1960s such as Amiri Baraka, Don Lee, and Maulana Karenga have targeted the eighteen- to thirty-five-year-old audience, and a large portion of the country's older population seems to have been deemed irrelevant to the revolution of that decade. This apparent, perhaps sometimes inadvertent, age bias seems to confirm what gerontologists Varghese and Medinger note in their research on fatalism among the minority aged: "[Aged] blacks and members of other minorities have lived most of their lives in the pre-civil rights era and therefore have not enjoyed the full benefit of the widening social and economic opportunities that have resulted from recent Civil Rights legislation" (104). However, in Gaines's hands, stereotypical roles such as the "bible-toting" preacher or Uncle Tom give way to roles that thrust old men into the forefront—demanding rather than acquiescing. Within the context of Gaines's novel, Baraka's plea to a generation of youthful recruits in the popular treatise "The Revolutionary Theatre" might be read to assume a new relevance: "And what we show must cause the blood to rush, so that pre-revolutionary temperaments will be bathed in this blood, and it will cause their deepest souls to move, and they will find themselves tensed and clenched, even ready to die, at what the soul has been taught" (*Home* 213). Both fictional and nonfictional accounts of the civil rights movement of the 1960s would have us believe that the typical freedom fighter was a young, aggressive black male. In "Alabama Centennial," 1960s poet Naomi Madgett expresses the generally held misconception that only the young black male is fit to represent blacks' struggle for freedom:

> Not all the dogs and hoses in Birmingham
> Nor all the clubs and guns in Selma
> Can turn this tide.
> Not all the jails can hold these young black faces
> From their destiny of manhood,
> Of equality, of dignity,
> Of the American Dream
> A hundred years past due.
> Now! (198)

Gaines begins to shatter myths of age and gender in his lively portrayal of Miss Jane Pittman. In *A Gathering* he continues to contradict the stereotypical image of revolutionaries as exclusively angry young men. His novel also rebuts the general notion that elderly black men have relinquished their role as defenders of civil rights to the young because of fear or apathy. Babb underscores the impact of the old men's revolt:

> Their collective confession has purged them of the impotent rage they have nurtured against the plantation system, but more importantly it has purged them of the self-loathing they have harbored for the majority of their lives. Through the telling of their stories, through the emotional truth of their symbolic if not actual killing of Beau Boutan, they confront their past and restructure their present and future. (131)

The sharecropper Mathu, more than seventy years old, is the primary example of the old black rebel whom Gaines offers as a contradiction to the more youthful stereotype. He is what Babb refers to as "a symbol for change because he is a repository of both the black and white pasts" (121). He has earned respect from his peers and from the whites around

Marshall plantation, particularly Sheriff Mapes, who considers him "a better man than most I've met, black and white" (74). Even though he is admired by his old comrades and by certain whites, he is humble in his realization that he cannot accept the label *hero,* for up to this moment he has been consumed by a bitter hatred for the very men who now idolize him: " 'I ain't nothing but a mean, bitter old man,' he said. 'No hero. Lord—no hero. A mean, bitter old man. Hating them out there on that river, hating y'all here in the quarters. Put myself above all—proud to be African. You know why proud to be African? 'Cause they won't let me be a citizen here in this country. Hate them 'cause they won't let me be a citizen, hated y'all 'cause you never tried. Just a mean-hearted old man. All I ever been, till this hour' " (182).

A Gathering mirrors an aspect of the revolutionary conflict of the 1960s in its depiction of Candy. She is the embodiment of the well-meaning but ineffectual white liberal who, though essentially benevolent, is in fact a deterrent to the cause of freedom. Revolutionary zealots of that era were keenly aware of the problem posed by an alliance with white liberals. Yet during the civil rights movement, numerous whites marched hand-in-hand with blacks and shared their struggle for economic and political freedom. The decision of blacks to cut ties with such whites often came as the result of a political backlash that focused on some of the most avid black advocates of civil rights. In order to be totally effective, political activists such as Eldridge Cleaver and Baraka went through agonizing dilemmas involving drawing away from white influence. Candy confuses her love for Mathu, who raised her from childhood, with a need to "protect him." When, in her innocence, she paradoxically implies that the old men cannot take charge of their own lives, even Mapes realizes that she has gone too far:

> "You've been trying to split us up all day," she said.
> "And you want to keep them slaves the rest of their lives," Mapes said back.
> "Nobody is a slave here," Candy said. "I'm protecting them like I've always protected them. Like my people have always protected them. Ask them." (174)

The climactic episode marking the conversion of each of the old warriors from manchild to revolutionary is their disavowal of Candy. Although Gaines allows Candy to think that she is in control for much of the novel, eventually the old men sever ties with her and become totally autonomous. At this point their metamorphosis is complete: they confer among themselves; they make decisions; they act as a unit; they are confident and unafraid of the fate awaiting them.

But Candy does not relinquish her role as guardian easily. She is, at first, the savior of the old men, ready to sacrifice her own reputation in order to defy any law that is unjust to them. As the group defines itself and gains strength, however, the men change their regard for her. Although their metamorphosis takes place right before her, Candy is stubbornly oblivious to the extent of their reversal of feelings. When she is faced with opposition from the group, her supposed loyalty to Mathu and to the other black families of the area turns to belligerence. She goes from being at the head of their ranks as their sole white defender to being excluded as a frightening reflection of the very same racism that Beau Boutan and his family represent.

Much like the precarious relationship between black and white comrades of the civil rights movement, the relationship between Candy and Mathu is one not easily explained. Candy's compulsion to take the blame for Mathu is not simply a manifestation of love for her father figure. Her feelings represent a symbolic emasculation masquerading as protectiveness—what Mary T. Harper calls "the child-protector syndrome, with the thirty-year-old plantation mistress paternalistically and benevolently caring for her seventy-plus-year-old men children" (300). Therefore, as Gaines's characters conquer other obstacles to physical and mental freedom, it becomes imperative that they not spare even Candy:

> "Y'all come on inside," Clatoo said to us. "Not you, Candy," he said to her.
> "Nobody's talking without me," Candy said, coming back toward the garry.
> "This time we have to, Candy," Clatoo said. "Just the men with guns."
> "Like hell," Candy said. "This is my place."
> "I know that, Candy," Clatoo said. "But we don't want you there this time." (173)

Through Candy, Gaines recalls similar love-hate relationships between the white female and the black male in previous literature (Ella Downey and Jim Harris in Eugene O'Neill's *All God's Chillun Got Wings;* Mary Dalton and Bigger Thomas in Richard Wright's *Native*

Son; Lula and Clay in Amiri Baraka's *Dutchman*). Out of either curiosity or a need to relieve their consciences of guilt they may feel for their race's treatment of blacks, these liberal white females enter into relationships with black men in which they behave in an overbearing manner. Yet, despite a similar love-hate relationship between Gaines's old men and their self-appointed guardian, they break Candy's protective hold and move one step closer to an affirmation of self. Through the symbolic exorcism of Candy's protective influence, Gaines gradually peels away various images of oppression. What remains is a newly tapped reservoir of strength that is potent enough to ensure that any changes effected by the group will remain in place for posterity.

For years the old black men who inhabit the Louisiana depicted in *A Gathering* sought temporary relief from their oppression by merely bemoaning their fates rather than actively seeking to change them. They unanimously attributed their despair to the Cajuns' greed for land and insensitivity to blacks, yet none of them has been willing to stage any sort of organized counterattack—individual, group, or otherwise—against the Cajuns' aggressive tactics. Medinger and Varghese describe similar thinking among the elderly who internalize their struggles. These scholars agree that repressed anxiety toward oppression among the elderly is "justified, instead of being simply a 'cop-out.' " They further contend that "[by] shifting blame for failure and low status onto forces outside of themselves, stigmatized people, including the minority aged, can relieve themselves of some of the self-recrimination that would otherwise follow their unsuccessful attempts to improve their position" (108). In *A Gathering,* Gaines depicts all the necessary ingredients by which society perpetuates the stereotype of elderly complacency and "system-blaming," but he also shows the abrupt reversal of such thinking.

The makeshift memorial service at the graves of the aged men's victimized relatives represents what is perhaps the second phase in a series of marked changes in the men's characters. This tribute to their dead becomes apocalyptic in its foreshadowing of the group's potential for retaliation. As they recall incidents of past cowardice, the reader understands the extent of the personal debts they owe their relatives for years of silence. By reminding the reader of the mutual sufferings of these men, Gaines prepares for the climax of their metamorphosis at Mathu's house.

The graveyard scene is important not only in suggesting that each of

these men has a motive for shooting Beau Boutan but also in providing an opportunity for Gaines to examine the characters as individuals.
Each has had a history of complacency. Each has been afraid to defend
a family member's life or honor. Each has had to decide whether to die a
hero or live and adopt means to cope with his resulting mental anguish.
So that the reader may see the men as individuals, Gaines significantly
slows down the pace of the novel when Candy's hastily appointed depu-
ties meet near the cemetery while awaiting several of their other aged
friends to join them.

The visits to their relatives' burial plots creates within the men a type
of bravery that transcends concern for their own safety and that seems
necessary for them to have if they are to redress a legacy of blatant
crimes by Fix, his vigilantes, and other such villains. The black men's
unrealized need to retaliate remained suppressed for years because of
aging bodies and dulled egos, yet now a fighting spirit is aroused in
them. Suddenly independent from Candy, they fuel their mission by gal-
vanizing the repressed anger stemming from the rape of their land and
the persecution of their people.

Perhaps the most dramatic example of the conversion from the manchild to revolutionary hero is Clatoo. During the course of the novel
he is transformed from a passive observer to an active participant in
changing the course of his people's lives. At first he spends his days with
his friend Mat at some quiet fishing site. Both men are characterized
by the messenger boy Fue, whom Clatoo considers "sissy-looking" and
who, in turn, feels they are unlikely to have been anybody's murderer:
"Y'all can go and do like she [Candy] say or y'all can go home, lock
y'all doors, and crawl under the bed like y'all used to" (28). This snide
remark from the child merely echoes community sentiments.

Clatoo must not only shed his lethargic image but also exorcise his
gnawing sense of being indirectly responsible for a family member's humiliation and insanity. When Myrtle Bouchard forces Janey and Bea
to name persons with possible motives for killing Beau, Clatoo's name
comes to mind first: She "[tries] to remember what Fix had done to
Clatoo" yet concludes that it "was not Fix, it was that crazy brother of
his, Forest Boutan, who had tried to rape one of Clatoo's sisters. She had
defended herself by chopping him half dozen times with a cane knife.
She didn't kill him, but he was well marked for the rest of his days.
And she was sent to the pen for the rest of hers, where after so many

years she died insane" (25). That Fix's brother is responsible for killing Clatoo's sister is not the elderly black man's major concern, however. Clatoo recognizes the more serious, universal problem. The enemy are all of Fix's kind who have abused them or their families.

Clatoo becomes the reincarnation of the revolutionary hero. Facing certain abuse and possible death, he opts to accept his fate. Thus he emerges as the unproclaimed leader of this revolt that marks the beginning of an era in which old black men will, as Amiri Baraka demands in "Poem for Black Hearts," "look up / black man, quit stuttering and shuffling, look up, / quit whining and stooping" (*Selected Poetry* 104). Clatoo becomes the organizer, the coach, the spokesman of the group. He encourages all of the men to shoot their guns at least once so that each gun may be regarded as the actual weapon that was used to kill Beau; he transports the group to the designated rendezvous in his truck; he even gives them a last-minute pep talk before proceeding to Mathu's house. Once there, he continues to coordinate the protest and even surprises Sheriff Mapes with his new defiance. He heckles Mapes from the crowd yet refuses to flinch when recognized, adding, "I'm old. . . . About time I had li'l trouble with the law before I died" (86).

Also featured in Gaines's character portrayals of members of this motley group are Uncle Billy, Gable, Tucker, and Johnny Paul. Although several of these octogenarians come from surrounding areas and have never before fraternized, they seem comfortable in the group. They bond instantly, overlooking the now inconsequential differences and shallow concerns of the past such as their complexions or their family name. They listen attentively and respectfully to each of the testimonies.

Uncle Billy is perhaps the oldest of the group and possibly the one with the most pathetic tale about Fix's cruelty to his family. Even as an elderly man, he recalls vividly his son's brutal beating: "They beat him till they beat him crazy, and we had to send him to Jackson. He don't even know me and his mama no more. We take him candy, we take him cake, he eat it like a hog eating corn. . . . His mama slice him a little piece and hand it to him, he let it fall on the table, and eat it like a hog eating corn" (80). Uncle Billy does not seem to mind that Mapes's deputy chooses him as the first of the elderly men to be interrogated, nor does he lose faith when Mapes smacks him. Despite Mapes's threats that he could die in the electric chair, the old man is not intimidated. Even after he fails miserably to prove that he is capable of aiming—much less shooting—his twelve-gauge shotgun, he backs away still echoing, "But I did it" (82).

Rivaling Uncle Billy's story of grossly inhumane treatment by whites is that of Gable. Despite his wife's warnings about his weak heart, he manages to testify about his mentally retarded son's torturous death by electrocution. Falsely accused of rape by a promiscuous young white girl, Gable's son was sentenced to die in a faulty electric chair. After failing to kill him on the first try, the white attendants kicked and tinkered with the machine until it finally worked. Gable is ashamed to have endured the horror of his son's death for so many years without retribution, and he senses that he has been given an opportunity to atone for his cowardice. Driven by his awareness of the imminence of his own death, he summons more than enough courage to avenge his son's death publicly and set things right within his own mind. His confession is accompanied by a bittersweet sense of relief.

As each of the elderly men's confessions reveals, old age heightens the sense of urgency. Old age has similarly increased their concern about the aggressive efforts of certain Cajun farmers to expand their landholdings at the expense of black families. Outrage over such ruthless encroachment brings both Tucker and Johnny Paul to the rendezvous at Mathu's house. Both know that even the graves they stop to survey en route to Mathu's are in jeopardy of being plowed under by wealthy Cajun farmers seeking more land to plant.

Their land possesses romantic as well as historical significance. Tucker and Johnny Paul are painfully aware of the hard labor that their ancestors put into land that is destined to be overtaken soon. Moved to lyrical sadness, these men voice opposition to the voracious Cajun plows. Tucker is deeply saddened when he remembers how his brother Silas was beaten to death for winning a contest that pitted his own two mules against a tractor. Helpless and frightened, Tucker could only stand by and watch the Cajuns "beat my brother down to the ground" (97). Johnny Paul voices his bitterness over the loss of the pastoral serenity that his ancestors once found on the land. Gone are the formerly vibrant little huts warmed with low chatter from front porches and the communal goodwill that existed despite their occupants' hard lives. In their place is a glaring vacuum of open space—land flattened by the tractor's plow. The ruthless aggression that destroyed his people's homes is the reason Johnny Paul offers for killing Beau: "I did it for them back there under them trees. I did it 'cause that tractor is getting closer and closer to that graveyard, and I was scared if I didn't do it, one day that tractor was go'n come in there and plow up them graves, getting rid of all proof that we ever was" (92).

Associated with a dwindling relationship between the Louisiana blacks of A *Gathering* and their land is a haunting sense of annihilation of the black man's cultural past. Like the American Indian, whose dwindling habitat led him to the cramped quarters of the reservation, these blacks resent the callous disregard for their past as well as their future. Both Tucker and Johnny Paul realize that the chances are slim that such a small group as theirs could make an effective protest, yet what other generation could be more suitable for calling attention to the plight of their people? Age and experience have endowed Tucker, Johnny Paul, and their comrades with the special ability to forge a link between an oppressed past and a promising future.

Gaines's novel depicts more than just a gathering of old men. He surpasses the impersonal connotations of the novel's title in his own delicate treatment of each character. He makes these men into more than examples of herd mentality, more than attention-seekers eager to share the limelight of the occasion. In addition to dispelling any notion of cowardice among these characters, Gaines shows that they are indeed conscientious men who display profound ties with the land, their communities, their families, and their ancestors. Although they gather to rally in Mathu's defense, their separate confessions reveal individuals suddenly awakening from the sleep of despair, fear, and ignorance of their own potential. Despite the many forces preventing unification of the black race, individual efforts have historically been the catalysts for great movements. By focusing on these individual heroes in A *Gathering*, Gaines draws attention to the possibility for effective group action.

Sterling Brown captures in his poem "Strong Men" the essence of such elderly black men as those in A *Gathering*. The men to whom Brown pays homage have learned to cope with insurmountable oppression by acknowledging it yet not succumbing to it. Fully aware of the weight of their burdens, they move steadily forward:

What, from the slums
Where they have hemmed you
What, from the tiny huts

They could not keep from you—
What reaches them
Making them ill at ease, fearful?
Today they shout prohibition at you
"Thou shalt not this"
"Thou shalt not that"
"Reserved for whites only"
You laugh.

One thing they cannot prohibit—
    The strong men . . . coming on
    The strong men gittin' stronger.
    Strong men. . . .
    Stronger. . . . (57–58)

Brown's treatment of resolution and strength against oppression is a fitting salute to a generation of old black men who have borne the shame of symbolic emasculation in America. His strong men, like those of *A Gathering*, have suffered lives of degradation but are able to affirm their dignity in their waning years. Thus Gaines's novel of protest among a group of old black Louisiana men is likely to stir the consciousness of elderly readers touched by reflections of their own private battles for respect. It is also likely to touch readers who are genuinely troubled by discrimination against older black men throughout the United States.

"The Sound of My People Talking": Folk Humor in *A Gathering of Old Men*

Milton Rickels and Patricia Rickels

Ernest J. Gaines creates his characters through their voices. He has said that in all his books he is trying to capture "the sound of my people talking" (Lecture).[1] *The Autobiography of Miss Jane Pittman* is the longest, most sustained of his voices, comparable in its aesthetic discipline to Mark Twain's *Adventures of Huckleberry Finn*.[2] *Bloodline,* too, presents its stories in a series of voices, from that of the small boy in "A Long Day in November" to that of old Felix in the title story. In *A Gathering of Old Men,* there are fifteen voices. Beginning with the child Snookum, just old enough to play mama and papa in the weeds with Minnie, they include five white voices and are most expressive in those of the old men. Their voices richly reveal their tragic communal history and their individual personalities, accustomed to enduring but at last finding strength to change their world.

The first critics of the book praised its humor. Reynolds Price perceived it as built "with large and singleminded skills, a dignified and calamitous and perhaps finally comic pageant" (15). The qualification "perhaps finally comic" reminds us that the categories of tragic and comic are not always helpful in categorizing twentieth-century novels. But despite the work's ambiguous mode, the voices—sometimes interior, sometimes articulated—are certainly rich in humor. Even in the most sombre scenes, varied tones of humor expand and deepen the meanings of character and action.

Colloquial repetition, with its pauses and reversals, characterizes the dialogue throughout the work, and at times this technique includes humor both to intensify meanings and simultaneously to modify and contrast relationships between characters. "Humor," Gaines said in a recent interview, "depends on that sense of pausing" (Gaudet and Wooton 91–92). Midway in the confrontation between the sheriff and the old men, all of whom claim to have shot the Cajun farmer, Johnny Paul engages Sheriff Mapes in a grueling dialogue. The men have begun recounting tales of terrible brutality inflicted on their families down through the generations. The survivors' choices were to die or to swallow their anger and suffering. As Mapes perceives a new pattern of defiance emerging, he says, "I see." "You see what?" old Johnny Paul asks. Then the Lejeune brothers interrupt, each to claim he has killed Beau Boutan. Again Mapes says, "I see. . . . I see." To this old Johnny Paul grunts, "No, you don't see"; and turning to address all the old men and women gathered in Mathu's yard, he invites, "Y'all look. . . . Look now. Y'all see anything?" "I see nothing but weeds, Johnny Paul," Mapes says. "Yes, sir," Johnny Paul says. "Yes, sir, I figured that's all you would see. But what do the rest don't see? What y'all don't see, Rufe?" (87–88)

What Johnny Paul is looking toward as he speaks is the weed-covered site of the house where his mother and father once lived. What he does not see are the houses and flower gardens that used to make up the quarters. Johnny Paul invites the members of his community not only to remember what is gone but to consider another indignity: the farmer Beau Boutan had threatened to plow up the old, largely unmarked cemetery. Johnny Paul presents his fear: "One day that tractor was go'n come in there and plow up them graves, getting rid of all proof that we ever was. Like now they trying to get rid of all proof that black people ever farmed this land with plows and mules" (92). If the cemetery is plowed off the face of the world, the dignity of the old work will be utterly destroyed and the life of the present further impoverished.

This weighty scene is serious but not solemn in its tone. The contrapuntal repetition of *see* throughout the dialog—"I see, I see," "No, you don't see," "What y'all don't see?"—is humorous, partly because of the strain and failure to communicate across cultures, partly because of the word's stubborn persistence, partly because of what Mapes would feel as its uppity defiance. The verbal repetition echoes the technique of the blues refrain; it savors the bittersweet life of suffering, anger, joy,

accomplishment, and endurance shared by the black community. Repetition emphasizes and deepens the symbolic weight of *seeing:* it takes on
complex accretions of knowing and feeling. The inarticulate lives that
rise to expression in the pressure of this encounter are commemorated
in the telling.

At the same time the sheriff, representative of the white man's law, is
forced to hear harrowing litanies of injustice and, simultaneously, is told
he will never be able to understand what he hears. Mapes can never see.
He feels the old men are pressing him to understand a point of view that
his culture has traditionally denied existed, a point of view he and his
community have in the past suppressed by force. With guns and voices,
the old men are, at a deep level, forcing Mapes to witness their turning
the world upside down. Mapes is a brutal, ordinary man, and what he
does not see further reduces his humanity. When Gaines reads this scene
aloud, Southern white audiences laugh with him in shared pleasure in
humor's ancient power to diminish the authority figure and to celebrate
man's capacity to thrash about and stand upright, even at the edge of
the grave.

In a later scene, middle-aged, white Miss Merle brings two baskets of
sandwiches to the murder site. Gathered there in Mathu's yard and on
his porch are all the old men; Candy Marshall, the plantation owner's
niece; Sheriff Mapes and his deputy Griffin; the black women Beulah
and Glo; Glo's three grandchildren; and Candy's fiancé, Baton Rouge
newspaperman Lou Dimes. Lou, who presents this scene, sees Miss
Merle drive up, get out with a covered basket, and say something to
Griffin. The deputy goes back to her car, then follows her into the yard,

with the basket in one hand and the gun in the other, and you could see
Mapes looking at him as if he were wondering if he actually needed Griffin
the rest of the day. Miss Merle didn't come up to Mapes, or Candy, or
me first, she started dishing out sandwiches to the first one she came to.
I supposed she felt that since we were all conspirators together, one was
no better than the others, so she just started dishing out sandwiches to the
first person she got to, fussing all the time.

"Just look at this, I mean just look at this—just look at it." Dishing out
sandwiches and fussing. "I hope you like ham and cheese because there
isn't anything else. Just look at that. I mean just look at that. Hurry up with
that other basket," she said over her shoulder to Griffin. Griffin brought
her the full basket, and she handed him the empty one. So Griffin was

standing there with an empty basket in one hand and a loaded revolver in
the other. "Can't you put that thing away for a second?" Miss Merle asked
him. "Who are you going to shoot, the hog?"
    "No, Ma'am," Griffin said.
    "Just look at that," Miss Merle said, looking at Griffin. Then she looked
at the rest of us. "Just look at that." (125–26)

Miss Merle's scandalized iteration of "Just look at that" in this passage expresses her boundless exasperation at this awful breach of decent
behavior by everybody she sees. At the same time, her incongruous hospitality introduces into the grim scene a traditional festive motif of folk
humor—communal eating. Nobody refuses the sandwiches, and with
Beau's blood drying on the weeds, they all eat. Lou observes that Miss
Merle does not follow the hierarchy of the local caste system in handing
out the sandwiches. Her failure of etiquette implies the world turned
upside down, the element of carnival in the complex web of meaning
around this murder. The humor in the above passage rests on the intrusion of Miss Merle's obsessive and indomitable hospitality into the
threatening confrontation, on her ineffectual attempts to correct and
control, and most fundamentally on the ancient comic celebration of life
itself: the irrational assertion that before law and order, before revenge
or justice or dignity or civilization, first comes life, the basic sacred thing.
    In addition to the technique of colloquial repetition, *A Gathering* has
other elements of traditional humor, notably a set of images from the
culture of oral folk humor. Sometimes these are characterizing details:
the fat, constantly sweating sheriff; the ever-present wet cigarette hanging from Dirty Red's mouth; the old men's nicknames: Clabber, Coot,
Chimley, Rooster. These nicknames—descriptive, derisive, affection-
ate—the gift of the whole community, must be endured, appropriated,
and finally celebrated. The play with names as identity or mask, with
naming as loving or hating, with meanings inside and outside the community, acquires complexity throughout the novel. By the concluding
courtroom scene, when the newspeople laugh at the old men's nicknames, the reader, now an insider, understands their laughter as missing
the point.[3]
    As a set, the images drawn from folk humor emphasize the physi-
cal ground of humanity, or as Mikhail Bakhtin maintains, the diversity
rather than the uniformity of human appearance. They voice the fact

that individuals are never, as classical aesthetics implies, harmonious, balanced, and complete, but rather are always in process (25ff). They are old or young, fat or thin, sick or well, flourishing or dying. As personalities, they are sometimes subservient and fearful, sometimes aggressive and threatening, sometimes wise, sometimes foolish. To Gaines, the varieties of humanity, the endless exfoliation of individual and community, are not threatening in their instability but rather exhilarating and, more often than not, promising.

This hope that Gaines holds for his characters, rising out of eternal renewal and change, pervades the novel so that, for all that it deals with oppression, suffering, violence, and death, A *Gathering* is comic in the most ancient sense of the term: its theme is rebirth, regeneration, resurrection. Not the Christian myth but an older and more elemental one is evoked in the image of Beau Boutan lying shot to death in the weeds, flies feasting on his blood, his face caked with dirt, and his hair full of dry grass seeds. Repeated twice early in the novel (51, 60), this image sets a tone of brutal realism yet holds within itself the germ of new life. In this most unpastoral of books, images from nature abound. Plants and animals, blood and dirt are recurrent motifs that establish the cultural and mythic meanings of Gaines's drama, as they are repeated, combined, and recombined with variations. Weeds are ubiquitous, having taken over the flower gardens and ditches of the quarters and now threatening to invade the graveyard. Neither beautiful nor useful, they represent natural vigor, the life force in its most primitive form, as the rows of sugar cane stand for man's regimented version of nature, harnessed for economic gain. The plant world teems on every page—grass, bloodweeds, bushes, turnips, beans, roses, four-o'clocks, palm-of-Christians (under which the plantation children play at lovemaking), oaks, pecans, willows, sycamores, and cypress. As Walt Whitman says of the grass in "Song of Myself," "The smallest sprout shows there is really no death" (34).

Blood is everywhere—on the grass by Beau's corpse; on the bodies of the dead and wounded; in the veins of the racist gang, who need a lynching "to pump blood back into their dying bodies" (143); and in the animals (which figure so prominently in Gaines's descriptions and metaphors) alive or killed by hunters, fishermen, or butchers. There are alligators, deer, wildcats, fish, horses and mules, rats, rabbits, chickens and chicken hawks, bears, hogs, possums, dogs, birds, flies, bedbugs, spiders, mosquitoes, mud daubers, rattlesnakes, and water moccasins.

As for dirt, it is the element that binds everything together. Soil that inspired the plantation system consumed at last the flesh of master and slave alike. Dirt, the great equalizer, represents the destruction of distinctions and illusions. The last in a line of plantation "aristocracy," Candy disposes of a weight of Southern legend by calling her family's plantation "a few miles of dirt" (176). Luke Will and his gang of bullies are called "the dirt-plant boys" because they work at the Dixie Gravel, Cement, and Dirt Company. Their hands are so filthy that at the bar grit lies in the bowl of ice after they reach into it (161). When the time of reckoning comes for black and white alike, Charlie says triumphantly, "We all in the dirt now, and it ain't no more Mister and no more Miss" (205).

A set of traditional abusive words, rooted in allusions to lower-body parts and functions, also appears from the culture of folk humor. These are carefully modulated. The most violent are used by Luke Will and his followers, a gang who decide to lynch Beau's killer. Luke Will calls Beau's brother, an LSU football star who refuses to take part in any lynching, "the All-American fart" (163). The youngest, most childish of Luke Will's followers is richest in his vocabulary of obscenities. After a few drinks, Leroy says, "Shit, I can't wait. Let's go kick some ass" (166). He accompanies Luke Will's mob to the Marshall plantation, only to find himself hiding with the others behind a tractor as the old black men fire at them from all angles. "Y'all didn't say they had all them guns," he says (202). "No shit," is the mock-sympathetic reply. When he threatens to give himself up, one of Leroy's companions says, "You walk out of here and I'll blow your back off. . . . You in it, fucker. You go'n stay here till the end" (202).

When used by the old black men, the vocabulary of abuse is markedly less frequent and less violent. During the encounter with the sheriff, Deputy Griffin is characterized by his impatient willingness to shoot somebody and by his slight build, focused in a traditional synecdoche. When he says he would not bear from the blacks what Mapes is tolerating, old Tucker asks, "And what would you do, you little no-butt nothing?"(94). In the opening scene of the novel, Snookum, on his errand to rouse the community, rides like Monty Python, "spanking my butt the way you spank your horse when you want him to run fast" (6). *Butt,* then, is established as a child's term, and when used by the old men, it connotes comically engaging politeness in its restraint of insult.

Later, after a long exchange with Johnny Paul, Griffin asks the sheriff how much he is going to take. Mapes orders him to go check the police radio, and old Rufe observes, "That little spare-butt, slack-pants deputy left the yard walking all tough" (100). At the end of the scene, Griffin again asks, "Why don't we just throw that old coon in the back of the car and take off?" (110). Old Yank, with humorous tolerance, observes, "He's sure got a big mouth for somebody with hardly any butt" (110).

This traditional synecdoche locates man's essential self, his biological life and the power to maintain it, in his buttocks. Yank's comment is a more rural, more decent version of the street-talk expression "His mouth has wrote a check his ass can't cash." The intent is judgmental and reductive, but the extravagance and incongruity of the imagery imply a shared humanity, not the detachment and intellectual superiority of satire. Yank's grotesque images are tolerant, not hateful, perhaps expressive of human brotherhood with even Griffin's narrow-hipped humanity.

The grotesque set of images throughout *A Gathering* includes many references to eating in incongruous places or under incongruous circumstances. Sometimes the eating is purely metaphoric, as when, early in the story, the sheriff asks old Clatoo if it isn't a little late for him to be "getting militant." Clatoo says, "I always been militant. My intrance gone sour, keeping my militance down" (87). Later Tucker ends the story of his brother's murder, which he witnessed, with an image of fear undigested: "Been in here all these years, boiling in me," hitting his chest. "Done spoiled my intrance. Fear. Fear. Done spoiled my intrance. I don't know how come I'm still alive" (96). This impassioned cry from a life imaged as a belly full of fear issues as a declaration of freedom: "Cause this is the day of reckonding and I will speak the truth" (94). The struggle against fear and its conquest is the source of both comic release and, as here, an eloquent lamentation, giving voice to the transformation old Tucker has achieved.

The episode of Miss Merle's distributing sandwiches, quoted above, serves as another example. Lawmen and confessed murderers munch their sandwiches together while the flies dine on the blood of Beau Boutan's corpse, the occasion for the macabre picnic. Some of these images of eating imply a mythic vision of man's union with the earth. As Chimley, Yank, Dirty Red, Mat, and some others walk through the old black cemetery, Cherry Bello, the narrator of this section, pauses at his own family graves. "After I knelt down and prayed over my own family plot, I wandered over to where Dirty Red was standing all by himself. He was eating a pecan and looking down at the weeds that covered the graves" (46). Cherry sees that some of the graves are sunken. " 'My brother Gabe there,' Dirty Red said." As Cherry watches, he notes, "As soon as he said it he cracked another pecan with his teeth." Cracking and eating pecans, Dirty Red says, "Graveyard pecan always taste good. . . . You tasted any of them?" (47). Dirty Red is closer to the earth than Mark Twain's raftsman who lauds the nutritious quality of Mississippi River water with an exemplum from cemeteries: "Trees won't grow worth shucks in a Cincinnati graveyard, but in a Sent Louis graveyard they grow upwards of eight hundred foot high. It's all on account of the water the people drunk before they laid up. A Cincinnati corpse don't richen a soil any" (24).[4] Mark Twain's humor rests on caste distinctions: the reader enjoys the raftsman's simplicity and his lack of sensitivity. Gaines's reader may enjoy his old men's responses in the graveyard also, but because the image here is food, not simply trees, and Red is eating what grows from his brother's grave, this image invites deeper symbolic interpretations. Humans literally grow out of their family, whose bodies nourish them. And although the individual dies, mankind is immortal, and our lives can be seen as part of a great, endless earthly cycle of birth and death and birth. Red's communion with the past and with his brother is direct and satisfying. He invites the rest of the community to eat with him. On the reader's reflection, the grotesque here disappears. Red's superficially comic breach of middle-class decorum reveals a grand if unspeakable truth.

Another set of images in Gaines's work deals with representation of God. Generally the imagery is anthropomorphic and consequently reductive of divine majesty. Miss Merle, passing out sandwiches, is "sure God had made a mistake putting her here at the same time He did Mapes" (127). Late in the book, Mapes learns that Fix Boutan, Beau's father, has had to learn from his football-playing son that Gil does not want the family's name in the paper for a lynching on the day before LSU's big game with Ole Miss. When the old men show disappointment at not getting to shoot at Fix, Mapes tells them it is their own fault for praying for integration: "Y'all wasn't satisfied Salt played at LSU on one side of town, and Pepper played for Southern on the other side of town. . . . Y'all prayed and prayed and prayed. . . . You told God you wanted Salt and Pepper to get together, and God did it for you. At the same time you wanted God to keep Fix the way Fix was thirty years ago so one day you would get a chance to shoot him. Well, God couldn't do both" (170–71). Mapes's folk-theological insight into the contradictory demands of Christians opens a valid problem, but his imputation of divine limitation is comically reductive. Mapes's baffled God recalls Miguel de Unamuno's witty praise of a humble God: "The greatest act of humility is that of a God who creates a world that adds not one whit to his glory, and then creates a human species to criticize his work" (55).

In black communities the preacher is often a personage of great dignity and power, but Reverend Jameson, alone of all the Marshall plantation men, crumples under pressure. Timid and fearful, he cuts a figure first pitiful, later comic. As the shoot-out begins, Coot recalls, "I could hear Jameson over by the house calling on God to have mercy on all of us. If it wasn't Jameson calling on God, it was Glo calling for her little grandson Snookum. Jameson, then Glo; Glo, then Jameson. I heard Dirty Red call to Rooster to go shoot Jameson and shut him up. Jameson musta heard it too. There wasn't another word from him" (198).

In some of Gaines's other works this comic treatment of religion and preachers embodies a very dark vision in imagery of the most wildly comic fantasy.[5] In the short story "Three Men" from *Bloodline*, Munford Bazille explains to a fellow prisoner how homosexuals came to be in the world: "I'll tell you. It start in the cradle when they send that preacher there to christen you. At the same time he's doing that mumbo-jumbo stuff, he's low'ing his mouth to your little nipper to suck out your manhood." Munford says that at his own baptism, although his whole family was there, only he saw what was really happening: "This preacher going 'Mumbo-jumbo, mumbo-jumbo,' but all the time he's low'ing his mouth toward my little private. Nobody else don't see him, but I catch him, and I haul 'way back and hit him right smack in the eye. I ain't no more than three months old but I give him a good one. 'Get your goddamn mouth away from my little pecker, you no-teef, rotten, egg-sucking sonofabitch. Get away from here, you sister-jumper, God-calling, pulpit-spitting, mother-huncher. Get away from here, you chicken-eating, catfish-eating, gin-drinking sonofabitch. Get away, goddamn it, get away' " (140). As Munford sees it, the black preacher helps to unman the black community. His dark vision is presented in the manner of a folk tall tale, the tale of a mythic hero in his cradle triumphing through quick wit, an Achilles-like voice, and Herculean physical strength. The comic myth is earthbound: one survives by his own resources and in spite of what is called spiritual help.

The climactic battle scene in *A Gathering*, for all its waste, is also part of the comic ground; it creates a distinctive tone that includes laughter and the exultation of liberation, yet is finally deeply human and paradoxically fruitful. By nightfall, the old men come to desire the violence under which their community has lived in fear. When they learn from Sheriff Mapes that Fix Boutan will not lead a lynch mob into the quarters to avenge his son's death, they feel disappointed. All day they have withstood both brutal and subtle attacks on their dignity with transforming grace, and now they want the ceremony completed. Even Rooster, whose wife has had to make him borrow a shotgun for the gathering, feels his new self uncompleted: "We had cranked usself up for a fight, and we wanted usself a fight" (170). Mapes's pleasure at the confrontation avoided is incomprehensible to Rooster, who is in another realm. "I had never seen a happier white man in all my born days" (171) is his ironic commentary.

Then suddenly Luke Will and his friends arrive to demand a lynch victim, as their culture dictates. But Big Charlie and the old men refuse to be victims any longer. Fired upon, they "bust out" of Mathu's house to find places in the weeds, ditches, and yards of the quarters to shoot back. For the black men it is a carnival of excitement: "I want to get that son of a bitch myself," Clatoo says, and Coot responds, "No more than I do. We didn't all get a chance at Beau, but we got a chance at him" (197). As they shoot, they express their high spirits, yelling "the way you holler at a rodeo when somebody's riding a bucking horse, 'Yahoo.'" Coot recalls, "They hooted and fired. You woulda thought you was listening to a bunch of Indians—Lord have mercy." With comic piety, this World War I veteran thinks, "I didn't know the last time I had felt so good. Not since I was a young man in the war. Lord have mercy, Jesus" (196–99).[6]

The men are well aware that they have undergone an October metamorphosis. Big Charlie, who finally returns from the swamps to claim responsibility for murdering Beau, says of himself, "A nigger boy run and run and run. But a man come back. I'm a man" (187). And, near the end, Mathu says, "I been changed. . . . I been changed. Not by that white man's God. I don't believe in that white man's God. I been changed by y'all. Rooster, Clabber, Dirty Red, Coot—you changed this hard-hearted old man" (182). Mathu's transformation is not the work of Reverend Jameson or of God, but of the community, which realizes its strength in a gathering of old sons of earth.[7]

The concluding violence focuses on Charlie. Rooster reports, "He had been running, and he had laid down on the ground. I could smell the sweat, the fields, the swamps in his clothes" (183). In his new courage, Charlie walks right toward the vigilantes, firing as he approaches. He kills Luke Will and is in turn killed. As he lies dying "like a big old bear," Dirty Red says, "I leaned over and touched him, hoping that some of that stuff he found back there in the swamps might rub off on me. After I touched him, the rest of the men did the same. Then the women, even Candy. Then Glo told her grandchildren they must touch him too" (209–10).[8] Through his contact with the earth, Charlie has been transformed and in death becomes himself a magic source of courage and power.

The trial scene with which the novel concludes is created in the voice of the reporter Lou Dimes. Here the powers of life and the powers of death, the powers of old orders and the powers of new orders appear reduced, in a subtly modified form comically domesticated. The heroic old men, who killed the symbol of brutal oppression, now return to the everyday, however well everyone in the community knows that things will never be the same again. The humor of the trial is tonally crafted to bring readers down from the high drama, culminating in three funerals. Everyone had taken baths and spiffed up so that in the courtroom "you smelled nothing but Lifebuoy soap and mothballs" (211). There is a good deal of laughter during the proceedings, mostly from the news people present, "who took the whole thing as something astonishing but not serious" (212). The best fun for all the spectators comes when the judge demands that Sheriff Mapes speak up. Full of impotent rage, Mapes finally admits that "the whole fight, I was sitting on my ass in the middle of the walk. Luke Will shot me, and I was sitting on my ass in the middle of the walk. Now, is that loud enough?" (213). At this even Judge Reynolds has a good laugh. In sentencing the old men, the judge says he is "putting all of them on probation for the next five years, or until their deaths—whichever came first" (213). Thus heroic old age becomes the occasion for a cruel reminder of human mortality, couched as "just a joke."

Like *Adventures of Huckleberry Finn* and that minor antebellum classic of American literature, Thomas Bangs Thorpe's "The Big Bear of Arkansas," *A Gathering* moves through comic realism into the realm of myth. Richard Slotkin argues that the myth of regeneration through violence is "the structuring metaphor of the American experience." What he calls "true myths" arise out of the individual and communal experiences of a people's history "and thus constitute part of that inner reality which the work of the artist draws on, illuminates, and explains" (4–5). For Gaines, the history of his own Pointe Coupee Parish people is the true myth, and their voices, painstakingly remembered and recreated, provide the medium for his artistic illumination of that myth.

Notes

1. For additional comments by Gaines on this element in his writings, see Gaudet and Wooton 7–12.

2. Miss Jane's is a "communal" voice. See Gates, "Criticism in the Jungle" 19.

3. Significantly, Mathu—the novel's center of dignity, wisdom, and power— is never "called out of his name," that is, addressed by whites by a patronizing title such as Uncle or a nickname. On naming, see Gates "Criticism in the Jungle" and Bentson. For a discussion of naming in *A Gathering*, see J. Griffin. To the reader familiar with the culture of south Louisiana, the abundance of nicknames is an added touch of realism. Among African Americans and Cajuns of Pointe Coupee and neighboring parishes, nicknames sometimes displace Christian names, even in telephone directories and obituary notices, where the deceased, the pallbearers, and even the officiating priest may be so designated.

4. For a full discussion of the forms and functions of the language of folk humor, see Bakhtin, especially chapters 3, 5, and 6. For a recent evaluation of his theories, see Kinser, especially 253–54. When the scene of eating in the cemetery is connected with the eating beside Beau Boutan's corpse, the carnivalesque tone of the image set is reinforced and deepened, ambiguously implying a new and better life may come from death. See Bakhtin 110–11, 218.

5. For a discussion of Gaines's treatment of religious leaders see Gaudet "Failure."

6. There are many episodes in African-American literature in which the element of celebration is incorporated into scenes of riot, destruction, and death. The best known of these is in chapter 25 of Ralph Ellison's *Invisible Man*. See

also Ann Petry's story "In Darkness and Confusion" and Langston Hughes's Jesse B. Simple sketch "Feet Live Their Own Life." According to Bakhtin, this is the laughter of "the awakened man who has attained virility" (67).

7. Gaines has said, "I think, in much black folklore and blues, that even when things are at their worst, there's often something humorous that comes through. . . . My characters are not usually 100 percent bitter, not hardened to the point that they cannot feel and give and change. Humor and joking are part of change" (Gaudet and Wooton 22).

8. The image of the bear, repeated four times on 207–9, is part of the large and ancient mythic tradition drawn upon also by William Faulkner in "The Bear" and by Ralph Ellison in his evocations of Brer Bear of African-American folklore in *Invisible Man*. The presence of the children here has a carnivalesque element: it emphasizes that the old world is dying and the youthful, new time is being generated out of death (Bakhtin 211). Contrast Cherry's tale of white men killing the "big pretty mulatto" girl on Mardi Gras Day, 1947 (45).

Gaines's Humor:
Race and Laughter

David C. Estes

When an interviewer asked Ernest J. Gaines if he saw himself as a humorist, he replied, "I don't tell jokes. Whenever I do tell a joke, no one laughs. . . . I think I am more of a listener, really. . . . I like to listen to the way that people talk, and I like to listen to their stories. Then when I get into a little room some place, I try to write them down" (Fitz Gerald and Marchant 333). Despite the self-deprecating modesty, his short stories and novels abound with funny characters and incidents. Only in *Catherine Carmier, In My Father's House,* and *A Lesson Before Dying* does he counterpoise no laughter against the disappointment and pain that overwhelm the central characters and their families. When humor appears in Gaines's fiction, it is intrinsic to the narrative. He does not elicit laughter by embellishing stories with superfluous scenes and characters intended merely to shift attention away from the bitter legacy of racial injustice that his characters face. Rather, the humor directly foregrounds issues of racism, so that through incongruities and ironic reversals, Gaines uses laughter as a weapon to retrieve the dignity of African Americans. In particular, his fiction repeatedly depicts the amusing qualities in people's behavior at times of crisis and also the more profoundly ironic reversal of the established racial hierarchy by the long-suffering oppressed. His two most widely acclaimed works, *The Autobiography of Miss Jane Pittman* and *A Gathering of Old Men,* reflect an essentially optimistic, comic view of the future in spite of the history of discrimination and racial tensions they portray.

228 The connection between racism and humor in Gaines's fiction matches what he observed while growing up in the region about which he writes. On the plantation in Pointe Coupee Parish, people responded to their deepest troubles with humor, and his own brother, so Gaines says, was particularly good at telling jokes about blacks and whites that fit the situation there: "A story can be tragic, and he [my brother] can make it very funny. You see, where I came from, my people were sharecroppers. . . . Their competitors were the Cajuns, the white people there. The people you make fun of more are the people who are closer to you. So when my people had to make fun of something, when they had to laugh, they made fun of the whites. You always make fun of your competitors. They are the people very close to you. And we had this relationship all the time" (Fitz Gerald and Marchant 333).

Despite the laughter directed at Cajuns in the oral traditions that have influenced Gaines's storytelling style, his own fiction relies primarily on African Americans, not whites, as comic figures. Many are universal humorous stereotypes. Others are modeled on stock depictions of blacks in popular humor dating back to antebellum blackface minstrelsy, images associated with a tradition of racist humor in America.[1] One of the consequences of stage minstrelsy, as Eric Lott notes, was "the dispossession and control by whites of black forms that would not be recovered for a long time" (229). Gaines is among those contemporary African-American writers employing some of the stock humorous stereotypes and situations of this tradition. Yet his work is not racist. He uses these emotionally charged character types intentionally as part of the social critique in his fiction. They always appear alongside fully developed black characters and are never the sole representatives of African-American culture in a text. Furthermore, over the course of his career, Gaines's comic figures have become increasingly complex reinventions of stereotypes and their conventional, demeaning connotations. His humorous stance subverts racist attitudes by conveying the full humanity and reality of African Americans and their experience. Gaines's movement away from simplistic duplication of humorous black stereotypes is related to significant changes in his treatment of comic white figures. These laughingstocks, who in early stories retaliate against blacks when humiliated by them, in later works must endure public scorn when seemingly impotent blacks subvert their accustomed authority and ability to punish. This difference is a measure of the comic vision that Gaines has come to develop more thoroughly in his fiction, a vision in which humor holds the promise of both humanizing and harmonizing the ethnic groups whose conflicts he chronicles.

In several of the early short stories, later collected in *Bloodline*, Gaines patterns a number of the characters on universal humorous types, but the laughter is never escapist. In these narratives of personal and community tension, Gaines's eye is on the humor that attends moments of crisis. Such a perception is, in his view, characteristically African-American: "I think, in much black folklore and blues, that even when things are at their worst, there's often something humorous that comes through" (Gaudet and Wooton 22). Much of the comedy in these stories comes from his attention to various male-female relationships. For example, "Just Like a Tree" tells of the farewell party for the revered old woman whose kin have decided to move her north to live with them. In the opening scene, a family is heading to the party down a dirt road in the rain. The circumstances are made even more miserable for the man driving by the back-seat driver, his mother, Aunt Lou. The vehicle is not an automobile but rather a two-mule cart. And Aunt Lou is in her own chair in the back of the wagon because, as her young grandson recollects, "she didn't ride in no wagon on nobody board, and if Pa liked it or not, that setting chair was going" (222–23). When her son whips her favorite mule, Mr. Bascom, for refusing to pull his share of the load, she interrupts, "That's right, kill him. . . . See where you get mo' money to buy another one." Pa ignores her, and she threatens to hit him. The old woman has the last word, however, and the youngster observes that his hen-pecked father is silenced: "Pa say something kind o' low to hisself, and I can't make out what it is."

Another stereotypically humorous woman is Eddie's meddlesome mother-in-law Rachel in "A Long Day in November." When Amy, his wife, moves back to her mother's home because her husband gives more attention to his car than to her, Rachel immediately invites a former boyfriend over to renew his proposals, and she presses the hesitant daughter to move in with him that very day. Eddie returns from the fields at lunchtime looking for his wife, and Rachel threatens to "get that butcher knife out of that kitchen and chop on your tail till I can't see tail to chop on" (33). Then she fires a shotgun over his head, scaring him out of the yard and into the road. His cowardice and her bravado are the stuff out of which television situation comedies are made. Finally Eddie's family problems make him the laughingstock of the quarters when, on the advice of the local conjure woman, he sets fire to his car to resolve the family crisis and bring his wife home.

Throughout his career Gaines has let young boys recount events from their own point of view, and their newfound interest in girls has frequently been an amusing part of narratives in which the thematic focus is on emergence into manhood. In "The Sky Is Gray" James must go to town for the dentist to pull his abscessed tooth. Standing beside his seated mother in the back of the bus, he notices a neatly dressed girl about his age. They keep glancing at each other and then feigning indifference. The girl's mother notices this posturing and "leans over and says something in her ear. 'I don't love him nothing,' that little old gal says out loud. Everybody back there hear her mouth, and all of them look at us and laugh" (92). For the rest of the journey they studiously avoid each other. Upon arrival in Bayonne, "she jugg her little old tongue out at me. I make 'tend I'm go'n hit her, and she duck down 'side her mama. And all the people laugh at us again." The first narrator in *A Gathering*, who carries the upsetting news of Beau's murder to the front house, is in a typical comic dilemma because of affection for a girl. His little brother discovered him and Minnie "playing pappa and momma in the weeds," and now Toddy is blackmailing him, enjoying the power that his promise not to tell their grandmother has secured. So when the narrator sees the bloody corpse lying in the weeds, he is relieved, not fearful as are others in the quarters: "I still had one thing on old Toddy. He didn't see what I saw" (9).

Of Love and Dust is the first novel into which Gaines incorporated humorous scenes and characters. Despite abundant comedy, the narrative pessimistically portrays racial conflict and the inevitable, violent reaffirmation of white supremacy, which finally drowns out the sound of laughter. Specifically African-American types appear alongside such universal comic figures as are found in the earlier short stories. The central character displays qualities of both the powerful "bad man" and the trickster of African-American folklore. However, Gaines treats his would-be hero ironically, and the novel ends tragically when Bonbon, the Cajun overseer, murders the new field hand Marcus, a ladies' man from the city, for seducing his wife. The mounting fear of those in the quarters that they will all suffer violence because of Marcus's behavior is justifiable. Still, Gaines at times presents their anxiety with a measure of levity by including characters who recall the comic caricature of the frightened black. The humor in *Of Love and Dust* is more complex than that in the short stories because the characters in the novel derive from both positive and negative representations of African Americans, by themselves as well as by whites, in folk and popular culture. In this novel Gaines takes up the artistic challenge of critiquing prejudice by using humorous stereotypes in what might seem unexpected ways. He not only undercuts the "bad man" and trickster qualities of the hero but also skillfully draws on the highly charged caricature of the frightened black, notwithstanding the racist notions implied by its presence in popular culture over the years.

After killing another black man in a fight over a woman in a Baton Rouge night club, Marcus is quickly bonded out of jail before trial by plantation owner Marshall Hebert. He must labor for five years on the white man's terms to earn back his freedom under this exploitative system. But Marcus is a cocky rebel who refuses to play the role of humble slave that is, in essence, the extralegal punishment for his crime. He fits Daryl Dance's definition of the "bad nigger": "The Bad Nigger of folklore is tough and violent. He kills without blinking an eye. He courts death constantly and doesn't fear dying. . . . He values fine clothes and flashy cars. He asserts his manhood through his physical destruction of men and through his sexual victimization of women" (224–25). As H. Nigel Thomas has noted, Marcus fits this stereotype in another important way: his presence arouses the fears of the black community for their own safety because he "is a reminder of their victim status" (76). Yet Gaines deftly balances the mounting fear in the quarters against several humorous scenes that satirize Marcus's confidence in his own menacing power, on which he can no longer rely in challenging unjust whites. Although he is, as Sherley Anne Williams explains, a streetman in Baton Rouge who is used to "controlling any game which he tries to run on others" (196), on the Marshall plantation he is a tenderfoot who must undergo a painful initiation. He becomes the laughingstock of both his fellow black laborers and the white overseer before learning the limits of overt physical prowess in a racist society and adopting the trickster's strategies of deceit and cunning to retaliate against his white oppressors.

His initial response to the realities of plantation life is comically inappropriate, suggesting his status as an immature outsider. Unconcerned that he must rise at 4:30 to begin harvesting corn, Marcus will not go to bed the first night until he finds nails and wire to hang up his clothes. The next morning Jim, the narrator, goes to wake him and sees that "he had everything hanging so pretty-like. He had his suits, his shirts, his ties all on a little line. Then he had six or seven pairs of dress shoes up against the wall in a nice little row. . . . And him? Sleeping. Laying there snoring like a six-month-old baby" (23). This wardrobe is unsuitable for work in the hot fields, but "Playboy Marcus," as Jim calls him, insists on wearing "a short-sleeve green shirt and a pair of brown pants. No hat—not even a handkerchief round his neck. He had on a pair of brown and white dress shoes" (25).

Deepening Marcus's comic humiliation are the homosexual field hands with whom he must work. Able to harvest more corn than any other men, they are stereotypically effeminate at other times. "In church on Sunday they shouted more than any two women," according to the narrator: "The funny thing about it, John and Freddie were ushers in church and they were supposed to look after the women when the women started shouting. But it always ended up with everybody else looking after John and Freddie. A couple of good-size women could hold down Freddie when he started shouting, but it always took seven or eight men to hold down big John" (25). On Marcus's first morning, they come to the field giggling, looking like "two little perfumed gals going to the dance" (33). It is Marcus, however, in his expensive shoes and work clothes, who ends up seeming less manly. He cannot match their pace at tossing ears of corn onto the trailer that Jim, driving the tractor, pulls along in front of them. At the end of the day, when Bonbon comes out on his horse, John and Freddie increase their speed and force Jim to drive faster so that Marcus, lagging behind, must stuff the corn from his row into the crocker sack Bonbon gives him. With the Cajun's arrival, the game played in the field is no longer a comic initiation of the tenderfoot. It becomes, rather, the brutal enslavement of a man. As Jim sees it, events exceed the punishment Marcus's vanity merits: "When I came home I saw Marcus laying on the gallery. He looked like somebody had beat him with an eight-plait whip and left him there to die" (43).

In retaliation, Marcus determines to seduce Pauline, Bonbon's mistress in the quarters. Accustomed to having any woman he chooses, he assumes that his conquest of her is assured. Pauline, however, publicly disgraces him by showing no interest in his advances. To the egotistical

Marcus, his decision to court Pauline is a personal reprisal against the overseer. To the other residents of the quarters, however, it is a reckless challenge to the racial hierarchy that will implicate all of them, hence the warning from Jim and the anxious silence of Pauline's neighbors when Marcus arrives at her gallery one evening. Here a stereotypically domineering wife's admonition to her husband provokes a smile that contrasts with the tension of the moment. Sitting on the porch they share with Pauline, Aunt Ca'line and Pa Bully must pretend for their own safety as if they witness nothing. Catching her husband "cutting his eyes toward the other side . . . where they had no business going" (61), she reproves him with her customary warning—"Mr. Grant"—just as she has been reprimanding him the last seven or eight years whenever he has given the slightest sign of noticing Bonbon during his visits to Pauline.

The fatal fight to which the novel builds is foreshadowed by a comic brawl Marcus starts at the house fair in the quarters on his first Saturday night. Valerie Babb has noted that, while serving no particular function in terms of developing the plot, this scene is "symbolically . . . a prelude to the chaos that will result from the random forces of interracial love within this society" (68). Moreover, it is an important turning point in Marcus's development. The proprietress, who has the house to herself only because Bonbon gets a cut of the profits, serves beer and gumbo to the gamblers and dancers, who find in this juke joint their only local entertainment. Marcus enters late, exhausted by the heavy work, angry about his unaccustomed powerlessness, and ready to release his pent-up frustration. The people, however, are wary, and their immediate silence makes him feel even more isolated. After he has a couple of drinks, his rage explodes. Without any provocation, he hits the closest person, who happens to be the toughest man at the poker table. Immediately, everyone present is trading blows in a free-for-all that is the most extended humorous episode in the novel.

This scene contrasts to literary works which evoke a racist laughter from violence directed against stereotypical black characters. Such humor appears frequently in the writings of antebellum Southern humorists, whose sketches were appearing in newspapers at the same time blackface minstrelsy was in vogue on the stage. However, there is an important difference. Unlike the humorists of the Old Southwest, Gaines has no white onlookers who find in the physical discomfort of blacks an amusing confirmation of the prejudiced view that they are sub-human. The brawl Marcus incites recalls the melee at Mrs. Turner's in *Their Eyes Were Watching God,* in which Zora Neale Hurston similarly renders physical discomfort humorously without evoking racist stereotypes. More complex than either of these, however, is the riot of the patients at the Golden Day in *Invisible Man,* in which Ralph Ellison plays the pandemonium in the bar against both Mr. Norton's and the narrator's mistaken notions of race and identity.

The comedy of the brawl in *Of Love and Dust* arises not out of the participants' race but rather from Gaines's technique as a writer—his skillful exaggeration, inversion, and pacing. Jim describes the fight from his point of view as an unwilling participant. He just wants to reach the door but keeps getting pulled back into the brawl, where he must finally use his fists to protect himself. When he grabs someone to keep from falling, the woman he clutches, thinking he is trying to take liberties with her, hits him until he finally drops to the floor. While he is down, "somebody picked up the tub of ice water that the beer had been in and dumped all that on my back" (104). Soon hot coals are knocked out of the stove onto the wet floor, and "the place was so full of steam and smoke you didn't know who was who now" (105). Such exaggerated confusion makes the scene humorous, as does the absence of serious consequences from the violence. The humor, however, is neither escapist nor incidental to the narrative. Its very extravagance underscores the significant reversal Marcus must make in his strategy for reclaiming his manhood. In just one week at Marshall, he learns to distrust direct physical confrontation, which he grew up thinking would assure him dominance over others. Now, he realizes a successful strategy of rebellion requires deception and the subversive powers of wit, after the fashion of the trickster in African-American folklore.

In a recent study of tricksters in antebellum black folklore, John W. Roberts argues that the African roots of the tradition explain why African Americans have considered the trickster to be a hero: "Despite the apparent rebelliousness of animal tricksters or even the brutality of their behavior in some tales, Africans had historically accepted the animal tricksters' characteristic actions as protecting their identity and values under certain types of situations" (21). Although tales of sacred tricksters did not continue to be passed down in antebellum America, stories existed about other tricksters that helped the slaves "maintain the value traditionally placed on native intelligence as a source of behaviors for protecting physical and social well-being" (35). These trickster tales did not offer "patterns of behavior capable of annihilating their real-life antagonists." Nevertheless, Roberts emphasizes, they "provide[d] a conception of behaviors which prevented physical and cultural annihilation" (43–44).

In contrast to the trickster's heroic possibilities, some nineteenth-century folk narratives in the John and Old Master tale cycle tell about the favorite slave's failure to outwit his owner, and they treat the disastrous consequences as humorous. As Roberts explains, "it is not surprising that as a 'trusty' of Old Master, John emerges as a numskull or flunky over whom Old Master triumphs in a number of tales. In these tales, John's blind allegiance to Old Master threatens both his well-being and, as often, other members of the community" (50). The stories of Master outfoxing John conform to a widespread folk narrative pattern known as "the trickster tricked" or "the biter bit." It has influenced literary humor in the South, most notably in fiction by the humorists of the Old Southwest, Mark Twain, and William Faulkner.

By structuring the narrative in *Of Love and Dust* so that the trickster is finally tricked himself, Gaines rejects Marcus as a champion of African-American rights. The young man acts with neither a full understanding of whites and their own ability to deceive nor a concern for the possible effects of his exploits on others in the quarters. Despite the sensible change from overt force to subversive craftiness in Marcus's strategy of reprisal, he never loses the self-centeredness that unfits him for leading an effective rebellion against racism. Unable to seduce Bonbon's black mistress, Marcus woos instead his wife, the lethargic and dissatisfied Louise. To him this cuckolding represents the ultimate repudiation of Bonbon and of Southern white culture, whose icon of the pure white woman is a token of its racial paranoia. However, the narrator, Jim, makes it clear that Louise is more than a willing participant. She, in fact, seduces Marcus, who, blinded by his rage, his ego, and his sexist view of women's limitations, cannot recognize her true, powerful role in establishing their relationship. Jim's early assessment of their growing interest in each other calls attention to the multiple comic reversals here: "But the funny thing about all this, Marcus didn't know Louise had been looking at him for a week already. If he had, I doubt if he would have wanted Louise. Because, you see, he wanted her only for revenge. He wanted to get to her, not her getting to him. . . . If they lynched him after, it wouldn't have meant a thing. Because, you see, they couldn't take away what he had got. No, he probably would have laughed at his lynchers" (116–17). By the end of the novel, Marcus is twice "the trickster tricked." Deceived by his apparent ease in gaining Louise's devotion, he tries to blackmail Marshall Hebert into providing them with a car and cash in order to run away from the plantation. But the owner turns the tables on him by informing Bonbon, who kills Marcus in a fight the reality of which is all the more grim after the slapstick comedy of the earlier brawl.

In contrast to this turn of events, in an early draft of the novel, Marcus and Louise drive away from the plantation, giving the narrative a comic ending. As Gaines has explained, Marcus was originally patterned after the trickster who could escape from difficult circumstances: "So he started bribing people; he started getting wine or whiskey or whatever at the grocery store. He knew they weren't going to kill him, so he went and got things on credit at the grocery store, and he started selling it to the people in the quarters. . . . He was something like my man, you know, Snopes, in 'Spotted Horses.' . . . He was playing all kinds of tricks on people" (Gaudet and Wooton 107). Gaines substantially reworked the narrative on the advice of his editor, E. L. Doctorow, because Marcus and Louise "escaped, but it was not working out. . . . The first part was tragic, but the second part was humorous." That humor came at the expense of Bonbon, who was doubly disgraced—by Marcus, who seduced his wife, and by Marshall Hebert, who condoned their liaison. In this version the narrative lacked balance because of the improbability of these reversals and the absence of effective reprisal by the white community. As the novel was published, however, it treats seriously the consequences of Marcus's personality and behavior. By following "the trickster tricked" pattern, it returns to whites the control of black lives, in conformity with the realities of race and power in rural south Louisiana at that time. Gaines would not be ready until later in his career to present whites as laughingstocks incapable of exacting revenge for their humiliation.

The published version of *Of Love and Dust* is, nevertheless, not without humor, even as the sense of impending doom grows. Gone are the lighthearted, escapist chuckles provoked by Marcus as trickster. Instead there are moments of laughter, touched with grim irony, that arise from the incongruous presence of humor in the frightening events of ordinary life. Thus Gaines tells a story true to the complexity of human experience. He recognizes that people's reactions to fear, even when they are authentic, may appear comic. This view challenges the demeaning implications of the kind of laughter that the "scared darky" stereotype has provoked in American popular culture. In three interesting ways, Gaines reinterprets this caricature so that it condemns, rather than supports, the dehumanizing ideology of racism.

Aunt Margaret, Louise's housekeeper, who is both afraid and angry because of the affair, can overhear the couple's energetic lovemaking in the bedroom as she keeps the young daughter Tite distracted. She reports on it in detail to Jim so that he will protect the community by stopping Marcus. Readers see the lovers through Aunt Margaret's eyes, or rather through her imagination; because of her strong feelings about the affair, she comically exaggerates their foreplay. "Looked like the whole place was coming apart, Aunt Margaret said. Looked like they overturned both the dresser and the armoire at the same time. Looked like Louise crawled under the bed and Marcus crawled under there after her; then halfway under he decided to stand up with the bed on his back and slam it against the wall" (181). The repetition of "Looked" ironically underscores the fact that Aunt Margaret can see nothing through the locked bedroom door. The sounds from the room, however, reverberate in her mind, creating a picture that matches the repercussions she anticipates the affair will have in that violent and segregated community. With firm control over tone, Gaines treats Aunt Margaret's immediate reaction with both the humor and the seriousness that are true to the complexity of fear. The first afternoon she hears the lovers in the bedroom, she hollers, "Come out of there, boy" and tries to break open the door, which has only a "little frail latch [that] would fly off even if Tite had hit that door hard enough" (159). But they have moved furniture in front of it. So when Aunt Margaret runs up against it with her shoulder, "like she had hit one of those oak trees out in the yard, she went falling back on the floor. 'What in the—.'" Ten more times she tries to break through, only to keep landing on the floor. At first she appears to be a slapstick comic taking a pratfall. Coming like a refrain after each of Marcus's seductive comments to the silent Louise is the comment "Aunt Margaret hit the door again. She hit it again, again, again" (160). Even though the action remains the same, the tone changes as she unflaggingly continues trying to intervene long after realizing she is too weak to do so. Thus Gaines moves the reader from laughter to empathy, affirming the appropriateness of Aunt Margaret's fear.

In contrast to Aunt Margaret, whose anger impels a physical reaction despite her fear, are two men whom fear incapacitates as events reach their tragic conclusion. Although the cowardice of both recalls the comic stereotype, they should be judged quite differently from each other. Derisive laughter is the appropriate response to Bishop, who has worked in the front house as Hebert's butler his whole life and selfishly wants to safeguard the plantation system. Befitting the caricature, he is "a little man with a shining bald head" and "steel-rim glasses with thick lenses" (213) that make "his eyes look bigger and sadder than they really were" (218). As he watches Hebert and Marcus come closer and closer to cutting a deal, he is paralyzed by anxiety about the consequences of Marcus's lack of deference to whites. A drinking glass slips from Butler's hand and breaks on the floor when he notices something ominous. And when Marcus comes up to the kitchen one evening to make final plans for his departure with Louise, Bishop is too terror-struck to open the door. He slumps to the floor when Hebert walks into the room, shutting his eyes and hiding "his face behind the basket that still hung on his arm" while the two men stand there talking (236). As tension mounts on the evening Marcus intends to leave, Bishop feels so weak that "he should have been laying down with a cold towel on his forehead" (255).

Similarly alarmed into exaggerated passivity is Sun Brown, accidental witness to Marcus's murder: Brown "ran all the way home. He didn't tell anybody what he had seen. He wouldn't tell anybody what he had seen for a whole week. He wouldn't even come out of his house" (276). "Scared speechless" is a frequent description of the comic black stereotype, yet Brown's silence in this context provokes no scornful laughter. Vengeful brutality against innocent blacks is a reality in this community, and his life could well be in jeopardy. His retreat into privacy, in contrast to Butler's self-indulgent wish for seclusion, arouses sympathy rather than satiric laughter. Brown is an important reinterpretation of the comic caricature because his response to fear, despite its extremity, remains a fully human one. It does not distort him into a buffoon. By presenting Brown's stereotypical behavior in a sympathetic rather than a humorous light, Gaines concludes *Of Love and Dust* with a firm refusal to let the coercive force of racist caricature limit the range of emotions and actions attributable to black characters in fiction. This book demonstrates technical skill at incorporating into serious fiction a variety of situations and characters familiar from popular and folk humor. It shows Gaines's innovative control over these materials, especially the humorous stereotype of the frightened black, which he has transformed into an effective tool for satirizing racism as well as for depicting the humanity of powerless African Americans.

Lacking the exuberant range of humorous scenes and characters found in *Of Love and Dust,* Gaines's next novel nevertheless presents an essentially comic rather than tragic view of race relations. Instead of depicting the futility of protest, *Miss Jane Pittman* ends with the hope that it will subvert white domination. Gaines communicates this vision through scenes of comic humiliation and through his narrator's own cheerful self-mockery. Miss Jane's self-deprecating humor paradoxically affirms the security of her own identity and respected status within the community.[2] The incongruous reversals in this book, unlike the ones in *Of Love and Dust,* do not imply the weakness of African Americans. From her point of view as storyteller, such incidents deserve full-throated laughter because they can compromise neither her dignity nor the strength of her people.

Miss Jane's sauciness throughout life toward those in authority, whether black or white, mocks racial injustice. Yet as storyteller, she constructs her reminiscences in order to satirize also the foolishness of her own impetuous speech and rash behavior. Such doubleness is particularly noticeable in the manner in which Miss Jane narrates incidents from her childhood. For example, when the master of the plantation announces to his gathered slaves that they are free, she butts in to assert that if he just points north, "I'll show y'all where to go" (11). The black driver, bewildered by the celebration going on around him, tells her to be quiet, and she talks back: "You ain't nothing but Nothing." Twice he knocks her down, and still she grabs a hoe, ready to attack him again: "Nigger, say your prayers. Maker, here you come." Only Uncle Isom can keep her from pursuing this unequal opponent. Later, on her journey north with young Ned, she encounters a white woman returning from Texas with her slaves. Jane saucily contradicts the woman's advice as well as her assertion that she does not beat her slaves, thus arousing the anger of the black driver Nicodemus. He refers to Jane as "little dried-up," tells her to "mind how you talk about white folks," and stands by rubbing his knuckles, ready to beat her should his mistress give permission (27–28). His uncomfortable and unaccustomed inability to punish a black child who talks back adds comedy to a scene in which Miss Jane mocks also her own foolhardiness in heading for Ohio. Impudently, the young girl rejects the woman's offer of assistance, lacking the wisdom at the time to distinguish between asserting her independence and protecting herself. As storyteller, Miss Jane clearly ridicules her own willfulness in trusting to illusions that put her and Ned in danger.

Miss Jane creates laughter at her own expense by the way she narrates several incidents in which white people perceive her as a stereotypically comic black. While her employers' smiles evoke racism's demeaning ideology, she can nevertheless laugh at herself because of the universal comic incongruity in these events. In her sixties, she is the victim of a dangerous practical joke planned by Robert Samson's black son Timmy with the help of his white half-brother Tee Bob. They scare her gentle horse when she is out riding for pleasure one evening, and she holds on tight as Rags runs through the field, down the back road, and up to the front gate: "Of course, I wanted to fall off, but fall where? . . . If I had hit that ground traveling a hundred miles an hour I would have busted open like a watermelon. So I didn't fall; I held on tight" (142). The scene recalls sketches by the humorists of the Old Southwest in which runaway horses produce comic chaos and practical jokes against the respectable abound. When told of the boys' rascality, Samson does not punish them. Greatly amused, he instead expresses disappointment at not having seen the distress of his servant. According to Miss Jane, he wanted to know "did my eyes get big and white, did they go up and down in my head? Could Miss Amma Dean hear my teeth hitting together?" (144).

From Miss Jane's point of view as storyteller, her self-deprecating humor is highly ironic; it enhances the racist comic stereotypes she uses in her narrative rather than diminishes her own dignity. When in middle age Miss Jane is first ordered to leave the fields and work in the big house, the elderly cook Molly, she recalls, unwilling to be replaced, "pitched me back outside [of the kitchen]. I fell flat on my face, my hands covered with chicken and guinea stuff" (85). Miss Jane does not realize that some of the "chicken stuff" is also sticking to the side of her face. When she goes into the dining room where the family is eating, one of the daughters tries to let her know but is too genteel to speak plainly and thus spare her servant embarrassment: "I could see her mouth working like she wanted to say something, then she pressed her lips tight. Then her nose worked a little bit like she was smelling something. All this time she was looking straight in my eye. She wanted me to guess what she didn't want tell me" (86). Only when one of the younger children yells "Caw-caw" does Miss Jane understand: "Then everybody else at the table looked at me, and all of them bust out laughing. I touched the spot they was looking at, and it was there, all right." She brings the scene to a close thus, ending abruptly but not ambiguously. To the white family around the table, this new servant comically fits the racist caricature of dirty, smelly blacks, just as they probably expected. To Miss Jane, on the other hand, this incident, narrated so as to emphasize its humor rather than any personal embarrassment, cannot compromise her inherent dignity. At a deeper level than they could understand, the story as she tells it prompts laughter at the expense of whites who judge blacks not on the basis of enduring inner qualities but rather on surface features, which may well occasionally be humorously inappropriate. Furthermore, it suggests that Miss Jane's sympathy for the misfortunes of others comes from a good-humored understanding of her own trials.

Miss Jane Pittman ends with a comic inversion of the racial hierarchy that has prevailed throughout the main character's long life. In contrast to the end of *Of Love and Dust,* the irony of the final scene is optimistic. The people from the quarters, gathered alongside the road to go to Bayonne for a civil rights demonstration, listen as Robert Samson commands them to go home. Miss Jane, who has talked back to him for years, now finally translates her sauciness into action, the political act of leading her people: "Me and Robert looked at each other there a long time, then I went by him" (246). This frail, century-old woman leaves him standing powerless and undoubtedly shamefaced in front of his tenants. As commentators have noted on the basis of details in the introduction, Samson does not evict her for this act of defiance, as he has done others. His authority, once lost, is unrecoverable. Unlike Miss Jane, he lacks the spirit of self-deprecating humor by which the dispossessed mock their disgrace and paradoxically establish their dignity. Her stories and narrative style are entertaining, but her humor is not escapist. Rather, it is a strategy of defiance that envisions a world made new by the truly comic power of subversion.

In *A Gathering of Old Men,* Gaines portrays militant protest for the first time, but the armed struggle against racism in this novel occasions a good deal of ironic humor, despite the ensuing deaths and injuries. The old men, who their whole lives have suffered the humiliation of allowing whites to think of them as docile Sambo types, gather in front of Mathu's house in the quarters as tricksters, ready now to subvert white authority by cunning. By evening, however, they have gained the courage to shed the trickster role, rely on their physical strength, and shoot back at the band of Cajuns and rednecks who attack them to avenge Beau Boutan's murder. During the unusually warm October afternoon, the old men rely on wit to thwart Sheriff Mapes and the legal system he represents, but the vigilantes challenge them to a physical confrontation that is the final test of their newfound manhood. By adopting both of these strategies of resistance, the black men succeed in overthrowing all their oppressors in richly comic scenes. Victims of public scorn, the whites lose their capability to maintain the community's tradition of white supremacy.

Miss Jane closes her autobiography by quickly and effectively humbling Robert Samson, a brave act congruent with the strong and self-reliant image her narrative voice projects. *A Gathering,* on the other hand, offers an extended depiction of the comic humiliation of white authority figures. In it, the irony of elderly men wresting control from whites is heightened because they have previously always acquiesced to racism's emasculation of them and, therefore, seem at first totally unfit for such a heroic task. Yet on this day they transcend the Sambo label they have accepted for years from white society. Instead of being laughingstocks themselves, the people in Mathu's yard ridicule the incongruous behavior of two stereotypical characters—one black, the other white. These men provide comic relief so that tension mounts effectively as the narrative progresses. Moreover, they are the points of reference readers need within the text in order to measure the growth of the old men and the debasement of Mapes.

Driving into the quarters to see what has happened, Miss Merle mistakenly concludes from the deserted houses that the people are behaving "just like frightened little bedbugs" (15). In reality, the men have gathered with their shotguns, each claiming to be the murderer. Only the unarmed Reverend Jameson, a "pathetic, bald, weary-looking little man," according to the white journalist Lou Dimes (61), fits the caricature of a frightened black, and the responses to his outbursts humorously disparage him. Jameson's frantic requests for the crowd to disperse and "the tears running down his face" (55), which Clatoo observes several times, contrast with the quiet resolve of the others, who try to ignore him as they wait for Mapes to arrive. Irritated, Rooster finally wonders aloud, "You think I ought to shoot him, Dirty Red?" The answer is to "let him slide. . . . He might change 'fore the shooting start" (56). Rooster asks the question a second time, when his wife Beulah, angry that Jameson has encouraged Mapes to end his interrogation and simply arrest the men, challenges the preacher to fight: "Come on, come on, you bootlicker. . . . You think Mapes knocked you down—you just come on here. Old possum-looking fool" (106). Dirty Red's answer is as demeaning as her epithets: "Let [the boy] Snookum beat him if he open his mouth again." The third time Jameson begins carrying on, however, Dirty Red does not even wait for the question to give his long-delayed assent. When the rednecks attack at dark, Jameson "over by the house [starts] calling on God to have mercy on all of us" (198). Coot says he "heard Dirty Red call to Rooster to go shoot Jameson and shut him up. Jameson musta heard it too. There wasn't another word from him." These men scorn the preacher because he does not come to master his fear as they do. While being interrogated by the sheriff in front of the others, Jameson seems "about to have a heart attack, he was so afraid" (70). Unlike them, he cannot look Mapes directly in the face and even falls flat on his back—twice—when Mapes slaps him. As Dimes points out, they show him no sympathy there on the ground, and their recollections satirize him as an embarrassing fool, a reminder of their former selves.

Just as Jameson is a gauge by which to measure the old men's manhood, the deputy Griffin is the index of the humiliating irony in Mapes's loss of authority. Although Mapes has only scorn for his ineffectual deputy, the people in the quarters will no longer obey the sheriff either. Contributing to the satire of Mapes is the physical incongruity between the two men. In Rooster's way of talking, the deputy is a "little no-butt nothing" (94), and Mapes is "too fat to catch him" when he starts backing away from the sheriff, afraid to follow the order to pull Candy off Mathu's porch (175). Dimes, with a reporter's eye for precise detail, notes that Griffin, in his early twenties, is about five feet eight inches tall and weighs probably 140 pounds. Mapes is in his late sixties and, like the former LSU basketball forward Dimes, "six three, six four, but he outweighed me by a hundred pounds at least" (63). An imposing man, Mapes is accustomed to relying on physical intimidation when questioning blacks. The deputy, however, is intimidated by the group that is waiting when they drive up. Afraid, he reaches back into the car for a gun but puts it back at Mapes's command. Dimes satirizes the spineless Griffin as a comic braggart who childishly loves to swagger. As the afternoon wears on and Griffin feels certain he is in no danger, he starts to bully the people with empty talk: "Left just to me, that old coon woulda been in jail an hour ago. And I'd shoot the first one tried to get him loose" (95). Knowing him to be harmless, however, the people mock him without fear of reprisal. They tell Mapes to "warn that boy . . . if you want him around much longer" (110).

Mapes himself shows nothing but disgust for his assistant. As Dimes observes, "you could see Mapes looking at him as if he were wondering if he actually needed Griffin the rest of the day" (125). Nevertheless, the day's events prove the sheriff's own sense of superiority to be as illusory as Griffin's, marking him, ironically, with the same stigma of impotence. The people sit still when he orders them to return home. He becomes red-faced in exasperation while interrogating one man after another. And at the end of the afternoon, right before Charlie returns to acknowledge his responsibility for the murder, the old men even laugh out loud at the sheriff's threats. Thus when Luke Will's gang attacks, it is fitting that Mapes is the first one wounded by a bullet. Young Snookum sees him "sitting out there on the walk, trying to get up. Rocking this way, that way like one of them big old scoiling kettles—trying his best to get up. But he was too big to make it by himself, and I sure wasn't going out there to help him" (200). Defeated, Mapes deputizes the astonished Dimes and relinquishes his command, a formality that events have rendered absurd.

Having outwitted the law, the men must still confront the community's self-appointed enforcers of white justice, whose assault tests their courage. The gunfight is the culminating irony of the narrative, suggesting the far-reaching effects of their miraculous transformation. In the morning they had cut across the field to Mathu's, as Cherry says, one "shuffling along, head down," another carrying his gun like a stick of wood, and another "nearly dragging his gun in the dust. . . . Neither one of them looked like he was ready for battle, that's for sure" (42–43). Later in the afternoon, Mapes orders Uncle Billy to prove that he can shoot, but "the gun was shaking so much you would have thought it was one of those divining rods that had just discovered water," according to Dimes (81). That night, however, they readily return fire, having surreptitiously loaded the guns that were originally intended only to baffle Mapes's investigation. They are elated by their courage, and Coot, the World War I veteran in his moth-eaten uniform, voices their satisfaction: "I didn't know the last time I had felt so good. Not since I was a young man in the war. Lord, have mercy, Jesus" (198). The five rednecks, on the other hand, arrive in drunken confidence but feel no gratification when they start shooting. The youngest, only seventeen, is terrified when he is winged by a bullet and will not stop "sniveling like some kinda gut-hanging dog," according to one of his companions (202). He is not, however, the only one who is afraid. Desperate for some assurance they will escape from their own raid, Sharp suggests that "Mapes won't let them niggers shoot us down like dogs." But the ringleader, Luke Will, clearly understands the new power relations between the races: "Mapes ain't in charge no more, Sharp. . . . We got to deal with Charlie now" (206). They are now on the offensive, a deeply humiliating position in their eyes because of the self-satisfied authority they maintained for so long over their African-American neighbors.

A *Gathering* concludes with a hilarious courtroom scene in which all the combatants, black and white, appear before Judge Reynolds, who "has a great sense of humor" (212). Readers, however, laugh at more than what the narrator, Dimes, relates, for his own words prove him to be an unwitting fool. Despite his sympathy for racial tolerance, he still does not comprehend the revolutionary implications of the events he witnessed in the quarters. Dimes relates the final episode from a condescending point of view, reducing all of the characters to simplistic, humorous figures. His account calls to mind the antebellum Southern humorists, who also focused on courtroom scenes. Moreover, Dimes adopts the same urbane perspective that emphasized their narrators' distance from the antics of the rural folk. Although the old men have earned dignity, Dimes and his fellow journalists at the trial think of them only as comic caricatures: "Every now and then one of the old black fellows, arm in sling, or forehead bandaged, knowing he was in the public eye, would go just a little overboard describing what had happened. Besides, he would use all nicknames for his compatriots— Clabber, Dirty Red, Coot, Chimley, Rooster. This would bring the court to laughing, especially the news people, who took the whole thing as something astonishing but not serious. No one else laughed nearly as much as the news people did" (212). This passage recalls Mat's comment earlier in the novel about nicknames. Chimley's friends call him that because he is smaller and blacker than they: "He didn't mind his friends calling him Chimley, 'cause he knowed we didn't mean nothing. But he sure didn't like them white folks calling him Chimley. He was always telling them that his daddy had named him Robert Louis Stevenson Banks, not Chimley. But all they did was laugh at him, and they went on calling him Chimley anyhow" (40). Although the racial hierarchy on the Marshall plantation has been completely reversed, the journalists have missed the story, and the last laugh is on them.[3] The old men's nicknames so neatly fit racist notions of black inferiority that the reporters are unable to think deeply about what they are witnessing. Although they are supposedly professionals, able to write about events objectively, they cannot break through stereotypical patterns to see the revolution in these men's character, their change from comic Sambos to complex humans.

The old men clearly revel in their prominence on the witness stand, where no brutality coerces them to testify. Mapes, on the other hand, is reticent in this public forum. On the third and last day, he must unwillingly attest to his humiliation, bringing into the light of day what only a few saw that night. Increasing his pain, the district attorney demands that he speak loudly so that all can hear his admission: "The whole fight, I was sitting on my ass in the middle of the walk. Luke Will shot me, and I was sitting on my ass in the middle of the walk" (213). At this point the laughter reaches its fullest pitch, and Mapes "stayed red all day, and would probably stay red for years to come."[4] Dimes correctly and effectively depicts the mortifying reversal of the sheriff's status but not the contrasting elevation of the elderly black men. Unlike Luke Will, Dimes does not yet recognize that they have emancipated themselves from the stereotypes still fettering his perceptions and that their dignity will compel him to change as well. He himself appears all the more foolish because of the thoroughness with which he satirizes Mapes. Dimes does not know that the men have "seen it" (208), in Charlie's words, and that their collective vision promises to make the world a radically new place for everyone.

As this discussion has shown, laughter is integral to Gaines's dramatization of the deep ironies in race relations. He has said that "humor and joking are part of change" (Gaudet and Wooton 22). Thus the laughter that occurs throughout his novels does not deny the intensity of racial conflict but rather provokes people to see each other, and themselves, differently. It is a weapon against racist misperceptions of weakness and power, of foolishness and dignity.

Nathan Huggins has argued that in the early twentieth century Negro ethnic theater was crippled because blackface minstrelsy had so strongly influenced the popular American imagination that writers were unable to deviate from the "Negro theatrical type" it had established (248). Gaines's fiction exhibits a creative surpassing of this barrier, erected by white popular culture, to a full, realistic representation of the complexities of African-American life in art. He has found ways of taking some of the stock characters and humorous situations that are part of minstrelsy's legacy and incorporating them with integrity into fiction with a social message that critiques the racist notions out of which that popular art form grew and which it in turn perpetuated. Gaines's humor originates in a double vision that ridicules conventional stereotypes of African Americans by revealing their complex humanity. His comic spirit holds forth the promise that, by possessing such a liberating double vision of themselves, they will become effective agents of change in society.

Notes

1. For background on black stereotypes in minstrel shows see Lott and Toll. In discussing the actor Thomas Dartmouth Rice and the development of the Jim Crow stage character, Dorman explains that the humor "lay in the incongruity of its situations and language, incongruity heightened by skillful burlesque of qualities believed characteristic of Negro speech, appearance, and behavior. . . . the burlesque was accepted as the real. The caricature became the stereotype" (121). Boskin traces the Sambo character from minstrelsy through the 1940s. For information on black stereotypes in American film through the 1980s, see Bogle.

2. Jones offers a corresponding interpretation of Miss Jane's character in a discussion of her speech patterns: "Miss Jane is neither a folk comedian nor a pathetic figure. Her language contributes to rather than detracts from the force of her personality" (165).

3. Mapes, on the other hand, recognizes the demise of the old hierarchies by

addressing Charlie as Mr. Biggs. J. Griffin has noted that Mapes does so "with sincerity," from the point of view of the journalist Lou Dimes, who is on the scene at the Marshall plantation. The renaming is significant because Charlie "has become a man, and that attainment has been recognized by the officer of the law" (95).

4. Sheriff Mapes's humiliation recalls the remarks made to followers by James Forman, Executive Secretary of the Student Nonviolent Coordinating Committee, following a demonstration in Selma in 1963: "We ought to be happy today . . . because [Sheriff] Jim Clark never saw that many niggers down there! . . . Yeah, there was Jim Clark, rubbin' his head and his big fat belly; he was shuffling today like *we* used to!" (Zinn 165).

Old-Fashioned Modernism: "The Changing Same" in *A Lesson Before Dying*

Valerie Babb

The term "modernism," broadly defined as a severing with traditions of the past and a quest for new forms of expression, seems particularly apt for describing a key element of African-American creativity. As peoples displaced from their own lands and cultures and forced to adapt to the culture of the United States, African Americans have a long history of revising and recreating, of taking alien conventions and transforming them into embodiments of their traditions and identities. In *Black Music*, Amiri Baraka coins the phrase "the changing same" to describe the relationship between tradition and evolving individual expression in African-American music (180–211). This coinage also applies to other forms of modernist African-American creativity that juxtapose the conventional and the novel. From creating new interpretations of the Bible, for example, a text often used to justify their oppression, to wedding the traditional Christian lexicon to the music and rhythms of Africa and creating the spirituals, African Americans have ensured their cultural survival by naturalizing foreign and sometimes hostile forms. In this sense they can be viewed as modernists who constantly revise established constructs to suit their needs.

One author whose work clearly exhibits the modernist character of African-American expression is Ernest J. Gaines. His fictive art consists of adapting literary conventions and making them suitable for voicing the experiences of rural Louisiana, the world that is the quintessence of his writings. Although Gaines frequently breaks with established conventions of novel writing, he does so to replace them not with new forms but with old ones steeped in the traditions of African-American oral culture. In his most recent novel, *A Lesson Before Dying,* Gaines's "old-fashioned" modernism is evident in both his unconventional narrative technique and his recreation of cultural history.

In its most basic sense, modernism often implies an alienation from traditional elements of Western culture and art. Notable breaks with traditional modes of expression can be found in post-World War I writers as varied as James Joyce, T. S. Eliot, and Langston Hughes. This epoch of change gave rise to the modernist impulse, and its impact on the imaginative mind is eloquently described by Houston A. Baker, Jr., in *Modernism and the Harlem Renaissance*: "Regardless of their strategies for confronting it . . . it was *change*—a profound shift in what could be taken as unquestionable assumptions about the meaning of human life—that moved those artists whom we call 'moderns' " (5).

New creative strategies emerged as writers sought to find forms appropriate for describing the experience of alienation and upheaval fostered by the war. In *The Waste Land,* for example, Eliot experiments with forms he felt were more capable of rendering the disorder he saw around him. Similarly, writers and poets of the Harlem Renaissance undertook the creation of artistic styles that drew their inspiration from heretofore devalued or ignored African-American sources. Hughes, for instance, in seeking to represent the pulse of his African-American community more appropriately, used elements of the blues and be-bop to inform the rhythms of poems such as "Dream Boogie" and "Same in Blues."[1]

In addition to breaking with forms of the past, modernism also embraces a break with accepted history, a questioning of the merit of old traditions and a consideration of the new ones that might possibly take their place. Many thinkers questioned the certainties that were assumed to be the bedrock of religious and social organization, in particular practices of racial inequality. The new racial order was eloquently articulated by scholars such as Alain Locke in *The New Negro* and W. E. B. Du Bois in *The Souls of Black Folks.*

These major attributes of modernism, a break from accepted history and an experimentation with artistic forms, characterize all the fiction of Gaines. He displaces traditional modes of ordering a novel with conventions rooted in African-American orality. He rejects the specious history of African Americans created by a culture that has sought to devalue them. Yet, modernist though he may be, in many ways Gaines is also a traditionalist. While he breaks with a history that devalues African-American culture, he substitutes in its place a rich communal folk history that validates and celebrates that culture. He stretches the possibilities of the novel by experimenting with forms that are rooted in the oral tradition of African Americans in remembered stories and shared histories.

The stories, values, and customs of Gaines's childhood Pointe Coupee Parish community influence each of his works, linking one to the next. Characters from Gaines's own youth—the elders of the parish, Cajuns who often have a tense relationship with African Americans, mulattos or Creoles of color who define their racial identity as neither black nor white, young black men who can no longer live within the racist protocol of their confining community, individuals who through personal dignity are capable of heroic acts—people all his literature and interact against a backdrop that recreates his native parish with striking verisimilitude. With a touch of old-fashioned modernism, he molds the occasions of their lives into an enduring fiction.

A Lesson Before Dying is no exception to the patterns Gaines has previously established in his fiction. Though set in the late 1940s and early 1950s, the narrative depicts racial relations that give it the same timelessness of all Gaines's texts. The novel chronicles the experiences of twenty-one-year-old Jefferson and his former teacher, Grant Wiggins, as both await Jefferson's pending execution for killing a Cajun shopkeeper. In the summation at Jefferson's trail, his defense lawyer pleads his client's innocence not on the basis of facts, which might prove that racist presumptions rather than evidence lead to Jefferson's conviction, but rather by likening his intellectual capabilities to those of a hog. This reference sets the novel's theme in motion, as Jefferson's godmother, Miss Emma, enlists Grant's help to persuade Jefferson that he is not an animal. She asks Grant to give him a lesson in dignity to prove the lawyer's remark untrue. The novel delineates both the evolving relationship of Grant and Jefferson in the final months of Jefferson's life and the impact Jefferson's sentence and mental condition have on the rest of his community.

From its earliest pages, the book reveals Gaines's modernist touch. Through questioning traditional histories and values, he discredits the defense attorney's racist assumptions and creates a nontraditional narrative strategy that explores issues of history, race, and caste. The lawyer's summation itself has all the earmarks of dogma used to devalue African Americans:

> Gentlemen of the jury, look at him. . . . do you see a man sitting here? Look at the shape of this skull, this face as flat as the palm of my hand— look deeply into those eyes. Do you see a modicum of intelligence? Do you see anyone here who could plan a murder. . . ? A cornered animal to strike quickly out of fear, a trait inherited from his ancestors in the deepest jungle of blackest Africa—yes, yes that he can do—but to plan? . . . What you see here is a thing that acts on command. A thing to hold the handle of a plow. . . . Mention the names of Keats, Byron, Scott, and see whether the eyes will show one moment of recognition. Ask him to . . . quote one passage from the Constitution or the Bill of Rights. . . . What justice would there be to take this life? . . . Why, I would just as soon put a hog in the electric chair as this. (7–8)

In these remarks Gaines condenses many common tenets used to justify maintaining African Americans in an inferior social status. The attorney's reference to the shape of Jefferson's skull recalls theories of phrenology popularized in the nineteenth century and used to argue that Africans and hence African Americans were not the cognitive equals of whites; the reference to the animalistic tendencies of those from "blackest Africa" recalls the persistent perceptions of blacks as no more than savages or beasts; describing Jefferson as a commodity conjures the history of slavery, during which African Americans were regarded as chattel; the allusions to Byron, Keats, and Scott evoke the tradition of literary creation from which African Americans were excluded because they were forbidden to read or write; and last, the mention of the Bill of Rights and the Constitution invokes the systematic denial of political enfranchisement to African Americans. These references represent a history of degradation that Jefferson's story is meant to repudiate. Toward the end of the novel, Grant says to Jefferson, "Do you know what a myth is? . . . A myth is an old lie that people believe in. White people believe that they're better than anyone else on earth—and that's a myth. The last thing they ever want is to see a black man stand, and think, and show that common humanity that is in us all. It would destroy their myth" (192). It is the aim of *A Lesson* to reveal the fiction of racial myths.

The setting of the novel reflects the legacy of the racial untruths the book seeks to subvert. Bayonne, a rural parish seat, is the locale, as it is, for all of Gaines's works except *In My Father's House*. It is a segregated city of six thousand, almost evenly split between black and white. It has a courthouse with a statue of a Confederate hero; a white Catholic church, a black Catholic church; a white movie theater, a black movie theater; a white elementary school, and a black elementary school. Situated in the rural areas are the Pichot plantation and the small tenant plots farmed by blacks, institutions that have essentially remained unchanged since the time of slavery. The challenge in *A Lesson* is to place these racial histories in a new context. Through the characters, Gaines offers revisionist interpretations of history and current events, and the composite of these views makes new meanings out of old forms and traditions.

The transformation from old to new is filtered through the eyes of Grant Wiggins, a somewhat existentialist character with tenuous ties to his past in the quarters. He is disconnected from members of his community because his values have become very different from theirs. He reminds readers of Gaines's earlier characters such as Jackson Bradley in *Catherine Carmier* and Marcus Payne in *Of Love and Dust*, those whose education—formal or otherwise—makes it impossible for them to inhabit the world they once knew.

Grant has gone to college and has returned to teach in the church that doubles as a schoolhouse on weekdays. Though he has a genuine affection for his students, his Tante Lou, and the elders of his community, he clearly feels apart from them and in some ways trapped by them. As he looks at his students chopping wood to warm the school, he questions his effectiveness as a teacher and reveals his frustration: "What am I doing? . . . They are acting exactly as the old men did earlier. They are fifty years younger, maybe more, but doing the same thing those old men did who never attended school a day in their lives. Is it just a vicious circle? Am I doing anything?" (62). Grant straddles the old and the new in balancing his education with his knowledge of the history of the quarters, in his affection for the community and his desire to flee it, and now in his role as Jefferson's former teacher, who will ultimately become a student himself, transformed by Jefferson's final steps toward personal dignity.

From Grant's perspective, which looks at once forward and backward, we come to know the community and its changing values. In the early scenes, racial relationships seem to conform to the Southern status quo of the 1940s. When Miss Emma goes to the landowner Henri Pichot to enlist his aid in making arrangements for Grant to see Jefferson in the parish jail, she and Grant must enter through the back door of his house. It is only her service to his family over the years that gains her an audience, and during the interchange between employer and former servant, Grant chafes at the rigid class and racial castes that have not changed. When asked by Pichot's maid whether he desires something to eat while they are kept waiting for an audience, Grant thinks, "I would not eat at Henri Pichot's kitchen table. I had come through that back door against my will, and it seemed that he and the sheriff were doing everything they could to humiliate me even more by making me wait on them. Well, I had to put up with that because of those in the quarter, but I damned sure would not add hurt to injury by eating at his kitchen table" (45–46).

Similar degradations are part of Grant's teaching experience. His students can attend classes for only the five and a half months from April to October when they are not needed to work the fields. When the school-district superintendent, Dr. Joseph Morgan, visits Grant's class, Morgan's apparent indifference is evident as he focuses less on the state of the children's academic education than on their personal hygiene and their flag drills. When Grant points out that he doesn't have the necessary materials to teach effectively, or even money to buy the toothbrushes Morgan seems to think are so essential, Morgan responds, "Can't they work? . . . Look at all the pecan trees. . . . Get them off their lazy butts, they can make enough for a dozen toothbrushes in one evening" (57–58). Grant inhabits a world where he is "supposed to grin" (47), is supposed to say "don't" instead of "doesn't" when using the third-person singular (48), and is considered "a little too smart for [his] own good" (49). He has witnessed his aunt, Miss Emma, and most others in the quarters work for whites for years without gratification or respect. These combined humiliations make Grant's greatest challenge avoiding both self-hate and contempt for his people, a fate which has befallen his former teacher, Matthew Antoine, a man who feels superior to any man blacker than he: "Those five and a half months you spend in that church each year are just a waste of your time. . . . You'll see that it'll take more than five and a half months to wipe away—peel—scrape away the blanket of ignorance that has been plastered and replastered over those brains in the past three hundred years" (64). These archaic social relationships cannot maintain themselves, however, and the transformation of Jefferson—from a youth who says of himself, "I'm a old hog" (83), to a young man who at the end of the novel bids Grant to "tell them im strong tell them im a man" (234)— illustrates inevitable change. Each session with Jefferson causes Grant to shift his attention away from the negative appraisals whites have used to degrade blacks to the ways in which blacks have been able to sustain their dignity. Eventually, as Grant reconnects with his traditions and history, he sees in them new meanings appropriate to his present life.

The change in Grant is depicted gradually through his ability to see his community in a new light. In a barroom gathering, Gaines shows the power of intraracial pride to change Grant's perceptions through the impact of orality. As he sits watching a group of older men reliving the escapades of Jackie Robinson, we note the power of storytelling to connect Grant to his people and make him see them in a new light:

> From where I stood, about halfway down the bar, all I could hear was Jackie this and Jackie that. Nothing about any of the other players. . . .
> I sipped my beer slowly while listening to them. And they were very good. They could recall everything Jackie had done in the past two years. . . . One of the men backed away from the bar to demonstrate how slow the pitcher was in throwing the ball. . . . Now the old man became Jackie— not running, but showing the motion of someone running. . . .
> Listening to them, I could remember back to the time before Jackie . . . when it was Joe Louis that everyone talked about. . . .
> I was only seventeen then, but I could remember it, every bit of it—the warm evening, the people, the noise, the pride I saw in those faces. (87–89)

Although this experience reawakens Grant's dormant pride in his people, in their history, and in their stories, it is not until he is able to balance his old world with the new one opened to him through his formal education that he sees the possibility for enacting real change.

Still seated at the bar, Grant recalls attending a lecture by a visiting Irish professor that first exposes him to the universality of human experience. The lecturer mentions James Joyce's "Ivy Day in the Committee Room,"[2] a story that reveals how talking about politics effects self-actualization for people largely marginalized by the world of policy-makers. After reading the story, Grant comments,

> I read the story and reread the story, but I still could not find the universality that the little Irishman had spoken of. . . . It was not until years later that I saw what he meant. I had gone to bars, to barbershops; I had stood on street corners, and I had gone to many suppers there in the quarter. But I had never really listened to what was being said. Then I began to listen, to listen closely to how they talked about their heroes, how they talked about the dead and about how great the dead had once been. I heard it everywhere. (90)

The fusion of histories and traditions in this barroom scene is characteristic of Gaines. It underscores his belief that knowledge of one's own history is vital to a healthy identity, but it also underscores his appreciation of the interconnectedness of human existence, of parallel human experiences that transcend races and cultures. The more Grant sees the similarities shared by all, the more he is able to create a new context for his and Jefferson's understanding of the racial dynamics that rendered Jefferson's trial a corruption of justice and make his impending execution inevitable. The more Grant's belief in human endurance is renewed, the more he is able to discover a means of helping a man in Jefferson's position.

Gaines's emphasis on the recreation of past racial and cultural histories is complemented by his treatment of religion and spirituality in the novel. Grant's psychic development suggests that old beliefs and traditions must be rethought, and one among them is religion. Just as Grant must transform his relationship to his community's social history, so too must he transform his relationship to its spiritual traditions. Although his aunt, Miss Emma, and many of the older members in the quarters can draw strength from their religion, Grant cannot believe as they do. He hears the " 'termination songs" sung by the elders in church every Sunday, he puts on the yearly Christmas pageant with the schoolchildren, but still he cannot wholly believe. Watching the children during the pageant, he notes resignedly that "the minister had offered the same prayer as always, Christmas or Sunday. The same people wore the same old clothes and sat in the same places. Next year it would be the same, and the year after that, the same again" (151). His battle with religious customs that seem to have no meaning in his life is represented in a manner to be found in other of Gaines's stories, as an ongoing tension between a young prodigal and an older minister. This war of wills recalls a similar one in "A Long Day in November," in which a father, Eddie, concludes that the aid of a hoodoo woman is more effective than the aid of the minister. It is also reminiscent of a scene in "The Sky Is Gray" in which the young protagonist, Sonny, overhears a debate between a minister and a student in the dentist's waiting room.

In *A Lesson*, the minister is Reverend Mose Ambrose, "a simple, devoted believer" (101) who wants Grant to "minister" not only to Jefferson's dignity but also to his soul. Although Reverend Ambrose sees Grant as a backslider who has lost his faith, and although Grant sees the minister as an archaic emissary of an impotent religion, it is actually the minister who shows Grant that to be effective, all beliefs, whether they are secular or religious, must stem from an understanding of the human experience they address. In an exchange that caps the ongoing contention between them, the minister states,

> You think you educated but you not. . . . You look down on me, because you know I lie. At wakes, at funerals, at weddings—yes I lie. I lie . . . to relieve pain. 'Cause reading, writing, and 'rithmetic is not enough. You think that's all they sent you to school for? They sent you to school to relieve pain, to relieve hurt—and if you have to lie to do it, then you lie. . . . She been lying every day of her life, your aunt in there. That's how you got through that university—cheating herself here, cheating herself there, but always telling you she's all right. I've seen her hands bleed from picking cotton. I've seen the blisters from the hoe and the cane knife. . . . And that's the difference between me and you, boy . . . I know my people. I know what they gone through. (217–18)

The minister's knowledge of his and his people's antecedents gives him his power within the quarters and differentiates him from the other leaders of orthodox religion in Gaines's fiction. Though his brand of knowledge seems impotent to help Jefferson, it is cast as the bedrock of the dignity Grant seeks to instill in Jefferson. Again Grant faces the challenge of transforming the old into something new, of creating an appropriate spirituality for Jefferson, one rooted in the past but able to answer convincingly the tough questions Jefferson poses: "You think I'm going to heaven?," "What I'm go'n pray for?," "You believe in God, Mr. Wiggins?," "You think He be there if I axe Him, Mr. Wiggins?,"

"Who make people kill people, Mr. Wiggins?" (221, 223). To answer these questions Grant realizes the need to draw on a theology that is more than an opiate for suffering, one that is connected to the wellspring of communal faith.

The rethinking of the old that Gaines represents through Grant's grappling with history and spirituality has a formulaic representation in the narrative devices of *A Lesson*. Gaines's modernist recreation extends to an experimentation with the traditional novel form. Throughout his career, Gaines has exhibited a talent for transforming the written word with a blending of strategies rooted in the oral tradition. Instead of direct dialogue, for example, he often uses indirect discourse, as in novels such as *Catherine Carmier* and *Of Love and Dust*. To underscore the many perspectives that make up oral history or oral tradition, he frequently employs the technique of communal narrative, as in *A Gathering of Old Men* and "Just Like a Tree." In his epic *The Autobiography of Miss Jane Pittman*, he recreates folk history by incorporating references to Jackie Robinson and Joe Louis, who have become heroes by surmounting racial impediments. The use of such techniques in *A Lesson* recreates the orality of Gaines's Louisiana community and accents the intertextuality between this work and the rest of his canon.

A Lesson is many novels in one. In some ways it is Grant's bildungsroman, in which he comes to a deeper understanding of himself and his community. In other ways it is a social novel examining the perpetuation of racial and economic inequity. In still other ways it is a historical novel using its characters to reveal the many legacies of slavery. And of course, as is true of all of Gaines's works, it is a regional novel in which the speech, settings, and customs of Gaines's Louisiana world are important.

While these traditional forms are present in *A Lesson,* from the outset Gaines indicates the ways in which he will mold the novel form to his own ends. *A Lesson* consists of three distinct narrative sections. Chapters 1 through 28 tell the story from the first-person point of view and interject elements of orality into a traditional novelistic form. The first-person narrative immediately establishes an intimacy between text and reader, and the reader is encouraged to interpret events primarily through Grant's eyes. Chapter 29 is a transcription of Jefferson's diary; in it Gaines crafts a unique voice to record the pivotal moments in Jefferson's psychic maturation. Chapter 30 is a communal narrative in which each section is given over to a different resident of the community, revealing the impact of Jefferson's destiny from a variety of perspectives. The final chapter returns to Grant's first-person narrative and gives a sense of closure, of coming full circle.

The book's opening, "I was not there, yet I was there" (3), suggests that Grant and Jefferson's story will have portions told in an atypical fashion, and throughout the novel are tags of the orality that is Gaines's trademark. Grant is not present for the courtroom drama that sets the novel in motion, and he hears of it later through the stories of his aunt and Miss Emma. Much of his knowledge of events comes in a twice-told fashion evident in the recurring phrase "I would hear later" (178). There is, as well, the sense of shared knowledge passed on orally as Jefferson's story circulates through the quarters. Many major events are accompanied by phrases such as "Just like everyone else in the quarter, I knew" (10) to reveal the communal nature of this narrative. Most of the residents receive information as does Farrell Jarreau, the caretaker for Henri Pichot: "To learn anything, he had to attain it by stealth or through an innate sense of things around him" (41). The information they obtain, they tell to their community. In addition, throughout this section we note the importance of perspective within oral tradition. When Gaines gives the responsibility of telling the story to a character, he often reminds the reader that this is one character's take on the situation, as in the section in which Jefferson's version of the shooting and the prosecutor's version are contrasted. The transition from one perspective to the next is carried out with the phrases "That was his story" and "The prosecutor's story was different" (6). All of the above devices recreate the orality of Gaines's world, and their overall effect is to make this a very realistic novel, one that reveals the complex motives of characters as they act and interact within the rigid confines of their racial and social classes.

In chapter 29, "Jefferson's Diary," Gaines makes a shift in narrative technique, and in an ironic twist we have an emphasis on writing to achieve self-actuality. This turn reminds us that though Gaines is deeply steeped in the oral tradition, he is still a writer, and the written word forms his fictional actuality. There is an ingenious stress on both the power of voice and the power of writing, for while Gaines crafts a language suitable to articulating the thoughts of a young man whose life is over before it has begun, it is the act of writing down these utterances that begins Jefferson's regeneration.

Gaines's representation of the diary breaks from standard orthography in an attempt to suggest Jefferson's handwriting, his thoughts, and ultimately his voice: "mr. wigin you say rite somethin but i dont kno what to rite an you say i must be thinking bout things i aint telin nobody an i order put it on paper but i dont kno what to put on paper cause i ain't never rote nothin but homework i aint never rote a leter in all my life cause nanan use to get other chiren to rite her leter an read her leter for her not me so i cant think of too much to say but maybe nex time" (226). In all the entries, thoughts are grouped in paragraphs, words are spelled phonetically, and sentences are not punctuated. The overall effect is that of a stream-of-consciousness portrayal of a young mind struggling to make sense of the events that have led to his sentence of execution, a mind struggling to find meaning in unfairness.

In a variety of ways, Jefferson's journal subtly reveals his nascent understanding of his social circumstances. In his earliest entry, when he notes, "i ain't never rote nothin but homework" (226), his internalization of the racist attitudes that have eroded his self-worth is evoked through the lower-case "i" he uses for the personal pronoun. That he has never written anything but homework is significant because it suggests that Jefferson has never had the opportunity to write expressively in order to develop his thoughts, only the opportunity to write in the proscribed manner dictated by an inequitable educational system. In the same entry he addresses Grant: "you say i must be thinkin bout things i aint telin nobody." Here we see evidence of the silencing of Jefferson's voice. Rendered invisible by a society that sees only the color of his skin, Jefferson is also rendered symbolically mute by doctrines that denied African Americans a social voice in the 1940s and '50s. This muteness is most keenly apparent in a justice system that does not heed his articulation of innocence simply because he is a black man who has presumably killed a white man.

As Jefferson continues keeping a record of his feelings, the act of writing takes on an urgency for him: "i coudn sleep las nite cause i kept dremin it and i dont want dreem it cause im jus walkin to somwher but i dont kno wher its at an fore i get to the door i wake up an i want to rite in the tablet las nite but you aint got no lite in yer but the moon so im ritin this monin soon is sunup but now i done fogot what i want to say" (227). Here writing fulfills two fundamental needs for Jefferson: it helps him to crystallize fleeting ideas, and, more important, it assists him in coming to terms with what is behind the door in his dreams—his death.

Eventually Jefferson does know what to write. He moves from awkward passages that depict portions of his day-to-day life—an inability to sleep, a visit from his godmother—to more eloquent passages, such as the following, in which he begins to question complex notions of spirituality and justice: "it look like the lord just work for wite folks cause ever sens i wasn nothin but a litle boy i been on my on haulin water to the fiel on that ol water cart wit all them dime bukets an that dipper . . . so i can git the peple they food an they water on time" (227). His final thoughts, the morning of his execution, are phrased almost poetically:

day breakin
sun comin up
the bird in the tre soun like a blu bird
sky blu blu mr wigin (234).

These words are a fitting prelude to his last injunction to Grant: "good by mr wigin tell them im strong tell them im a man good by mr wigin" (235). Writing has a transformative effect on Jefferson, most probably because this is the first time he has a document of his experience and also a reader to value that document. Seeing his thoughts written down lends them a permanence that allows him to investigate and evaluate them.

This portion of the novel might seem to place an inordinate importance on the written word, one particularly uncharacteristic of an author so heavily steeped in the oral tradition, yet it is in actuality a segment that strikes a balance between the written and the oral. It is the power of the written word that assists in transforming Jefferson, but as is clear in the preceding quotations, this is a written word strongly overlaid by the oral cadence of Jefferson's speech. It is a written word that reveals to Jefferson his possession of a voice, and through that voice he is able to effect a psychic renaissance. His voice transforms him from the status of a brute, for through his language he is able to express thoughts about the people around him, pass judgments on the judicial system that has convicted him, and understand the social system that will not take his protestations of innocence seriously because he is a black man who has been charged with killing a white.

The chapter that follows "Jefferson's Diary" consists of a sequence of vignettes, each revealing individual reactions to the impact of Jefferson's impending fate. Each segment has a distinct voice. For example, Grant's is matter-of-fact and reportorial, revealing his new ability to focus less on himself and more on his community: "My aunt did not sleep at the house the night before. Like many of the other older people in the quarter, she spent the night with Miss Emma" (236). The tone of the sheriff's segment suggests his remorse for being party to the upcoming execution: "As the sheriff ate, he talked to his wife, but he avoided looking her directly in the face most of the time. He told her he wished this day had never gotten here, but now that it had, he had to do what he had to do" (238). Fee Jenkins, a prisoner jailed for a month and responsible for cleaning the sheriff's offices and the rest rooms, has a voice that reveals the status of observer, one who goes about cleaning the facilities yet remains unnoticed by those who use them: "Fee could hear the man with the cowboy hat talking to another man through the window. . . . Out in the corridor, more people were coming in for work. They all wanted to know if the first ones had seen it. . . . And a woman said she wished she had played sick and stayed home today" (241). Other people are depicted as they encounter various signs of what is to happen: the clearing of the bottom floor of the prison's storeroom, a truck carrying ominous cargo to the prison, a prisoner overhearing snippets of conversation from prison employees, the sight of people keeping a quiet vigil, a loud noise coming from the direction of the prison. Thus, in classic Gaines fashion, communal narrative and history are recreated. The novel's final events are not rendered directly but are quilted together through the stories and reminiscences of a variety of characters.

The final chapter returns to the first-person narrative of Grant Wiggins, and it is here that we learn of Jefferson's lasting impact. In a tellingly symbolic scene, Grant and the white deputy Paul, a young man whom those from the quarters refer to as "quality," illuminate Jefferson's significance. Their shared response, their budding friendship, and Grant's invitation to Paul to come to the school to tell the children how brave a man Jefferson was end this novel on the positive note characteristically present even when Gaines deals with the most deterministic subject matter. In many of his works, in spite of unchanging poverty, in spite of unchanging racial hierarchies, a ray of hope exists, usually manifested through simple acts of human decency that transcend mores of race, class, and history.

Much in *A Lesson Before Dying* links this work to Gaines's others: the interaction between African Americans and Cajuns, the theme of racial self-hatred, the probing of systems of religious belief, the contrast between formal and folk education, the recreation of oral expression, the symbolic manifestations of individual dignity, and, of course, the setting. In this novel as in the others, the community, customs, and people of Pointe Coupee Parish endure, providing a modernist interpretation of a rich and remarkable legacy.

Notes

1. For additional information on modernism and its effect on African-American literature, see Baker and also de Jongh.

2. Gaines has often cited Joyce as a profound influence on his work. See Babb 4, 16. For a discussion of Gaines's relationship to Joyce, see Werner.

Works Cited

Andrews, William L. " 'We Ain't Going Back There': The Idea of Progress in *The Autobiography of Miss Jane Pittman.*" *Black American Literature Forum* 11 (1977): 146–49.

Aubert, Alvin. "Ernest J. Gaines's Truly Tragic Mulatto." *Callaloo* 1.3 (1978): 68–79.

———. "Self-Reintegration Through Self-Confrontation." Rev. of *In My Father's House*, by Ernest J. Gaines. *Callaloo* 1.3 (1978): 132–35.

Auerbach, Nina. *Communities of Women: An Idea in Fiction.* Cambridge: Harvard UP, 1978.

Babb, Valerie Melissa. *Ernest Gaines.* Boston: Twayne, 1991.

Baker, Houston A., Jr. *Modernism and the Harlem Renaissance.* Chicago: U of Chicago P, 1987.

Bakhtin, Mikhail. *Rabelais and His World.* Trans. Hélène Iswolsky. Cambridge: MIT P, 1968.

Baraka, Amiri (LeRoi Jones). *Black Music.* New York: William Morrow, 1967.

———. *Selected Poetry of Amiri Baraka/LeRoi Jones.* New York: William Morrow, 1979.

———. *Home: Social Essays.* New York: William Morrow, 1966.

Bates, E. Stuart. *Inside Out: An Introduction to Autobiography.* Oxford: Basil Blackwell, 1936.

Beckham, Barry. "Jane Pittman and Oral Tradition." *Callaloo* 1.3 (1978): 102–9.

Benjamin, Walter. "Theses on the Philosophy of History." *Illuminations.* Ed. Hannah Arendt. Trans. Harry Zohn. New York: Harcourt, Brace, and World, 1968.

Bentson, Kimberly W. "I Yam What I Am: The Topos of (Un)naming in Afro-American Literature." *Black Literature and Literary Theory.* Ed. Henry Louis Gates, Jr. New York: Methuen, 1984. 151–72.

Blake, Jeanie. "Interview with Ernest Gaines." *Xavier Review* 3 (1983): 1–13.

Blasing, Muthu Konuk. *The Art of Life: Studies in American Autobiographical Literature.* Austin: U of Texas P, 1977.

Bloom, Harold. *Anxiety of Influence: A Theory of Poetry.* New York: Oxford UP, 1975.

Bogle, Donald. *Toms, Coons, Mulattoes, and Bucks: An Interpretive History of Blacks in American Films.* 2nd ed. New York: Continuum, 1991.

Boskin, Joseph. *Sambo: The Rise and Demise of An American Jester.* New York: Oxford UP, 1986.

Brown, Sterling. *The Collected Poems of Sterling Brown.* Ed. Michael S. Harper. New York: Harper and Row, 1980.

Bryant, Jerry H. "Ernest J. Gaines: Change, Growth, and History." *Southern Review* 10 (1974): 851–64.

———. "From Death to Life: The Fiction of Ernest J. Gaines." *Iowa Review* 3.1 (1972): 106–20.

Burke, William. "*Bloodline:* A Black Man's South." *College Language Association Journal* 19 (1976): 545–58.

Butler, Robert N. *Why Survive? Being Old in America.* New York: Harper and Row, 1975.

Byerman, Keith E. "Afro-American Folklore and the Shape of Contemporary Black Fiction: The Example of Ernest Gaines's *The Autobiography of Miss Jane Pittman.*" *Designs, Patterns, Style: Hallmarks of a Developing American Culture.* Ed. Dan Harkness. New York: American Studies P, 1983. 49–50.

———. "Ernest Gaines." *Dictionary of Literary Biography.* Vol. 33. *Afro-American Writers: 1955–Present.* Ed. Thadious M. Davis and Trudier Harris. Detroit: Gale Research, 1984. 84–96.

———. *Fingering the Jagged Grain: Tradition and Form in Recent Black Fiction.* Athens: U of Georgia P, 1985.

Callahan, John F. "Hearing is Believing: The Landscape of Voice in Ernest Gaines's *Bloodline.*" *Callaloo* 7.1 (1984): 86–112.

———. "Image-Making: Tradition and the Two Versions of *The Autobiography of Miss Jane Pittman.*" *Chicago Review* 29 (Autumn 1977): 45–62.

———. *In the African-American Grain: The Pursuit of Voice in Twentieth-Century Black Fiction.* Urbana: U of Illinois P, 1988.

———. "One Day in Louisiana." Rev. of *A Gathering of Old Men,* by Ernest J. Gaines. *New Republic* 26 Dec. 1983: 38–39.

Carby, Hazel V. "The Politics of Fiction, Anthropology, and the Folk: Zora Neale Hurston." *New Essays on "Their Eyes Were Watching God."* Ed. Michael Awkward. Cambridge: Cambridge UP, 1990. 71–93.

———. *Reconstructing Womanhood: The Emergence of the Afro-American Woman Novelist.* New York: Oxford UP, 1987.

Carter, Tom. "Ernest Gaines." *Essence,* July 1975: 52–53, 71–72.

Clark, Arthur Melville. *Autobiography: Its Genesis and Phases.* Edinburgh: Oliver and Boyd, 1935.

Dance, Daryl Cumber. *Shuckin' and Jivin': Folklore from Contemporary Black Americans.* Bloomington: Indiana UP, 1978.

Davis, Thadious M. "Ernest J. Gaines." *African American Writers.* Ed. Valerie Smith. New York: Scribners, 1991. 129–45.

——. "Headlands and Quarters: Louisiana in *Catherine Carmier.*" *Callaloo* 7.2 (1984): 1–13.

de Jongh, James. *Vicious Modernism: Black Harlem and the Literary Imagination.* Cambridge: Cambridge UP, 1990.

Dorman, James H. "The Strange Career of Jim Crow Rice." *Journal of Social History* 3 (1969/70): 109–22.

Doyle, Mary Ellen. "Ernest J. Gaines: An Annotated Bibliography, 1956–1988." *Black American Literature Forum* 24 (1990): 125–50.

——. "Ernest Gaines' Materials: Place, People, Author." *MELUS* 15.3 (1988): 75–93.

——. "The Heroines of Black Novels." *Perspectives on Afro-American Women.* Ed. Willa D. Johnson and Thomas L. Green. Washington: ECCA, 1975. 112–25.

——. "A *MELUS* Interview: Ernest J. Gaines—'Other Things to Write About.'" *MELUS* 11.2 (1984): 59–81.

Duncan, Todd. "Scene and Life Cycle in Ernest Gaines' *Bloodline.*" *Callaloo* 1.3 (1978): 85–101.

Eakin, Paul John. *Fictions in Autobiography: Studies in the Art of Self-Invention.* Princeton: Princeton UP, 1985.

Ensslen, Klaus. "History and Fiction in Alice Walker's *The Third Life of Grange Copeland* and Ernest Gaines' *The Autobiography of Miss Jane Pittman.*" *History and Tradition in Afro-American Culture.* Ed. Gunter H. Lenz. Frankfurt: Campus Verlag, 1984. 147–63.

Erikson, Erik. *Childhood and Society.* 2nd ed. New York: Norton, 1963.

——. *Identity: Youth and Crisis.* New York: Norton, 1968.

Fabre, Michel. "Bayonne ou le Yoknapatawpha d'Ernest Gaines." *Recherches Anglaises et Américaines* 9 (1976): 208–22. [Trans. Melvin Dixon and Didier Malaquin, *Callaloo* 1.3 (1978): 110–23.]

Faulkner, William. *Absalom, Absalom!* 1936. New York: Vintage, 1990.

Fitz Gerald, Gregory, and Peter Marchant. "An Interview: Ernest J. Gaines." *New Orleans Review* 1 (1969): 331–35.

Foley, Barbara. "History, Fiction, and the Ground Between: The Uses of the Documentary Mode in Black Literature." *PMLA* 95 (1980): 389–403.

Forkner, Ben. Rev. of *A Gathering of Old Men. America* 2 June 1984: 425.

Fox-Genovese, Elizabeth. "Between Individualism and Fragmentation: American Culture and the New Literary Studies of Race and Gender." *American Quarterly* 42 (1990): 7–34.

Fuller, Charles. "Scenes from 'The Sky Is Gray.'" *The American Short Story.* Vol. 2. Ed. Calvin Skaggs. New York: Dell, 1980. 437–42.

Fuller, Hoyt W. Rev. of *The Autobiography of Miss Jane Pittman,* by Ernest J. Gaines. *Black World* Oct. 1971: 87–89.

Gaines, Ernest J. "Auntie and the Black Experience in Louisiana." *Louisiana Tapestry: The Ethnic Weave of St. Landry Parish.* Ed. Vaughn B. Baker and Jean T. Kreamer. Lafayette: Center for Louisiana Studies, 1982. 20–29.

———. *The Autobiography of Miss Jane Pittman.* 1971. New York: Bantam, 1972.

———. *Bloodline.* 1968. New York: Norton, 1976.

———. "Bloodline in Ink." *CEA Critic* 51.2–3 (1989): 2–12.

———. "Boy in the Double Breasted Suit." *Transfer* 3 (1957): 2–9.

———. *Catherine Carmier.* 1964. New York: Random House, 1993.

———. "Chapter One of *The House and the Field,* A Novel." *Iowa Review* 3.1 (1972): 121–25.

———. *A Gathering of Old Men.* 1983. New York: Random House, 1984.

———. "Home: A Photo-Essay." *Callaloo* 1.3 (1978): 52–67.

———. *In My Father's House.* 1978. New York: Norton, 1983.

———. Lecture. Southern University, Baton Rouge, La. 15 March 1972.

———. *A Lesson Before Dying.* New York: Knopf, 1993.

———. *A Long Day in November.* New York: Dial, 1971.

———. "Miss Jane and I." *Callaloo* 1.3 (1978): 23–38.

———. "Miss Pittman's Background." *New York Times Book Review* 10 Aug. 1975: 23.

———. "My Grandpa and the Haint." *New Mexico Quarterly* 36 (1966): 149–60.

———. *Of Love and Dust.* 1967. New York: Norton, 1979.

———. Personal Interview. Conducted by Mary Ellen Doyle. 13 July 1983.

———. "The Turtles." *Something in Common: Contemporary Louisiana Stories* Ed. Ann Brewster Dobie. Baton Rouge: Louisiana State UP, 1991. 89–97.

———. "A Very Big Order: Reconstructing Identity." *Southern Review* 26 (1990): 245–53. [Simultaneously published as "The Autobiography of Mister Ernest Gaines." *Cultural Vistas* (Spring 1990): 4–6, 15–16.]

Gates, Henry Louis, Jr. "Criticism in the Jungle." *Black Literature and Literary Theory.* Ed. Henry Louis Gates, Jr. New York: Methuen, 1984. 1–24.

———. *Figures in Black: Words, Signs and the Racial Self.* New York: Oxford UP, 1987.

————. *The Signifying Monkey*. New York: Oxford UP, 1988.

Gaudet, Marcia. "The Failure of Traditional Religion in Ernest Gaines' Short Stories." *Journal of the Short Story in English* 18 (1992): 81–89.

————. "Miss Jane and Personal Experience Narrative: Ernest Gaines' *The Autobiography of Miss Jane Pittman*." *Western Folklore* 51 (1992): 23–32.

Gaudet, Marcia, and Carl Wooton. *Porch Talk with Ernest Gaines: Conversations on the Writer's Craft*. Baton Rouge: Louisiana State UP, 1990.

Giles, James R. "Revolutions and Myth: Kelley's *A Different Drummer* and Gaines' *The Autobiography of Miss Jane Pittman*." *Minority Voices* 1.2 (1977): 39–48.

Giovanni, Nikki. "'Jane Pittman' Fulfilled My Deepest Expectations." *New York Times* 3 Mar. 1974, 2:17.

Griffin, Joseph. "Calling, Naming and Coming of Age in *A Gathering of Old Men*." *Names* 40 (June 1992): 89–97.

Griffin, Lloyd W. Rev. of *Bloodline*. *Library Journal* July 1968: 2689–90.

Harper, Mary T. "From Sons to Fathers: Ernest Gaines' *A Gathering of Old Men*." *College Language Association Journal* 31 (1988): 299–308.

Harrington, Stephanie. "Did 'Jane Pittman' Show Us Black History?" *New York Times* 10 Feb. 1974, 2:17.

Harris, Trudier. *Black Women in the Fiction of James Baldwin*. Knoxville: U of Tennessee P, 1985.

Henderson, Harry B., III. *Versions of the Past: The Historical Imagination in American Fiction*. New York: Oxford UP, 1984.

Hicks, Granville. "Sound of Soul." *Saturday Review* 17 Aug. 1968: 19–20.

Hicks, Jack. *In the Singer's Temple*. Chapel Hill: U of North Carolina P, 1981.

————. "To Make These Bones Live: History and Community in Ernest Gaines's Fiction." *Black American Literature Forum* 11 (1977): 9–19.

Hogue, W. Lawrence. *Discourse and the Other: The Production of the Afro-American Text*. Durham: Duke UP, 1986.

Holloway, Karla F.C. *The Character of the Word: The Texts of Zora Neale Hurston*. Westport: Greenwood, 1987.

Huggins, Nathan Irvin. *Harlem Renaissance*. New York: Oxford UP, 1971.

Hunter, Charlayne. "'Jane' Show: Tale of Hope and Efforts." *New York Times* 31 Jan. 1974: 68.

Hurston, Zora Neale. *Their Eyes Were Watching God*. 1937. New York: Harper and Row, 1990.

Ingram, Forrest L. *Representative Short Story Cycles of the Twentieth Century: Studies in a Literary Genre*. The Hague: Mouton, 1971.

Ingram, Forrest, and Barbara Steinberg. "On the Verge: An Interview with Ernest J. Gaines." *New Orleans Review* 3 (1973): 339–44.

Jackson, Blyden. "Jane Pittman Through the Years: A People's Tale." *American*

Letters and the Historical Consciousness: Essays in Honor of Lewis P. Simpson. Ed. J. Gerald Kennedy and Daniel Mark Fogel. Baton Rouge: Louisiana State UP, 1987. 255–73.

Johnson, Charles. *Being and Race: Black Writing Since 1970.* Bloomington: Indiana UP, 1988.

Jones, Gayl. *Liberating Voices: Oral Tradition in African American Literature.* Cambridge: Harvard UP, 1991.

Kael, Pauline. "Cicely Tyson Goes to the Fountain." *New Yorker* 28 Jan. 1974: 73–75.

Kanin, Joseph. "Peripheral Vision." *Atlantic* April 1974: 117–18.

Katz, Ephraim. *The Film Encyclopedia.* New York: Crowell, 1979.

Kennedy, J. Gerald. "Toward a Poetics of the Short Story Cycle." *Journal of the Short Story in English* 11 (1988): 9–25.

King, Richard H. *A Southern Renaissance: The Cultural Awakening of the American South, 1930–1955.* New York: Oxford UP, 1980.

Kinser, Samuel. *Rabelais's Carnival.* Berkeley: U of California P, 1990.

Laney, Ruth. "A Conversation with Ernest Gaines." *Southern Review* 10 (1974): 1–14.

Locke, Alain, ed. *The New Negro.* New York: Albert and Charles Boni, 1925.

Lott, Eric. " 'The Seeming Counterfeit': Racial Politics and Early Blackface Minstrelsy." *American Quarterly* 43 (1991): 223–54.

Lukács, Georg. *The Historical Novel.* Trans. Hannah and Stanley Mitchell. Lincoln: U of Nebraska P, 1983.

McDonald, Walter R. " 'You Not a Bum, You a Man': Ernest J. Gaines's *Bloodline.*" *Negro American Literature Forum* 9 (1975): 47–49.

MacKethan, Lucinda Hardwick. *The Dream of Arcady.* Baton Rouge: Louisiana State UP, 1980.

Madgett, Naomi. "Alabama Centennial." *The Black Poets.* Ed. Dudley Randall. New York: Bantam, 1971. 198.

Mann, Susan Garland. *The Short Story Cycle: A Genre Companion and Reference Guide.* Westport: Greenwood, 1989.

Mansell, Darrell. "Unsettling the Colonel's Hash: 'Fact' in Autobiography." *The American Autobiography: A Collection of Critical Essays.* Ed. Albert E. Stone. Englewood Cliffs: Prentice Hall, 1981. 61–79.

Marx, Leo. *The Machine in the Garden.* New York: Oxford UP, 1964.

Mills, Gary B. *The Forgotten People: Cane River's Creoles of Color.* Baton Rouge: Louisiana State UP, 1977.

Morris, John N. *Versions of the Self: Studies in English Autobiography from John Bunyan to John Stuart Mill.* New York: Basic Books, 1966.

Ngugi, wa Thiong'o. *Decolonizing the Mind: The Politics of Language in African Literature.* London: James Currey, 1986.

O'Brien, John. "Ernest Gaines." *Interviews with Black Writers.* Ed. John O'Brien. New York: Liveright, 1973. 79–93.

Olney, James. "Autobiography and the Cultural Moment: A Thematic, Historical, and Bibliographical Introduction." *Autobiography: Essays Theoretical and Critical.* Ed. James Olney. Princeton: Princeton UP, 1980. 3–27.

———. *Metaphors of Self: The Meaning of Autobiography.* Princeton: Princeton UP, 1972.

Pascal, Roy. *Design and Truth in Autobiography.* Cambridge: Harvard UP, 1960.

Pecile, Jordon. "On Ernest J. Gaines and 'The Sky Is Gray.'" *The American Short Story.* Vol. 2. Ed. Calvin Skaggs. New York: Dell, 1980. 452–58.

Pettis, Joyce. "The Black Historical Novel as Best Seller." *Kentucky Folklore Record* 25 (1979): 51–59.

Potter, Vilma Raskin. "*The Autobiography of Miss Jane Pittman:* How to Make a White Film from a Black Novel." *Literature/Film Quarterly* 3 (1975): 371–75.

Price, Reynolds. "A Louisiana Pageant of Calamity." *New York Times Book Review* 30 Oct. 1983: 15.

Ramsey, Alvin. "Through a Glass Whitely: The Television Rape of *Miss Jane Pittman.*" *Black World* Aug. 1974: 31–36.

Rickels, Patricia. "An Interview with Ernest J. Gaines: September 22, 1978." *The Southwestern Review* 4.5 (1979): 33–50.

Roberts, John W. *From Trickster to Badman: The Black Folk Hero in Slavery and Freedom.* Philadelphia: U of Pennsylvania P, 1989.

———. "The Individual and Community in Two Short Stories by Ernest J. Gaines." *Black American Literature Forum* 18 (1984): 110–13.

Rowell, Charles H. "The Quarters: Ernest Gaines and the Sense of Place." *Southern Review* 21 (1985): 733–50.

———. "'This Louisiana Thing That Drives Me': An Interview with Ernest Gaines." *Callaloo* 1.3 (1978): 39–51.

Saeta, Elsa, and Izora Skinner. "Interview with Ernest Gaines." *Texas College English* 23.2 (1991): 1–6.

Shelton, Frank. "Ambiguous Manhood in Ernest J. Gaines's *Bloodline.*" *College Language Association Journal* 19 (1975): 200–209.

———. "*In My Father's House:* Ernest J. Gaines after Jane Pittman." *Southern Review* 17 (1981): 340–45.

Simpson, Anne K. "The Early Life of Ernest Gaines," *Louisiana Literature* 7 (1990): 71–87.

———. *A Gathering of Gaines: The Man and the Writer.* Lafayette: Center for Louisiana Studies, 1991.

Slotkin, Richard. *Regeneration Through Violence: The Mythology of the American Frontier, 1600–1860.* Middletown: Wesleyan UP, 1973.

Smith, Rick, and Ruth Laney. *Ernest J. Gaines: Louisiana Stories.* Videotape. Distributed by Louisiana Public Television. 1993.

Sollors, Werner. "Modernization as Adultery: Richard Wright, Zora Neale Hurston, and American Culture of the 1930s and 1940s." *Hebrew University Studies in Literature and the Arts* 18 (1990): 109–55.

Spector, Judith A. "Gender Studies: New Directions for Feminist Criticism." *College English* 43 (1981): 374–78.

Taylor, Anne Robinson. *Male Novelists and Their Female Voices: Literary Masquerades.* Troy: Whitston, 1981.

Thomas, H. Nigel. *From Folklore to Fiction: A Study of Folk Heroes and Rituals in the Black American Novel.* New York: Greenwood, 1988.

Toll, Robert C. *Blacking Up: The Minstrel Show in Nineteenth-Century America.* New York: Oxford UP, 1974.

Tooker, Dan, and Roger Hofheins. *Fiction: Interviews with Northern California Novelists.* New York: Harcourt, 1976.

Toomer, Jean. *Cane.* 1923. New York: Liveright, 1975.

Twain, Mark. *Life on the Mississippi.* 1883. Vol. 12 of *The Writings of Mark Twain.* New York: Gabriel Wells, 1923.

Unamuno, Miguel de. *The Life of Don Quixote and Sancho.* Princeton: Princeton UP, 1967.

Varghese, Raju, and Fred Medinger. "Fatalism in Response to Stress Among the Minority Aged." *Ethnicity and Aging: Theory, Research, and Policy.* Ed. Donald Gelfand and Alfred Kutzik. New York: Springer, 1979. 96–116.

Walker, Alice. "The Black Writer and the Southern Experience." *In Search of Our Mothers' Gardens: Womanist Prose.* New York: Harcourt Brace Jovanovich, 1983. 15–21.

Weintraub, Karl Joachim. *The Value of the Individual: Self and Circumstance in Autobiography.* Chicago: U of Chicago P, 1978.

Welty, Eudora. *The Eye of the Story: Selected Essays and Reviews.* New York: Random House, 1978.

Werner, Craig Hansen. *Paradoxical Resolutions: American Fiction since Joyce.* Urbana: U of Illinois P, 1982.

Wertheim, Albert. "Journey to Freedom: Ernest J. Gaines' *The Autobiography of Miss Jane Pittman.*" *The Afro-American Novel Since 1960.* Ed. Peter Bruck and Wolfgang Karrer. Amsterdam: Gruner, 1982. 219–35.

White, O. Z. "Our Prejudice Against the Elderly." *The Elderly: Victims and Deviants.* Ed. Carl Chambers. Athens: Ohio UP, 1987. 1–12.

Whitman, Walt. *Leaves of Grass.* Ed. Harold W. Blodgett and Sculley Bradley. New York: Norton, 1965.

Williams, Sherley Anne. *Give Birth to Brightness: A Thematic Study in Neo-Black Literature*. New York: Dial, 1972.

Woods, Frances Jerome. *Marginality and Identity: A Colored Creole Family Through Ten Generations*. Baton Rouge: Louisiana State UP, 1972.

Wright, Richard. *Uncle Tom's Children*. 1940. New York: Harper and Row, 1965.

Zinn, Howard. *SNCC: The New Abolitionists*. 2nd ed. Boston: Beacon, 1965.

Contributors

Valerie Babb is associate professor of English at Georgetown University. She is the author of *Ernest Gaines* and of articles on twentieth-century African-American novelists.

Keith E. Byerman is professor of English at Indiana State University. He serves as managing editor of the *African American Review*. A specialist in African-American literature, he is the author of *Fingering the Jagged Grain: Tradition and Form in Recent Black Fiction,* an annotated bibliography of criticism of Alice Walker, and a book on W. E. B. Du Bois.

Mark J. Charney is associate professor of English and assistant head of the English department at Clemson University. He is the author of *Barry Hannah* and has recently completed *Red to the Rind,* a videotape about ritual at the annual New Orleans Jazz Fest.

Mary Ellen Doyle is associate regional leader of the southern region of the Sisters of Charity of Nazareth and also adjunct associate professor of English at Christian Brothers University in Memphis. She has twice received the Woodrow Wilson National Fellowship and Teaching Internship and NEH summer research grants. In addition to articles on African-American literature, she has published *The Sympathetic Response: George Eliot's Fictional Rhetoric.*

David C. Estes is associate professor of English at Loyola University in New Orleans. He has received an NEH Fellowship for his ethnographic research in urban black folk religion. A specialist in southern literature and folklore, he has published a critical edition of Thomas Bangs Thorpe's humorous and sporting sketches of the Old Southwest.

Marcia Gaudet is associate professor of English at the University of Southwestern Louisiana. A widely published folklorist, she has written *Tales from the*   275

Levee, a book on Louisiana folklore. She is the co-editor of *Porch Talk with Ernest Gaines: Conversations on the Writer's Craft.*

Joseph Griffin is associate professor of English at the University of Ottawa. He is the author of *The Small Canvas: An Introduction to Dreiser's Short Stories* and has published articles on Gaines and other twentieth-century American novelists.

Karla F.C. Holloway is professor of English and African-American literature at Duke University. Her most recent book is *Moorings and Metaphors: Figures of Culture and Gender in Black Women's Literature.* Her teaching and research focus on the intersections among linguistics, literature, and cultural studies.

Robert M. Luscher is associate professor of English, chair of the English department, and director of the honors program at Catawba College. He is the author of *John Updike: A Study of the Short Fiction* and of articles on the short story sequence.

Milton Rickels is professor emeritus of English at the University of Southwestern Louisiana. A specialist in southern literature and humor, he is the author of *Thomas Bangs Thorpe: Humorist of the Old Southwest* and *George Washington Harris.*

Patricia Rickels is director of the university honors program and professor of English at the University of Southwestern Louisiana. She is a specialist in the folk traditions of Louisiana and has edited *1776–1976: Two Hundred Years of Life and Change in Louisiana.* Along with her husband, Milton, she has written *Richard Wright* and *Seba Smith.*

Sandra G. Shannon is associate professor of African-American literature at Howard University. She has received an NEH Fellowship to complete a book-length study of August Wilson, about whom she has published widely.

Frank W. Shelton is associate dean for academic affairs and professor of English at the University of South Carolina at Salkehatchie. He has published numerous articles on Gaines and on modern southern fiction.

David Lionel Smith is professor of English and chair of Afro-American Studies at Williams College. He has held fellowships from the American Council of Learned Societies, National Humanities Center, and NEH. He is co-editor of the *Encyclopedia of African-American History and Culture.*

Daniel White is a graduate student in American literature and poetics at the University of New Mexico. His poetry has appeared in various journals, and he is co-author of the Edward Abbey episode of the radio documentary series *Writing the Southwest.*

Index